WILDERNESS SURVIVAL

0 11557 03292 5

WILDERNESS SURVIVAL

SECOND EDITION

Gregory J. Davenport

STACKPOLE
BOOKS

Published by
STACKPOLE BOOKS
5067 Ritter Road
Mechanicsburg, PA 17055
www.stackpolebooks.com

Printed in the United States

10 9 8 7 6 5 4 3 2 1

Although *Wilderness Survival* provides extremely valuable information, it
cannot guarantee survival. Misuse of some of the information in this book
may lead to both physical and equipment damage, for which the author
disclaims any liability.

Cover Design by Caroline A. Stover
Illustrated by Steven Davenport and Ken Davenport

Library of Congress Cataloging-in Publication Data

Davenport, Gregory J.
  Wilderness survival / Gregory J. Davenport.— 2nd ed.
    p. cm.
  Includes index.
  ISBN-13: 978-0-8117-3292-5 (alk. paper)
  ISBN-10: 0-8117-3292-4 (alk. paper)
  1. Wilderness survival—Handbooks, manuals, etc. I. Title.

GV200.5.D38 2006
613.6'9—dc22

2005036234

This book is dedicated to the
USAF SERE
(Survival, Evasion, Resistance, & Escape) cadre—
especially Robert Milks, Joe Sitterly,
Rick Arnold, and William Frye.

Contents

Introduction   ix

BEFORE YOU GO   **1**

1. Climates of the Globe   2
2. Weather   11
3. Gear   16
4. Survival and Medical Kits   33
5. Predeparture Survival Plan   38

THE SURVIVAL ALGORITHM   **41**

6. Three Steps to Wilderness Survival   42

MAINTAINING LIFE   **47**

7. Health   48
     General Health Issues   48
     Traumatic Injuries and Their Treatment   50
     Environmental Injuries and Illnesses   57
     Survival Stress   70

8. Personal Protection   74
     Clothing   74
     Shelter   90
     Fire   112

9. Sustenance   137
     Water   137
     Food   155

RETURNING HOME   **203**

10. Signaling   204

11. Travel and Navigation   220

IMPROVISING TO MEET YOUR NEEDS   **267**

12. Improvising   268

SURVIVAL SKILLS FOR CHILDREN   **277**

13. Children and Survival   278

Index   285

Introduction

The elk he'd been tracking was nowhere in sight; he wondered why he'd kept following it for so long. Less than forty-eight hours ago, he'd been comfortably sleeping in a warm king-size bed. Now he lay in a fetal position under a sparsely covered pine tree. The tree provided little protection from the cold, damp snow that flurried around him. His clothes were soaked. He was shivering and couldn't seem to stop.

Earlier attempts at starting a fire had failed when his wet matches wouldn't light. "Why didn't I carry more emergency survival gear?" he asked himself. Before leaving the comforts of home, he'd filled his car with all the modern camping necessities: a large Coleman stove, an ornate kerosene lamp, a colorful expensive tent, and a top-of-the-line down sleeping bag. He hadn't bothered to pack an emergency survival or first-aid kit. He had never needed one before.

For Mark, the day had started like so many others. At 5 A.M. his friend Jake could be heard rustling around the camp, breaking wood and starting a fire. He counted on Jake to build a hair-singeing fire every morning. Jake loved fires so much that Mark often wondered if he was a closet pyromaniac. He didn't use matches, opting to use a metal match instead. Mark thought it seemed silly to use such a primitive device when both matches and lighters were available. But Jake, sticking true to his convictions, often said, "Matches and lighters run out, but a metal match will last forever." Secretly, Mark often wished he had Jake's talent for building fires.

Mark hated getting out of his sleeping bag in the morning, especially on a cold day like this. He waited until the fire crackled and then jumped from his bag and ran toward it as fast as his bare feet could safely take him. Sitting on a wet, cold log, Mark attempted to put on his socks and boots. The leather boots had been left out all night. They were slightly frozen and stiff, and he was unable to get them over his thick wool socks. Although he knew better, Mark decided to wear a thin pair of cotton socks that he'd brought along for the ride home. He was sure they wouldn't get wet.

Breakfast was quick—a peanut butter-and-jelly sandwich washed down with a coffee mug full of beer and tomato juice, a long-standing tradition. After eating, Mark began packing his gear. Staying close to the fire in order to keep warm, he organized a small fanny pack full of all the things he felt were necessary for a day of hunting: a bag of red licorice, four granola bars, matches, ammunition, a knife, and a quart of water. Mark always traveled light, believing it was necessary to conserve his strength to pack out the elk he intended to kill. He would laugh at Jake, who carried a small summit pack full of gear; it seemed unreasonable to carry so much.

Mark said good-bye to Jake as he left camp, feeling high on the morning air and sure today would be his day to return with an elk in tow. When Jake asked for his itinerary, Mark said he was going to play it by ear and really didn't have any special plans for the day. He felt so comfortable with his knowledge of the surrounding terrain that he didn't even carry a map or compass. He often bragged about this to his friends and made fun of them for carrying a compass and map into the same old forest where they'd hunted for so many years.

Within minutes of departing camp, Mark spotted a majestic seven-point elk feeding on the dew-fresh grass of a nearby meadow. Caught unprepared, he was unable to chamber a round before the elk spooked and cascaded into the surrounding forest. Sure of his tracking skills, he excitedly headed into the woods after the evasive creature. Several hours of searching passed before Mark stopped and suddenly realized he'd lost track of his location. Unwilling to abandon the hunt, he decided to continue until 3 P.M. If he was unable to locate the elk by then, he thought, he'd get to high ground and look for a familiar landmark by which to find his way back to camp.

At around 2 P.M., the weather began to change drastically. The temperature quickly dropped below freezing, and a thick fog descended. Mark felt as if he'd been placed inside a large cooler without lighting or windows; the cold air was bone-chilling, and he couldn't see more than five feet ahead of him. The elk he'd been tracking was long gone. He was still unaware of his present location, and as there were no visible landmarks, the way back to camp was uncertain. Shortly after the fog settled, Mother Nature decided it was time to show her teeth and delivered an unyielding downpour of rain and snow. Mark wished he had brought his rain gear. As the temperature continued to drop, Mark started to sense his predicament and began to frantically wander around in circles looking for a landmark or any sign of his hunting party. Panic began to set in, and the rhythmic beat of his pounding heart was so loud he thought his head would explode.

Darkness fell. In an attempt to alert his comrades of his desperate situation, Mark fired three rounds from his rifle every five minutes until his ammunition was gone. Cold, wet, and freezing, he crawled under a large lodgepole pine and tried to keep warm, but to no avail. His attempts to build a fire failed because his matches had become wet. He had no matches, no fire, no change of clothing, no navigational tools, and no improvising skills with which to meet his needs.

Crying and scared, he recalled how he'd read of a hiker who had died two years earlier from the effects of hypothermia while camping under conditions similar to these. When reading the article, he'd wondered how it could have happened and questioned the experience of the hiker. He now understood his own vulnerabilities and wished he'd been better prepared. As the hours passed, hypothermia's overwhelming cloud began to take hold, and Mark started drifting off to sleep. His thoughts became peaceful—wondering if his family would miss him; if his body would be found before Christmas; and if another hunter might read of his death and question, as he'd done of the hiker, his experience as a wilderness traveler.

Although extreme, this scenario is not unheard of. Every year wilderness travelers make one or more mistakes similar to those made by Mark, and for some it may even lead to death. Learning to survive in the wilderness is a skill not only for hunters but also for those who raft, fish, hike, climb, ski, four-wheel drive, forage, and so on. You can't predict where or when you might find yourself in a survival situation, and that's why preparation is of paramount importance for all backcountry travelers. If people like Mark had prepared properly and known a few basic survival skills, they might have lived. *Wilderness Survival* covers these principles and has been written to aid all backcountry travelers regardless of the climate and environment they might be in. This book explores the survival process, which begins before leaving home and ends with a successful return. It outlines basic environment and climate issues, provides a comprehensive predeparture checklist and survival kit, and promotes a far-reaching survival thought pattern.

BEFORE YOU GO

1

Climates of the Globe

Knowledge is power—know your climate before departing, and use this information to decide what you need to bring in order to meet your trip and survival needs. As always, prepare for the worst so that if things go bad, you'll have what you need to decrease the severity of the situation and increase odds of a good outcome.

SNOW CLIMATES

LOCATION
Snow climates are located in the interior continental areas of the two great landmasses of North America and Eurasia that lie between 35 and 70 degrees north latitude. The pole side usually meets with the tundra climate and its southern side with a temperate forest.

DISTINGUISHING CHARACTERISTICS
There are two snow climates: the continental subarctic, where freezing temperatures occur six to seven months of the year and the ground is frozen to a depth of several feet; and the humid continental climate, which has only 10 to 40 inches of precipitation (primarily snow) and far fewer temperature extremes than the continental subarctic. Both have seasonal extremes of daylight and darkness.

The continental subarctic climate presents vast extremes. Temperatures can have large swings from –100 degrees F to 110 degrees F. Temperature may fluctuate up to 50 degrees in several hours. These climates are most often seen from Alaska to Labrador and Scandinavia to Siberia. They are cold, snowy forest climates most of the year with short summers. Winter is the dominant season.

Humid continental climates are generally located between 35 and 60 degrees north latitude, and are located in central and eastern parts of continents of the middle latitudes. Seasonal contrasts are strong, and the weather is highly variable. In North America, this climate extends from New England westward beyond the Great Lakes region into the Great Plains and into the prairie provinces of Canada. Summers are cooler and shorter than in other temperate zones. A high percentage of precipitation is snow.

AVERAGE TEMPERATURE
During the coldest months, the temperatures are often less than 26.6 degrees F; during the warmest months, the temperature is often greater than 50 degrees F.

AVERAGE PRECIPITATION
Precipitation may range from 10 to 40 inches.

LIFE FORMS
Vegetation is similar to that found in the temperate climates. The inland animals are migratory yet obtainable. Most shorelines are scraped free of vegetation and animals by winter ice. The larger game (caribou, reindeer, goats, musk oxen, etc.) migrate in these climates. Small animals like snowshoe hare, mice, lemming, and ground squirrels are prominent. Many birds breed in snow climates.

PROBLEMS FOR THE SURVIVOR
Extreme cold, difficulty traveling on snow and ice, and problems with battery-operated equipment due to the low temperature.

ICE CLIMATES

LOCATION
Most ice climates are located north of 50 degrees north latitude and south of 45 degrees south latitude.

DISTINGUISHING CHARACTERISTICS

Ice climate terrain varies greatly. Ice climates can be broken into three separate, distinct categories: marine subarctic, noted for its high precipitation and strong winds; tundra, which has a layer of permafrost (permanent ground frost) over most of its underbrush; and the ice cap.

Marine subarctic climates are found between 50 and 60 degrees north latitude and 45 and 60 degrees south latitude. They commonly have persistent cloudy skies, strong winds, and high rainfall. They exist on the windward coasts, on islands, and over wide expanses of ocean in the Bering Sea and North Atlantic, touching points of Greenland, Iceland, and Norway. In the southern hemisphere the climate is found on small landmasses.

Tundra climates are north of 55 degrees north latitude and south of 50 degrees south latitude. The average temperature is below 50 degrees F. Proximity to the ocean and persistent cloud cover keep summer air temperatures down despite abundant solar energy at this latitude near the summer solstice. Shrubs, herbs, and mosses are found in the shrub tundra zone; wooded tundra includes a variety of tree species; and bogs are characterized by large peat moss mounds.

Ice-cap climates are located in Greenland, Antarctic continental ice caps, and the larger area of floating sea ice in the Arctic Ocean.

AVERAGE TEMPERATURE

Warmest months are less than 50 degrees F.

AVERAGE PRECIPITATION

Extremely variable.

LIFE FORMS

Animal life is poor in species but rich in numbers. Common large animals, birds, and fish can be found. However, in the Antarctic, animals are virtually nonexistent. Most common are seals and penguins along with sea birds.

PROBLEMS FOR THE SURVIVOR

Extreme cold, difficulty traveling on ice, problems with battery-operated equipment due to the low temperature, and scarcity of fuel for starting a fire.

DESERT CLIMATES

LOCATION

There are approximately twenty deserts around the world covering about 15 percent of its total land surface. Most dry climates (deserts) are between 15 and 35 degrees latitude on each side of the equator.

DISTINGUISHING CHARACTERISTICS

Approximately 20 percent of the world's deserts are covered in sand that often resembles unmoving ocean waves. About 50 percent of deserts are gravel plains (an extensive area of level or rolling treeless country) created by the wind removing ground soil, leaving only loose gravel (pebbles and cobbles). The remaining desert terrains include scattered barren mountain ranges, rocky plateaus (often seen as steep-walled canyons), and salt marshes (flat desolate areas with large salt deposits). Deserts are classified by their location and weather pattern as high-pressure deserts, rain-shadow deserts, continental deserts, and cool coastal deserts.

High-pressure deserts occur at the polar regions and between 20 and 30 degrees latitude on both sides of the equator. These deserts are located in areas of high atmospheric pressure where ongoing weather patterns cause dry air to descend. As the dry air descends, it warms up and absorbs much of the moisture in the area. Polar region deserts are often overlooked as deserts due to the cold temperatures. In reality these deserts have an annual precipitation of less than 10 inches a year. However, a polar desert rarely has temperatures over 50 degrees F and often has day and night temperature changes that cross over the freezing point of water. On the flip side, a high-pressure desert located between 20 and 30 degrees latitude north and south of the equator is hot as a result of its proximity to the equator and the wind's weather pattern (see above). Most of the world's deserts are located in this area. Unlike the cold deserts, these hot deserts have been known to reach temperatures as high as 130 degrees F.

Rain-shadow deserts occur where the prevailing winds meet a mountain range. As wind travels over a mountain range it cools and dumps its moisture in the form of rain or snow. As its elevation decreases (on the other side of the mountain range) the wind becomes very dry and warm. Unless moisture is obtained through other means, a rain-shadow desert will form on the protected side of the mountain range as a result.

Continental deserts occur in the center of large continents. As inland winds travel from the sea over land, they lose moisture (rain), and by the time they reach the center of a large continent, they are very dry.

Coastal deserts are the result of the cold ocean currents that parallel the western coastline near the Tropics of Cancer and Capricorn. At these locations, the cold ocean current touches a warm landmass, and as a result, almost no moisture is transferred from the ocean's cold water to the air that flows over the adjoining coastline. The descending air mass, which is already dry, becomes even drier. These deserts are some of the driest in the world.

AVERAGE TEMPERATURE
Deserts may be both hot and cold and may or may not have seasonal rainfall. However, most deserts have large temperature swings between day and night as a result of low humidity and clear skies (lack of cloud cover). In addition, desert winds increase the already prevalent dryness in the atmosphere.

AVERAGE PRECIPITATION
Although deserts get less than 10 inches of rainfall a year, don't count on it coming throughout the year. Rain is usually seen in big bursts and at irregular intervals. In some instances these intervals have been known to extend through several years. The desert surface is often so dry that even during hard downpours the water often runs off and evaporates before soaking into the ground. In addition, most deserts lie in high-pressure zones where limited cloud cover makes the earth's surface vulnerable to the sun's radiation. As a result of constant sun exposure, the area heats up, quickly causing high temperatures. As a result of high temperatures, what surface water there is quickly evaporates. In areas with strong winds the rate of evaporation is greatly increased.

LIFE FORMS
A lack of water and temperature extremes creates a hostile environment for most plant life. Plants that survive do so by drought escaping (rapid reproduction when rain arrives), drought resistance (storing water in their stems and leaves), and drought enduring (efficiency in absorption), or

Gobi Desert

accessing water from sources other than precipitation. The sun's unrelenting heat can also be an issue for desert vegetation; to compensate, many of these plants have small leaves oriented in a near vertical position. To avoid herbivore consumption, most desert plants have thorns, spines, and chemical compounds (tannins and resins). A wide assortment of wildlife can be found in the various deserts. In order to survive, most creatures avoid the temperature extremes. Most small game live in burrows during the day and come out at night, and some even remain dormant during the rainless seasons. Larger game is often active during the day but routinely seeks shade during the hottest hours. Most desert creatures have learned to compensate for a lack of water by developing the ability to meet this need from the food they metabolize (metabolic water).

PROBLEMS FOR THE SURVIVOR
Deserts present a survivor with a myriad of problems that include water shortages, intense heat, wide temperature ranges, sparse vegetation, sandstorms, and surface soil that is potentially irritating to the skin.

RAIN FOREST

LOCATION
Most tropical rain forests are between 23.5 degrees north latitude and 23.5 degrees south latitude in South and Central America, Asia, Africa, and Australia. The largest rain forest is located in the Amazon River basin in Brazil and neighboring countries of South America. Other rain forests can be found in Asia (examples include Borneo, Republic of the Philippines, New Guinea, and Northern Australia) and Africa (along the Atlantic coast and the Congo River Basin). Small temperate rain forests exist in the northern and southern hemispheres. An example of this type of rain forest can be found in the Olympic Peninsula of Washington state, where rainfall and humidity are high and the winters are mild.

DISTINGUISHING CHARACTERISTICS
Rain forests typically have an abundance of lush vegetation, high temperatures, and excessive rainfall. Although only 7 percent of the earth is covered by rain forests, 50 percent or more of the earth's animal and plant life exist there. The vegetation can be from three to five stories with an upper canopy of trees ranging from 150 to 180 feet high. The density of the underlying layers depends upon how much sun penetrates the upper canopy. The more sun that gets through, the greater the density.

AVERAGE TEMPERATURE
Temperatures are greater than 64.5 degrees F with a monthly average of close to 80 degrees F. The actual temperature in a rain forest depends on its distance from the equator and its altitude (rain forests are rarely seen above 3,000 feet).

AVERAGE PRECIPITATION
Rainfall is greater than 80 inches per year and exceeds annual evaporation. As a general rule, at least four inches of rain falls each month. There are no true dry seasons.

LIFE FORMS
Rain forests have more plants and animals than any of the other world habitats. The rain forest's understory and midstory plants often have large

leaves, allowing them to catch as much sunlight as possible. The upper-story plants have smaller leaves that spread out so that they touch plants around them, creating a canopy. Plants on the forest floor feed themselves by collecting falling debris or trapping animals and insects in their leaves. Almost 90 percent of the rain forest animal species are insects, and of these, most are beetles. In fact, one rain forest tree can host up to 150 species of beetles. The rain forest has an abundance of various mammals that can be found on the ground and in the trees. Most are nocturnal, choosing to sleep during the hot days. Almost half the rain forest mammals are bats. Ground dwellers of the rain forest include gorillas, elephants, tapirs, rodents, and wild pigs.

PROBLEMS FOR THE SURVIVOR
Insects, steep terrain, extreme moisture, and difficulty finding an appropriate signaling site.

TEMPERATE FORESTS

LOCATION
Most temperate zones are between 23.5 and 66.5 degrees latitude on each side of the equator. Temperate forests occur in eastern North America, northeastern Asia, and western and central Europe.

DISTINGUISHING CHARACTERISTICS
Temperate forests can be classified into five categories based on the seasonal distribution of rainfall. Moist coniferous and evergreen broad-leaved forests have wet winters and dry summers. Dry coniferous forests exist in higher elevations and have low precipitation. Mediterranean forests exist in areas with mostly winter precipitation. Temperate coniferous forests exist in areas of mild winters but high annual precipitation. Temperate broad-leaved forests exist in regions with mild, frost-free winters and high precipitation.

AVERAGE TEMPERATURE
Both winter and summer seasons are usually without extremes and can have temperatures that range between –20 and 85 degrees F.

AVERAGE PRECIPITATION
Varies from 10 to 300 inches, depending on which temperate climate you're in.

LIFE FORMS
Temperate forests can support broad-leaved deciduous trees and coniferous trees alone or in combination. Deciduous trees have broad leaves (that are lost annually) and include oak, hickory, beech, hemlock, maple, basswood, cottonwood, elm, and willow. Coniferous trees have thin leaves (needles), produce cones, and most are evergreens, which do not lose their needles and therefore are green year-round. Coniferous trees include pines, firs, junipers, and spruces. Most temperate forests have a dense canopy that allows enough penetrating light to create enough ground vegetation to support a moderately diverse animal population, such as squirrels, rabbits, skunks, birds, and deer.

PROBLEMS FOR THE SURVIVOR
The temperature, abundance of resources for improvising, and edible vegetation and game make the temperate environment one of the best for the survivor to meet his needs.

2

Weather

Weather (including wind) is a result of the sun's variable heat along with the differences in the thermal properties of the land and ocean surfaces. How weather forms is a complicated process beyond the scope of this book. However, taking the time to check the weather report before departing and understanding a few basics about predicting its change is extremely helpful.

WEATHER REPORTS

The weather report often includes information about the wind, temperature, atmospheric pressure, and fronts. Wind and temperature often relate to present conditions. Atmospheric pressure and fronts, however, help predict what the future weather will be. Knowing a few basic rules about pressure systems and fronts is helpful when deciding if you should go on a trip or put it off until another time. Pay attention to this information!

PRESSURE SYSTEMS

Atmospheric pressure at the earth's surface directly impacts weather. Air located in an area of high pressure will compress and warm as it descends, inhibiting cloud formation. This warming process inhibits the formation of clouds, often creating bright, sunny days with calm weather. In areas of low pressure, light warm air tends to rise and form clouds that often lead to precipitation. When you look at a weather map that has a blue "H" and red "L," they indicate the areas with high and low pressure.

FRONTS

Warm and cold fronts (boundaries) occur at the point where two air masses, of different density, meet. These masses seldom mix. Instead, the

11

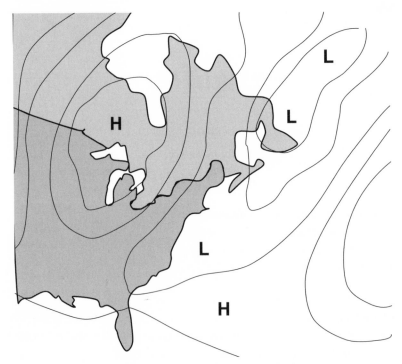

High- and low-pressure centers on a weather map

lighter air mass is pushed up and over the denser mass, often resulting in foul weather.

If you are looking for a trip filled with sunny days, avoid low-pressure systems and areas closely associated with any warm or cold front. Instead, try to find a stable area where a high-pressure system exists.

PREDICTING THE WEATHER

Once you are in the field, weather reports may not be available. You may, however, still be able to predict upcoming conditions by using a barometer or simply observing the clouds.

FORECASTING USING BAROMETRIC PRESSURE

Weathermen have used barometric pressure since the beginning of meteorology to predict the weather. You can too! An aneroid barometer (without fluid) is an instrument used for measuring atmospheric pressure. The device's pointer will raise or fall as the pressure of the atmosphere increases or decreases. Atmospheric pressure is affected by high- and low-pressure systems (see above) along with your elevation (air pressure decreases as you gain altitude). At sea level, barometric pressure is normally 29.92 inches of mercury (although it varies throughout the year and with weather changes). As you increase elevation, the air gets lighter and barometric pressure decreases. When using a barometer to predict weather, remember, as a general rule, that when the air pressure drops, bad weather is immanent.

FORECASTING USING CLOUDS

Clouds have a direct role in our weather. In addition to bringing precipitation, clouds warm the earth by preventing its radiant heat from escaping and cool the earth by blocking it from the sun. Clouds are usually classified by height and type.

Cloud Heights

The height of a cloud is indicated in the prefix used to describe it. Clouds above 20,000 feet (high-level) have the prefix "cirro" assigned to their name. Cirrus clouds usually contain ice crystals and are typically very thin and translucent. Clouds at 6,500 to 23,000 feet (mid-level) have the prefix "alto" assigned to their name. Alto clouds usually contain liquid water droplets in summer and a liquid droplet–ice crystal mix during the winter. Precipitation-producing clouds will often have the prefix "nimbo" or suffix "nimbus" assigned to their name. These clouds will typically be big and black with ragged dark edges.

Cloud Types

The two basic cloud groups are stratus and cumulus. Stratus clouds look similar to a high fog, often covering most of the sky with their gray uniform appearance. These clouds are associated with warm, mild weather and mist or drizzle. Cumulus clouds are an isolated group of clouds that look similar to a cotton ball with flat bases and fluffy tops. Large areas of blue sky appear between each cloud, and the clouds are normally (but not always) associated with fair weather.

Clouds are named by adding the height prefix (or suffix) to the cloud type. Identifying the cloud is helpful provided you understand what type of weather is often associated with it.

Cirrostratus

Thin, high-level (above 20,000 feet) stratus clouds that form a milky white sheet covering the whole sky. These clouds are so thin that the light rays from the sun and moon pass through them, forming a visible halo around the sun and moon. Cirrostratus clouds often indicate the arrival of rain or snowfall within twenty-four hours secondary to an approaching warm or occluded front.

Cirrocumulus

High-level (above 18,000 feet) isolated groups of cumulus clouds that look like rippled sand or globular masses of cotton (without shadows). As with most cumulus clouds, fair weather is often present or expected when these clouds are prominent in the sky. A storm, however, may be approaching when these clouds are present.

Altostratus

Thin, mid-level (between 6,500 and 23,000 feet) stratus clouds that form a gray sheet covering the sky. The sun can be seen under thin sections of altostratus clouds as a dim round disk, often referred to as a watery sun. Although the sun might be seen, the clouds will not allow enough rays through to produce a visible shadow on the ground. Altostratus clouds often indicate an impending storm with heavy precipitation.

Altocumulus

Mid-level (between 6,000 and 20,000 feet) isolated groups of cumulus clouds with the typical flat-based cotton ball appearance often in parallel waves or bands. These clouds typically support a darkened area (often at their flat bases) that is a key feature that helps set them apart from the higher cirrocumulus clouds (see below). Although these clouds usually indicate good weather, when they appear as "little castles" in the sky, afternoon thunderstorms may follow, especially when the clouds are associated with a warm humid summer morning.

Nimbostratus
Low-level (below 6,500 feet) stratus clouds are dark gray and usually associated with continuous light to moderate precipitation. This cloud formation provides no information about impending weather since it has already arrived. The sun and moon will not be visible through these clouds.

Cumulonimbus
These high, mountainous clouds are more commonly known as thunderstorms. The towering clouds will often look like the top of an anvil, which is a classic appearance for thunderstorm clouds. When these clouds are present, bad weather can be expected in the immediate area.

Stratocumulus
Low-level (below 6,500 feet) stratus clouds are white to dark gray and can be seen in rows, patches, or as rounded masses with blue sky in between individual cloud formations. Although these clouds can be associated with strong winds, precipitation is rarely seen.

3

Gear

When traveling into the wilderness, the type of gear you carry can either help or hamper your efforts. Specific gear will depend on many factors, which include the environment, weight, and cost. Whenever possible, try to bring gear that has multiple uses. A durable space blanket is a good example: It can be used as an added layer of clothing, a signal (orange side in winter; silver side in summer), water collection device, and shelter. A military poncho, thick-ply garbage bag, and parachute line are a few other examples of multi-use items. When bringing gear that operates on batteries, make sure to protect it from cold, soaking moisture, salt corrosion, and sand by wrapping it with a good insulating material and placing it in a waterproof bag.

This chapter does not include all items you might consider taking on a wilderness outing. Many additional items can be found throughout this book or within the recommended survival and medical kits.

BACKPACKS

The type of pack you carry depends on your personal preference. As a general rule, however, internal frame packs provide better balance and are used for cold days, off-trail hikes, and rough terrain, while external frame packs provide better airflow between the pack and your back and are used for hot days, trail hikes, and level terrain. For both, use the following guidelines when packing them for a trip.

ON TRAIL

When hiking on trail, organize your gear so that the heavier items are on top and close to your back. This method focuses most of the pack's weight on your hips, making it easier to carry.

Internal frame packs allow better balance for off-trail travel.

OFF TRAIL

Organize the pack so that the heavy items are close to the back (from the pack's top to its bottom) so that the majority of the pack's weight is carried by your shoulders and your back, giving you better balance.

The size of your pack will depend on its use. For overnight trips, 3,000 to 5,000 cubic inches is appropriate, whereas for long trips, you'll need 5,000 or more cubic inches. When selecting a pack, make sure it fits your back's length and contour and has strong webbing and thick shoulder and waist padding.

Regardless of which packing method you use, make sure to pack your larger survival items so they can be easily accessed and carry a smaller survival kit on your person. In addition, pad items that might gouge your back or can easily break.

An external frame pack allows better circulation between the pack and your back.

If a pack is not available, using a bedroll to carry gear is a good option. Lay a poncho or other large square piece of waterproof material flat on the ground. Place all gear on the edge of the material. Pad any sharp or hard items. Roll the material over the gear and continue until all the material is used. Tie the resulting roll at each end and every 12 inches in between with any available line or rope. Finally, tie both ends securely together and slide the roll over your head and onto either shoulder.

CAMELBAK

The CamelBak was a great innovation that not only insures you'll stay hydrated but also allows you to carry more emergency gear. I have several sizes, and all allow me to carry 100 ounces of water and have a drinking nozzle located over the shoulder strap, allowing ease of access. When in camp, I always have it on. On the trail, it is securely placed on top of my large pack, and the water bladder's hose is draped over my pack's shoulder strap. By doing this, I have easy access to my water and can quickly get into my emergency gear when I stop. My favorite CamelBak, the HAWG, can carry 1,203 cubic inches (1,020 in the cargo pocket) and weighs 1.9 pounds empty and approximately 8.2 pounds when its 100-ounce water reservoir is filled. It measures 9 by 7 by 19 inches in size. The HAWG CamelBak costs approximately $100.

TENTS

The majority of tents are made of nylon held up with aluminum poles. A balance—or trade-off—between weight and strength is often foremost in people's minds. When choosing a tent, you'll have to decide which is more important: less weight on your back or more durability and comfort in camp. A tent's size, strength, and weight will all factor into your decision of which one to use. A tent provides shade during the day, warmth at night, and protection from precipitation. Adding a full-coverage rain fly increases the amount of protection it offers. Most tents are classified as either three-season or four-season. Three-season tents are normally lighter and often have see-through mesh panels that provide ventilation (ideal in hot environments). Four-season tents are made from solid panels and in general are heavier and stronger. Typically they have stronger poles and seams are reinforced (ideal in many cold environments).

BIVOUAC BAGS

Bivouacs original concept was to allow the backpacker an emergency light-weight shelter. However, even though these shelters are made for just one person, many travelers now carry them as their primary three-season shelter. A good bag will be made from a waterproof/breathable fabric like Gore-Tex or Tetra-Tex, with a coated nylon floor. In addition, a hoop or flexible

Bivouac bag

wire sewn across the head area of the upper along with nonremovable mosquito netting is advised for comfort and venting when needed.

SLEEPING BAGS

There are many types of sleeping bags available, and the type used by individuals varies greatly. However, there are several basic guidelines you should use when selecting a bag. The ideal bag should be compressible, have an insulated hood, and be lightweight (but not to the point of failing to keep you warm). How well the bag keeps you warm will depend on the amount and type of insulation and loft, design, and method of construction.

INSULATION

Sleeping bags use either a down or synthetic insulation material. Down is a very lightweight, effective, and compressible insulation. The greatest downfall to this insulation is its inability to maintain its loft and insulating value when wet. In addition, it is very expensive. Synthetic material provides a good alternative to the down bag. Its greatest strength is its ability to maintain most of its loft and insulation when wet, along with its ability to dry relatively quickly. On the flip side, it is heavier and doesn't compress as well as down. Lite Loft and Polarguard are two great examples of a synthetic insulation.

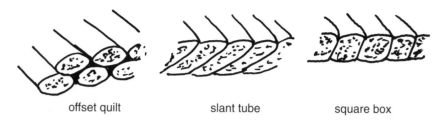

offset quilt   slant tube   square box

Sleeping bag construction designs

DESIGN
Without question, the hooded, tapered mummy style is the bag of choice for all conditions. In cold conditions, the hood can be tightened around your face, leaving a hole big enough for you to breathe through. In warmer conditions, you may elect to leave your head out and use the hooded area as a pillow. The foot of the bag should be somewhat circular and well insulated. Side zippers need good insulated baffles behind them.

METHOD OF CONSTRUCTION
There are three basic construction designs for sleeping bags: slant tube, offset quilt, and square box. Each design has its benefits, and the type you choose will depend on many factors, including weight, temperature, and compressibility. However, of these options, the slant tube and offset quilt are more comfortable and provide better insulation from the ground.

SLEEPING PADS
A sleeping pad is essential for insulating you from the hot or cold moist ground. Most commercial pads are closed-cell foam or open-cell foam. Closed-cell foam pads provide excellent insulation and durability but are bulky to carry. They may or may not have an outer nylon shell covering. Open-cell foam pads are often self-inflating pads (using a high-flow inflation valve) that offer the benefit of compression and rebound. This makes them ideal when space is a concern. Open-cell foam pads are usually inside a durable, low-slip polyester fabric.

PONCHO

A poncho (or tarp) is a multi-use item that can meet shelter, clothing, signaling, and water procurement needs. Its uses are unlimited, and you should consider bringing it on most outdoor activities. The military Rip-stop nylon poncho measures 54½ by 60 inches and features a drawstring hood, snap sides, and corner grommets. For shelter variations using a poncho, refer to chapter 8.

EMERGENCY ALL-WEATHER BLANKET

Don't waste your money or risk your life carrying one of those flimsy foil emergency blankets. Instead carry a durable waterproof 10-ounce, 5- by 6-foot all-weather blanket. The blankets are made from a four-ply laminate of clear polyethylene film, a precise vacuum deposition of pure aluminum, a special reinforcing fabric (Astrolar), and a layer of colored polyethylene film. The blanket will reflect moisture and help retain over 80 percent of the body's radiant heat. In addition to covering the body, these blankets have the added benefit of a hood and inside hand pockets that aid in maintaining your body's heat. When compressed down, these blankets take up about twice as much space as the smaller foil design, but the benefits far outweigh the size issue. The all-weather blanket is a multi-use item that can be used as an emergency sleeping bag, signal, poncho, or shelter. Its uses are unlimited.

FLEECE OR QUILTED BLANKET

A blanket can be used to increase the insulating quality of your lightweight sleeping bag or carried as emergency gear when taking day hikes in the desert. A fleece blanket is soft, comfortable, and durable, and some say it provides more warmth pound per pound than wool. The biggest downsides are its inability to repel wind and lack of compressibility. The Enhanced Infantry Thinsulate Poncho Liner (lightweight quilted blanket) measures approximately 91 by 60 inches and can be used for emergency and general survival needs.

KNIVES

I often carry a folding pocketknife for the majority of my cutting work and a larger fixed-blade knife and saw for the bigger projects. I consider the pocketknife one of my most important tools. I use it in virtually all of my improvised tasks, including cutting line, improvising shelter, preparing fire, and skinning game. For most of my big projects, such as cutting dead small branches or prepping the larger stages of firewood, I use a large fixed-blade knife. A simple blade is all you will need. Avoid those that have multiple modifications to the blade that supposedly allow you to do the unimaginable (it is just a bunch of marketing hype). The SCOLD acronym—sharp, clean, oiled, lanyard, and dry—can help you remember to properly care for your knives.

SHARP
A sharp knife will be easier to control and use, decreasing the chance of injury. Two methods of sharpening a knife are outlined below, followed by a general guideline on obtaining a proper angle for sharpening your knife blade.

Push and pull
In a slicing fashion, repeatedly push and pull the knife's blade across a flat sharpening stone (if a commercial sharpening stone isn't available, use a flat, gray sandstone). For best results, start with the base of the blade on the long edge of the stone, and pull it across the length of the stone so that when you're done its tip has reached the center of the stone. To obtain an even angle, push the other side of the blade across the stone in the same manner. Each side should be done the same number of times.

Circular
In a circular fashion, repeatedly move the knife blade across a circular sharpening stone or gray sandstone. Starting with the base of the blade at the edge of the stone, move the knife in a circular pattern across the stone. To obtain an even angle, turn the blade over and do the same on the other side. Each side should be done the same number of times.

To establish the best sharpening angle, lay the knife blade flat onto the sharpening stone and raise the back of the blade up until the distance between it and the stone is equal to the thickness of the blade's back side.

CLEAN
Dirt and sand that get into the joint can destroy it and cause it to either freeze closed or open, or even break. Dirt and sand can be harmful to the

blade's steel and can lead to its deterioration. To clean a knife blade, use a rag and wipe it from the back side to avoid cutting yourself. Never run it across your pants or shirt since that will transfer the dirt into the pores of your clothing or even cut your clothes. Use a twig to help get the cleaning rag into those hard-to-reach joints.

OILED

Keeping the blade and joint of your knife oiled will help protect the joint and steel and decrease the chances of rust.

LANYARD

Before even thinking of using a knife make sure you have it lanyarded to your body. The lanyard's length should allow you to hold the knife in your hand with 6 inches to spare when your arm is fully extended over your head. This length allows you full use of the knife and decreases the risk of cuts due to a lanyard that is too short.

DRY

Keeping your knife dry is a way to prevent rust that can impact the blade and the joint.

The knife is one of the most versatile tools a survivor can carry.

A knife has many uses and is important for a survivor to carry. However, using a knife isn't without risk. The potential for injury is high, and every precaution should be taken to reduce this risk. Cutting away from yourself and maintaining a sharp knife will substantially reduce your potential for injury.

SAWS

The Pocket Chain Saw and Sven Saw are two great items to consider taking into cold climates. Although I wouldn't consider them a replacement for the ax, both will help break down bigger sections of wood into a more workable size.

POCKET CHAIN SAW

The 31-inch heat-treated steel Pocket Chain Saw weighs only 6.2 ounces when stored inside a small 2¾-inch-diameter by ⅞-inch-high tin can. The saw has 140 bidirectional cutting teeth that will cut wood just like a chain saw; the manufacturer claims it can cut a 3-inch tree limb in less than 10 seconds. The kit comes with two small metal rings and plastic handles. The rings attach to the saw's far ends, and the handles slide into the rings, providing a grip that makes the cutting process easier. In order to save space, however, I don't carry the handles and simply insert two sturdy branches, about 6 inches long and 1 inch in diameter, into the metal rings. The Pocket Chain Saw costs around $20.

SVEN SAW

The lightweight Sven Saw has an aluminum handle and 21-inch steel blade that folds inside the handle for easy storage. When open, the saw makes a triangle measuring 24 by 20 by 14 inches, and when closed, 24 by 1½ by ½ inches. The saw weighs 16 ounces and costs about $22.

AX

An ax is a must when traveling into cold weather environments. The ax allows you to access the larger dry deadwood necessary to sustain a fire. Rhythm, not brute force, is the key to properly using an ax. In addition, remember that a sharp ax requires less energy to use than one that is dull. The last thing you want is a broken handle caused by a misguided forceful swing. The weight of a sharp and properly aimed ax is all that is required to get the job done. An ax can be used to fell a tree, cut poles, or split wood.

FELLING TREES

If possible, always fell the tree in the direction of its naturally occurring lean. For safety, make sure to clear the area within the scope of your swing from all debris and obstacles. Make the first cut (wedge) on the tree's downward leaning side and as close to the ground as can safely be done. The second cut should be on the opposite side and just slightly higher than the first. Use caution! Since trees often kick back at the last minute, make sure you have a clear escape route established. When cutting the tree's limbs, start at the bottom and always stand on the side of the tree that is opposite of the side you are working on.

Felling a tree

Cutting poles

CUTTING POLES

When cutting poles, hold the wood in your left hand, and let it rest on top of and perpendicular to a downed log. With the ax in your right hand, strike the pole in a controlled downward motion. Note: If you are left-handed, switch hands. Not only does this technique help prevent physical injury, but it also decreases the chances of damaging your ax.

SPLITTING POLES

When splitting a pole, hold it firmly in your left hand while, at the same time, holding the ax in your right hand. The pole and ax should be parallel to one another, and the sharp side of the ax head should be on top of and at the far end of the pole. Swing both the pole and the ax together, striking them on top of and perpendicular to a downed log.

A sharp ax is easier to use and thus decreases the chances of injury. A file is often used to sharpen an ax. To do this, work the file from one end of the cutting edge to the other—in a controlled motion—an equal number of times on each side. To help prevent accidental injury you should file away from—not toward—the cutting edge. Once the edge is regained, a honing stone can be used to smooth out the rough edges.

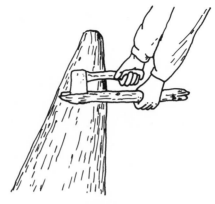

Splitting wood

BACKPACKING STOVES

When selecting a stove, you should consider its weight, altitude and temperatures of where you are going, ease of operation (even in cold, wet, or windy conditions), and fuel availability. The two basic styles are canister and liquid fuel. Canister designs use butane, propane, or isobutane cartridges as their fuel source. The most common types of liquid fuels used are white gas and kerosene.

WHITE GAS

White gas has a high heat output and is highly available in the United States. Although the fuel quickly evaporates, it is highly flammable if spilled. A white gas stove often does not require priming in order to start.

KEROSENE

Kerosene gas has a high heat output and is available throughout the world. Unlike white gas, when spilled this fuel evaporates slowly and will not easily ignite. The stove requires priming in order to start.

BUTANE/PROPANE

This canister allows for a no-spill fuel that is ready for immediate maximum output. These canisters are available throughout the United States and most of the world. I like these types of stoves for their ease of use and unmatched performance. The biggest problems are that some versions do not perform well in temperatures below freezing, you must dispose of the used canisters, and fuel may not be readily available.

The exact use of each stove will depend upon the manufacturer's recommendations and the type of fuel you use. Generally, a windshield is a must, preheating the stove helps it work better, and stoves that have a pump perform better when pumped up. For safety purposes, don't use a stove in a tent or enclosed area except when absolutely necessary. If necessary, make sure the area is vented, and do everything in your power to avoid fuel leaks. In addition, always change canisters and lines, fill fuel tanks, and prime the stove outside the shelter. Plan on ¼ quart of liquid fuel per person per day if you need to melt snow for water. Plan on ⅛ quart per person per day if water will be available.

HEADLAMPS

Headlamps have become a great alternative and replacement to the old handheld flashlights. The greatest benefit of headlamps is that they free up your hands so that you can use them to meet your other needs. When selecting a headlamp, you should consider its comfort, battery life history, durability, weight, water resistance, and whether or not it has a tendency to turn on while in a pack. I personally prefer the newer headlamps, which provide a compact profile with the battery pack directly behind the bulb.

COOKING POTS

A cooking pot is a luxury item that can be used to cook food and boil water. There are many types available, and the one you choose may depend on your needs. Cooking pots come in aluminum, stainless steel, titanium, and composite. Aluminum is cheap and the most common material used by backpackers. However, unless you buy it with a nonstick coating on the inside of the pan, plan on scorching your food. Stainless steel is far more rugged than aluminum but weighs considerably more. Titanium is lighter than aluminum, but the cost may be prohibitory. It does have a tendency to blacken your food unless you constantly stir it. Composite cooking pots have the benefits of aluminum and stainless steel to create a durable yet lightweight pot. The inside of the pan is made from steel to reduce scorching, and aluminum on the outside decreases its weight. A good cookware set includes a frying pan that doubles as a lid, several pots, and a pot gripper (handle).

GLOBAL POSITIONING SYSTEM (GPS)

A Global Positioning System (GPS) is a tool that can augment solid navigation skills but should *never* replace them. Learn how to use a map and compass before ever laying hands on a GPS! With that said, a GPS is a great tool that you should consider adding to your gear. It is a worldwide radio-navigation system that helps individuals, cars, boats, ships, and aircraft identify their locations. It uses satellites that rotate around the earth while sending a signal traveling at the speed of light to a ground unit that includes the exact time it was sent. The ground stations use this information to calculate a satellite's location by applying it to the dead-reckoning formula: rate × time = distance. The ground station is constantly monitor-

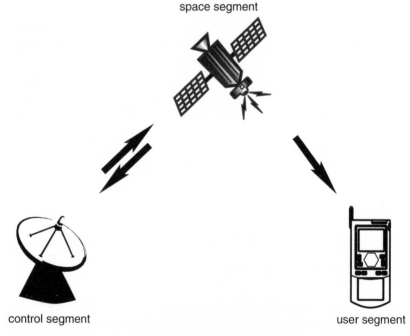

The Global Positioning System

ing the satellite's location (orbit, altitude, and speed) and forwarding this information to a master control station. In turn, the master control station sends this updated information to the satellite, and the satellite relays it to the GPS receiver (the device you are using). The GPS receiver knows the satellite's distance by using the dead-reckoning formula.

Once the system locks into three satellites, it can use the three imaginary lines (from known satellite location in line with where it would meet the earth—distance) to triangulate and identify your approximate location (latitude and longitude). Using three satellites produces a potential error similar to what is experienced when triangulating with a compass (see navigation chapter). To better pinpoint location and identify latitude, longitude, and altitude requires locking into four satellites. Using a fourth satellite creates three additional triangulations, making it much more accurate.

GPS receivers equipped with a differential beacon receiver and beacon antenna are often accurate to within three meters. This feature allows the system to receive differential GPS correction signals transmitted from a network of towers. Simply put, the towers receive GPS satellite signals, correct small errors, and then transmit the corrected signal by beacon transmitters. Without this feature, the accuracy of the GPS is perhaps to within 15 meters. Once the GPS receiver's position is known, it can calculate other information like bearings and distances.

ALTIMETER

A digital altimeter can provide information about your elevation that, when used along with a map and the terrain, can help you pinpoint your location. Since an altimeter reading is based on air pressure (just like a barometer), it is affected by changes in weather. With this in mind, you'll need to set its elevation from a known point when you start and on a regular basis as new known points are reached.

SNOWSHOES

Snowshoes are an outstanding aid when traveling on snow and are especially helpful when carrying a pack. They make travel easier by dispersing your weight over a greater surface area, which in turn decreases the posthole effect. When compared to cross-country skis, they are superior in snow-covered areas that also have brush or rocks. In addition, they are easier to use than skis for those who are inexperienced. Modern snowshoes are made of an oval-shaped lightweight tubular frame that supports a durable decking material. Most bindings are easy to attach to your boot and come with cramponlike metal plates at the toe and heel to aid in traction. The type of snowshoe you use will depend upon how you use it and your weight. The smaller shoe allows greater maneuverability, whereas the larger one provides greater flotation.

OTHER ITEMS TO CONSIDER

For winter travel, consider bringing crampons, Nordic and mountaineering skis, a sled to transport gear, ice ax, snow shovel, mountaineering pole, probes, avalanche transceiver, AvaLung, and clinometers. For desert travel, add a few nylon anchors to weigh down tent edges. On the water, carry antinausea medication or a ReliefBand device (wristwatch-style device that controls nausea) and an adequate personal flotation device.

SURVIVAL TIPS

In order to cut down on weight, try to bring gear that meets multiple purposes.

Protect your batteries from moisture, salt water, sand, and cold by putting them in a sealable plastic bag and, during extreme cold, between the layers of your clothing.

4

Survival and Medical Kits

A survival and medical kit should be one of the most important items you carry. Sadly, they are often the first item compromised when trying to decrease your pack's load. Better to carry a little extra weight than to have a debilitating blister forming and be without moleskin, or find yourself without a means of starting a fire during harsh wet and cold conditions.

SURVIVAL KIT

As a bare minimum a survival kit should carry the ten essentials (see table). I advise, however, that you consider carrying much more. Take the time to review the five survival essentials (covered throughout this book) and consider potential problems when putting your kit together. Try to create a kit that will meet your needs under all situations. Put together several kits: a large one for your pack, a medium-size one for your Camel-Bak, and a small one that you always have on your person.

THE SEMIESSENTIALS

Other items you might consider in addition to the ten essentials include a tent or shelter material, paracord for improvising, signaling devices (signal mirror, ground-to-air panel, flares, etc.), water-purifying system, snare wire and fishing gear, wristwatch, note paper and a pencil, toilet paper, and a plastic bag.

I carry my survival gear using a complete yet scattered design. My pack is filled with items that will meet my everyday and emergency needs. In addition, I carry a smaller yet fairly complete kit in my CamelBak

TEN ESSENTIALS OF A SURVIVAL KIT

Essential Items	Five Survival Essentials Category
map	navigation
compass	navigation
knife	improvising, fire, etc.
water and food	sustenance
rain gear and proper clothing for warmth	personal protection (clothing)
headlamp or flashlight	health (avoid traumatic injuries at night)
first-aid supplies	health (environmental and traumatic injuries)
matches or spark source	personal protection (fire)
tinder	personal protection (fire)
sunglasses and sunscreen	health (environmental injuries)

(which goes everywhere with me, including on top of my pack during long trips) and a smaller yet comprehensive kit in the cargo pocket of my pants. When carrying my pack, I have safety gear. If I take my pack off and walk around camp with just the CamelBak on, I am covered. Finally, if for some odd reason I find myself separated from my pack and CamelBak, the kit in my cargo pocket covers me. A list of my smaller cargo pocket kit is provided. Take a look and see how it might work for you.

SMALL CARGO POCKET KIT ITEMS

Survival Category	Items	Potential Uses
personal protection	needle	sewing, splinter removal
	dental floss	floss teeth, sewing, gear repair
	duct tape	clothing repair, gear repair, medical tape, signaling, note paper
	knife	cutting applications, metal match striker, screwdriver, digging, skinning
	parachute cord	lashing shelters/tools, gear repair, inner strands for sewing, snares
	Vaseline/cotton tinder	tinder, lip balm, moisten dry skin
	metal match	fire starter, nighttime signal device
	candle	match saver/fire starter, light source
	matches	fire starter
signaling	mirror	ground/air signal, ground/ground signal
	whistle	audible signal
	survey tape	ground signal, trail marker, note paper, gear repair
	coins	pay phone, ground/air signal, fishing lure
	marker	note taking, writing messages
sustenance	condoms	water bladder
	water purification tablets	water purification
	water purification container	air/water tight container
	tubing	water bladder hose, sling shot, snare device, tourniquet

SMALL CARGO POCKET KIT ITEMS (continued)

Survival Category	Items	Potential Uses
	safety pin	secure tubing to clothing, clothing repair, gear repair, splinter removal, secure arm sling
	bread ties	secure top of water bladder, keep small gear organized
	aluminum foil	water scoop for condom, fire base on wet ground, wind block for small fires, cooking, signaling
	snare wire	snares, gear repair
	fishing line	fishing, gear repair, sewing, shelter lashing, all cordage applications
	fishing hooks	fishing, sewing, gear repair
	fishing sinkers	fishing
	fishing float	fishing, trail marker
travel	button compass	
medical	medical tape	secure dressings, gear repair, clothing repair, all tape applications
	Band-Aids	small wound dressings
	antibiotic cream	small wound care, chapped lip/skin balm
	moleskin	blister prevention/repair
	alcohol preps	disinfect skin/needles
	Ziploc bag for picture of loved ones	relieve stress, motivation to succeed
miscellaneous	Ziploc bags	keep small essentials dry/organized
	PSK pouch	carry survival gear
	three-step approach card	guidance for a survival scenario

MEDICAL KIT: SUGGESTED ITEMS

antibiotic ointment	routine medications
antihistamine	scissors
aspirin	snake bite kit
Band-Aids	soap
bee sting kit	sunscreen
Chapstick	tincture of benzoin
matches	triangular bandage
medical tape	tweezers
moleskin	various dressings
roller gauze	water purification tablets

5

Predeparture Survival Plan

A trip plan should be completed and left with a reliable friend prior to your departure. Your friend should notify the sheriff or rescue organization if you fail to return as scheduled. Plans are not filed with the sheriff's office, so unless your friend notifies them, they will not start a rescue mission. To avoid unnecessary searches, be sure to notify your friend of any delays and upon returning.

Person Reported Overdue

Name _____ Phone _____

Address _____

_____

_____

Survival Equipment

Cell phone and number _____

Flares _____ Signal mirror _____ Smoke signal _____

Other signals _____

Trip Expectations

Depart from _____

Departure date _____ Time _____

Going to _____

Arrival date _____ Time _____

Expected camping sites, water sources, and expected arrival dates:

	Date	**Site (latitude and longitude)**	**Water source**
1.			
2.			
3.			
4.			
5.			

If you have not arrived/returned by:

Date _____ Time_____

Call the sheriff or local authority at the following number:

_____

Vehicle Description

License no. _____ Make _____

Model _____ Color _____

Where is vehicle parked?_____

_____

Persons on Trip

Name	**Age**	**Phone**	**Medical conditions**

Additional Information

_____

_____

_____

_____

_____

_____

_____

_____

THE SURVIVAL ALGORITHM

6

Three Steps to Wilderness Survival

The ability for a person to prevail in a survival situation is based on three factors: survival knowledge, equipment, and will to survive. All are important, but the most important is the will to survive. Unfortunately the will to survive cannot be taught in a book. Increasing your knowledge of survival skills and understanding of related gear, on the other hand, can. One method of increasing your skills and knowledge is through others. It's with this end in mind that this book has been written. For most of the last twenty years I have used a simple three-step approach to help overcome most survival scenarios. Understanding and using this approach keeps the survivor organized, reduces stress, and ultimately increases the will to survive. It can do the same for you.

GREG DAVENPORT'S THREE-STEP APPROACH TO WILDERNESS SURVIVAL

As an outdoor educator and wilderness survival expert, I believe a survivor's needs remain constant regardless of his or her circumstances (climate, terrain, or health). In fact, the only thing that changes in how these needs are met is how they are prioritized and how well you improvise to meet them. The three steps are stop and recognize the situation for what it is; identify and prioritize your five survival essentials for the situation you are in; and improvise to meet your needs (using man-made and natural resources).

STEP 1
Stop and recognize the situation for what it is. If you think you're lost, you probably are. Stop trying to find that familiar road or rock. Walking when lost burns up daylight and moves you beyond the probable search-and-

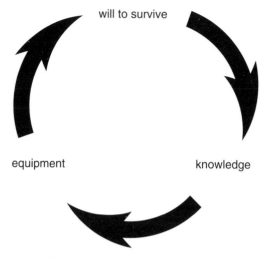

will to survive

equipment   knowledge

Factors that influence survival

rescue zone. This common scenario often leads to a cold and frustrating night for both you and search-and-rescue teams. Once you recognize that you are lost, stop wandering around! Use your time to identify and meet your five survival essentials, making a safe and rapid rescue more probable.

STEP 2
Identify and prioritize your five survival essentials. Once you've recognized the situation for what it is, it's time to identify your five survival essentials and prioritize them in order of importance. Take the time to write down your order of preference and be willing to adjust the order as mandated by your constantly changing scenario. The five survival essentials are:
1. Personal protection (clothing, shelter, fire)
2. Signaling (man-made and improvised)
3. Sustenance (identifying and procuring water and food)
4. Travel (with and without a map and compass)
5. Health (mental, traumatic, and environmental injuries)
    Health, personal protection, and sustenance needs relate to maintaining life. Signaling and travel relate to returning home. Although these needs are constant, your situation and the environment will dictate the exact

order and method used to meet them. To better understand the five survival essentials, each is explained in greater detail in the following chapters.

STEP 3
Improvise to meet your needs (using man-made and natural resources). Tap water, refrigerators, heaters, and a nice bed are not part of an outdoor adventure. These needs can often be met, however, with a little imagination, your gear, and what Mother Nature provides.

Since it's unlikely you'll have all the necessary resources in your gear, you'll need to improvise using what you have and what Mother Nature can supply. Sometimes this task is easy, and other times it may stretch your imagination to its limits. Using the following five-step approach to improvising will help in the decision process.

STOP
Identify & Prioritize

Personal Protection   **Signaling**   **Sustenance**   **Travel**   **Health**

Clothing   Shelter   Fire   Water   Food   Mental   Environment   Traumatic

Improvise

Greg Davenport's three-step approach to global survival

1. Determine your need (shelter, signal, heat, etc.).
2. Inventory your available man-made and natural materials.
3. Consider the different ways you might meet your need (tree-well shelter, snow cave, etc.).
4. Pick the one that best utilizes your time, energy, and materials.
5. Proceed with the plan, ensuring that the final product is safe and durable.

The only limiting factor is your imagination! Don't let it prevent you from creating a masterpiece that keeps you comfortable while in your survival situation.

No matter what your circumstances, these three steps will help you during a time when you are uncertain of what tomorrow brings. They keep you organized, on task, and focused on a safe return home.

MAINTAINING LIFE
Meeting Your Health, Personal Protection, and Sustenance Needs

7

Health

Survival medicine is simply first aid and CPR with a twist. Ultimately, the environment and the amount of time before you return to civilization may have the biggest impact upon any health issues that arise. The weather may be bad, and the nearest medical facility may be miles from your location. It's highly advisable that you receive adequate first-aid and CPR training, and in no way should you consider this chapter a replacement for that instruction.

GENERAL HEALTH ISSUES

Your ability to fend off an injury or infection plays a significant role in how well you handle any given survival situation. Proper hydration, nutrition, hygiene, and rest all impact your ability to ward off opportunistic problems found in the wilderness.

STAYING HYDRATED

Without water, you'll die in approximately three to five days. In addition, dehydration will directly affect your ability to make logical decisions about how to handle any given problem. Fluids are lost when the body works to warm itself, when sweating or doing intense activity, and when you urinate or defecate. As dehydration starts to set in, you'll begin to have excessive thirst and become irritable, weak, and nauseated. As your symptoms advance, you'll get a headache and become dizzy, and eventually your tongue will swell and your vision will be affected. Prevention is the best way to avoid dehydration. This can be accomplished by drinking at least 2 quarts of water during minimal activity and 4 to 6 (or more on extremely hot days) during more intense activity. If you should become dehydrated, decrease your activity, get out of the sun, and drink enough potable water

While climbing in northwestern Washington, Greg Davenport takes time to rest and rehydrate.

to get your urine output up to at least 1 quart in a twenty-four-hour period. Hopefully you'll have the ability to procure enough water.

NOURISHMENT

Nourishing foods increase morale, provide valuable energy, and replace lost nutrients (salt, vitamins, etc.). Although food is nice, it's not normally necessary; you may be able to go without it for several weeks.

CLEANLINESS

Not only does staying clean increase morale, but it also helps prevent infection and disease. Different methods of staying clean include taking a bath or sunbathing. A sunbath should last from 30 minutes to 2 hours a day. Keeping your hair trimmed, brushing your teeth and gums, monitoring your feet, and cleaning your cooking utensils after each use are also important tasks that will decrease the risk of illness or infestation.

REST

Providing the body with proper rest helps ensure that you have adequate strength to deal with the stress of initial shock and subsequent trials associated with a survival situation.

TRAUMATIC INJURIES AND THEIR TREATMENT

Traumatic injuries are extremely taxing on a survivor—keeping your composure may mean the difference between surviving or not. The treatment of traumatic injuries should therefore follow a logical process. Treat the most life-threatening injuries first: Concentrate on breathing, bleeding, and shock. In general, a six-step approach can be taken when evaluating a victim.

SIX STEPS FOR A LIFE-THREATENING EMERGENCY

1. Take charge of the situation: If in a group, the person with the most medical experience should take charge.
2. Determine if the scene is safe to enter: Is there a risk to the subject or rescuer? If so, don't enter until the area is considered safe.
3. Treat life-threatening injuries: If necessary, the subject should be moved to a safe area. Perform a head-to-toe evaluation using the ABCD format and in that order.

    A = Airway
    B = Breathing
    C = Circulation and C-spine
    D = Deadly bleeding

4. Treat for shock: Shock can lead to death, and thus early intervention is a must. Appropriate body positioning, dry clothing, insulation, pain control, and comforting words are all part of shock treatment.
5. Secondary evaluation: Once life-threatening issues have been addressed, perform a secondary survey evaluating all injuries. Treat each injury.
6. Treatment plan: How to prevent the subject's condition from worsening should be discussed and an appropriate treatment plan implemented.

AIRWAY, BREATHING, CIRCULATION (ABCs)

To be successful when treating someone who has a compromise of his or her airway, breathing, or circulation, you must know CPR, and I'd advise you learn this prior to departing for the wilderness. In cold-water submersions or drownings, CPR can be successful even when the subject has been submerged for up to one hour.

BLEEDING (HEMORRHAGE)
There are three types of bleeding, and contrary to popular belief, color is not always the best indicator of its source. An arterial bleed is the most serious of the three and is normally bright red spurting blood. A venous bleed can also be very serious and is usually identified as a steady stream of dark red blood. Capillary bleeds are minor, and since the vessels are so close to the skin's surface, the dark red blood typically oozes from the site. Basic treatment options are direct pressure, pressure points, and rarely a tourniquet.

Direct pressure
Do not delay in applying pressure, even if you have to use your hand or finger. If materials are available, use a pressure dressing. To apply a pressure dressing, pack the wound with several sterile dressings, and wrap it with a continuous bandage. Make sure the bandage is snug, but not so snug as to cut off circulation to the rest of the extremity. (To insure this doesn't occur, regularly check for pulses and sensations of the extremity beyond the wound site.) If the dressing soaks through, apply subsequent dressings directly over the first. Leave in place for two days. Thereafter, change it daily. If on an extremity, elevate it above the heart level. In most cases, applying direct pressure for ten minutes will stop the bleeding.

Pressure points
Applying pressure to a blood vessel between the heart and the wound will decrease the amount of blood loss from the injury site. To be effective it must be applied for about ten minutes. Refer to the following diagram for examples of different pressure points.

Tourniquet
A tourniquet is rarely necessary and should only be utilized when direct pressure, elevation, and pressure points have failed or it's deemed necessary to save a life. The likelihood of losing an extremity from tourniquet use is

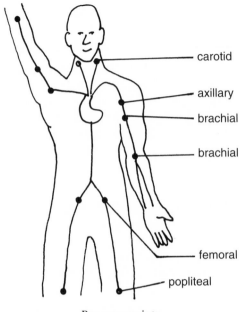

carotid

axillary

brachial

brachial

femoral

popliteal

Pressure points

high; however, once it has been applied, never loosen it. To use a tourniquet, apply a 3- to 4-inch band 2 inches above the wound so that it is between the wound and the heart. After wrapping the band around the limb several times, tie it into a square knot with a sturdy stick placed in the knot's center, tighten the tourniquet by turning the stick until the blood flow comes to a stop, and secure the stick in place. Finally, mark the victim's head with a big "T" and note the time when the tourniquet was applied.

SHOCK
Shock is a direct result of the body's inability to provide a sufficient blood supply to the vital organs. If not corrected, it could ultimately lead to death. Signs and symptoms of shock include pale, cold, and clammy skin; a weak, rapid pulse; and feelings of restlessness, disorientation, and faintness. All injuries, no matter how small, can potentially lead to shock, and all victims should be treated as if it is present. To treat, control the patient's heat loss by covering him with any form of dry insulating material and provide insulation from the ground, and if hypothermia is present,

treat it. If conscious, lay the victim on his back. If unconscious, lay him on his side (in case of vomiting). Elevate lower extremities 8 to 12 inches, except when there is a serious head, neck, chest, or abdomen injury. For head or chest injury: raise the victim's upper torso about 15 degrees toward a sitting position.

INJURIES TO THE HEAD
Signs and symptoms of a head injury include bleeding, increasing headache, drowsiness, nausea, vomiting, unequal pupils, and unconsciousness. To treat, immobilize the neck if a neck injury is suspected, monitor for any change in the victim's mental status, and if the victim is conscious, treat him for shock by slightly elevating the head and keeping him warm. If the victim is unconscious, treat him for shock by laying him on his side (to avoid aspiration of vomit).

INJURIES TO THE SPINE
Signs and symptoms of a spinal injury include pain, numbness, tingling, decreased sensation or lack of feeling in extremities, and the inability to move the body below the injury site. To treat, immobilize the neck and body if spinal injury is suspected (any firm flat surface will do) and treat for shock.

INJURIES TO THE ABDOMEN
Signs and symptoms of an abdominal injury include bleeding, abdominal wall bruising, pain, drowsiness, nausea, and vomiting. An open wound where intestines are exposed should be covered and care taken to prevent drying. To treat an open intestinal wound, rinse away any dirt and debris with a mixture of sterile water and salt (1 quart of sterile water mixed with 1 teaspoon of salt). After cleaning the area, cover it with a clean, wet dressing, using the above solution. It's extremely important to prevent the intestines from drying out. Both open and closed abdominal injuries should be treated for shock (see Shock).

INJURIES TO THE CHEST
Signs and symptoms of a chest injury can vary tremendously depending on the cause or problem. As a general rule subjects may have pain, cough

and shortness of breath, irregular breathing pattern (rapid or slow), anxiety, and cyanosis (bluing around lips and fingers). An open chest wound should be covered with a piece of plastic or other airtight material (dressing may be used but it isn't as effective). Tape the covering on three sides, allowing air to escape but not enter the opening. If the subject's breathing pattern worsens, remove the patch. Both open and closed chest injuries should be treated for shock.

CLOSED FRACTURES
Signs and symptoms of a closed fracture include site deformity, swelling, pain, and an inability to bear weight on the effected extremity. To treat, clean all open wounds and apply a splint that immobilizes the extremity one joint above and below the fracture site. A splint can be improvised by using strong branches that are held in place with 1-inch-wide bands of clothing or similar material. Once you have applied a splint, monitor for any changes in circulation or sensation. When in doubt about whether something is broken or not, treat it as if it is.

OPEN FRACTURES
An open fracture has all the signs and symptoms of a closed fracture with the addition of bone protruding through the skin. Don't push bone ends back in or handle them during the treatment process! To treat, rinse away any dirt and debris with a mixture of sterile water and salt (1 quart of sterile water mixed with 1 teaspoon of salt). After cleaning the bone and the surrounding area, cover the end of the bone with a clean, wet dressing, using the above solution. It's extremely important to prevent the bone ends from drying out. Secure the dressing in place, splint the fracture, and monitor the extremity for any changes in circulation or sensation.

Suspected fractures should be splinted and immobilized.

DISLOCATIONS OF THE SHOULDER

Signs and symptoms of dislocations of the shoulder are shoulder pain with a depression below its anterior tip. In addition, the affected arm is usually rotated slightly outward, with the elbow held away from the side of the body. Attempts to bring the elbow or forearm into the body are met with resistance.

If pain medication is available, use it. It's important to find a rock or other formation that allows the victim to lie on his belly with his arm dangling toward the ground at 90 degrees to his body. Tape or tie a 10- to 20-pound weight to the victim's arm (be sure you don't cut off his distal circulation), and let it pull his arm down toward the ground as he lies flat on the rock or other formation. After fifteen to thirty minutes, the muscle should loosen and allow the bone to slip back into its socket. Sling both the upper arm and forearm close to the body so that the arm and shoulder are completely immobilized.

SPRAINS AND STRAINS

A sprain (area of pain over a joint) will present similar to a closed fracture and should be treated as if a fracture exists. A strain (area of pain over a muscle) will present as localized muscle tenderness and is usually a result of overuse or trauma. To treat, apply moist heat and discontinue the activity that seems to make it worse.

BURNS

Burns are rated by depth as first, second, or third degree, with each showing deeper penetration, respectively. A first-degree burn causes superficial tissue damage (similar in appearance to a sunburn), sparing the underlying skin. A second-degree burn causes damage into the upper portion of the skin, with resultant blister formation surrounded by first-degree burn damage. Third-degree burns cause complete destruction of the skin's full thickness (and beyond). In addition, first- and second-degree burns are usually present. To treat burns, cool the skin as rapidly as possible and for at least 45 minutes. This is extremely important, since many burns continue to cause damage for up to 45 minutes even after the heat source has been removed. Remove clothing and jewelry as soon as possible, but don't remove any clothing that is stuck in the burn. Never cover the burn with grease or fats, as they will only increase the risk for infection and are of no value in the treatment process. Clean the burn with sterile (if available) water, apply antibiotic ointment, and cover it with a clean, loose dressing. To avoid infections, leave the bandage in place for six to eight days. After that time, change the bandage as necessary. If the victim is conscious, fluids are a must. Major burns cause a significant amount of fluid loss, and ultimately the victim will go into shock unless these fluids are replaced. If pain medications are available, use them. Burns are extremely painful.

FOREIGN BODIES IN THE EYE

Most eye injuries encountered in the wilderness are a result of dust or dirt blown into the eye by the wind. Signs and symptoms include red and irritated eye, light sensitivity, and pain in the affected eye. To treat, first look for any foreign bodies that might be causing the irritation. The most common site where dirt or dust can be found is just under the upper eyelid, and it's worth inverting the lid and trying to isolate and remove the irritant. If unable to isolate the cause, rinse the affected eye with clean water for at least ten to fifteen minutes. To avoid contaminating the uninjured eye, make sure the injured eye is lower during the rinsing process. If available, apply ophthalmic antibiotic ointment to the affected eye.

WOUNDS, LACERATIONS, AND INFECTIONS

Clean all wounds, lacerations, and infections, and apply antibiotic ointment, dressing, and bandage daily.

BLISTERS

Blisters result from the constant rubbing of your skin against a sock or boot. The best treatment is prevention. Monitor your feet for hot spots or areas that become red and inflamed. If you develop a hot spot, apply a wide band of adhesive tape across and well beyond the affected area. If you have tincture of benzoin, use it. It will make the tape adhere better, and it also helps toughen the skin. To treat a blister, cut a blister-size hole in the center of a piece of moleskin, and place it on the area of concern so that the hole is directly over the blister. This will take the pressure off the blister and place it on the surrounding moleskin. Try to avoid popping the blister; if it does break open, treat it as an open wound by applying antibiotic ointment and a bandage.

THORNS, SPLINTERS, AND SPINES

Thorns and splinters are often easy to remove. Cactus spines, however, hook into the skin, and in most cases you'll need a pair of tweezers or pliers to get them out. If you can't pull the spines out, don't panic. They often come out on their own over a several-day period. Regardless of removal, prevent infection by applying antibiotic ointment, a dressing, and a bandage.

FISH HOOK INJURIES

A fish hook can be left in place for short periods of time, provided rescue is coming. If rescue is not expected within several hours, however, it should be removed. The easiest way to do this is to advance it forward until the barb clears the skin, cut the barb off, and reverse the hook back out.

ENVIRONMENTAL INJURIES AND ILLNESSES

The environment challenges us in many different ways, and it needs to be respected. Realize it cannot be conquered. Adapting and being properly prepared will play a significant role in surviving nature's sometimes awesome power.

HEAT INJURIES

Heat injuries can be broken down into heat rash, sunburn, muscle cramps, heat exhaustion, heat stroke, and hyponatremia.

Heat rash

Heat rashes often occur in moist, covered areas. These red bumpy irritants can be pretty uncomfortable. To treat, keep the area clean and dry and air it out as much as you can. If you have 1 percent hydrocortisone cream, apply a thin layer to the rash twice a day.

Sunburn

Sunburns should be prevented by wearing protective clothing and using a strong sunscreen whenever necessary. If a burn occurs, apply cool compresses, avoid further exposure, and cover any areas that have or may become burned.

Muscle cramps

Muscle cramps are a result of excessive salt loss from the body, exposure to a hot climate, or excessive sweating. Painful muscle cramps usually occur in the calf or abdomen, while the victim's body temperature is normal. To treat, immediately stretch the affected muscle. The best way to prevent reoccurrence is to consume 2 to 3 quarts of water with minimal activity and 4 to 6 quarts of water when in cold or hot environments or perhaps even more during heavy activity.

Heat exhaustion

Heat exhaustion is a result of physical activity in a hot environment and is usually accompanied by some component of dehydration. Signs and symptoms include feeling faint or weak, cold and clammy skin, headache, nausea, and confusion. To treat, rest in a cool, shady area and consume plenty of water. Since heat exhaustion is a form of shock, the victim should lie down and elevate his feet 8 to 12 inches.

Heatstroke

Heatstroke occurs when the body is unable to adequately lose its heat. As a result, body temperature rises to such high levels that damage to the brain and vital organs occurs. Signs and symptoms include flushed dry skin, headache, weakness, lightheadedness, rapid full pulse, confusion, and in severe cases, unconsciousness and convulsions are common. Heatstroke is a true emergency and should be avoided at all costs. Immediate treatment is imperative. Immediately cool the victim by removing his clothing and covering him with wet towels or by submersion in cool but not icy water. Fanning is also helpful. Be careful to avoid cooling to the point of hypothermia.

Hyponatremia

Hyponatremia is potentially fatal and can occur under extremely hot conditions. Hyponatremia is caused by a lack of sodium in the blood and frequently occurs when someone drinks too much water while losing high levels of body salt through sweating. Symptoms are dizziness, confusion, cramps, nausea, vomiting, fatigue, frequent urination, and in extreme conditions, coma and even death. To treat, stop all activity, move to a shaded area, treat for shock, and have the victim eat salty foods along with small quantities of lightly salted water or sports drinks. If the victim develops an altered mental alertness or alertness decreases, seek immediate help!

COLD INJURIES

Hypothermia

Hypothermia is a result of an abnormally low body temperature. Heat is lost through radiation, conduction (touch), evaporation, convection (air movement across body), and respiration. Signs and symptoms of hypothermia include uncontrollable shivering, slurred speech, abnormal behavior, fatigue and drowsiness, decreased hand and body coordination, and a weakened respiration and pulse. The best treatment is prevention through avoiding exposure and early recognition. Dressing appropriately for the environment and maintaining adequate hydration can help you avoid most problems with hypothermia. If hypothermia does occur, it should be treated without delay. First stop continued heat loss. Get out of the wind and moisture, and put on dry clothes, a hat, and gloves. If you have a sleeping bag, take off your clothes, fluff the bag, and climb inside. If it's an extreme case, someone else should disrobe and climb inside the bag with you. If conscious, the victim should consume warm fluids and carbohydrates.

Frostbite

The best treatment for frostbite, which commonly affects toes, fingers, and face, is prevention. Using the COLDER acronym (covered in chapter 8) and understanding how heat is lost are two methods of ensuring frostbite doesn't occur. The two types of frostbite are superficial or deep. Superficial frostbite causes cold, numb, and painful extremities that appear white or grayish in color. To treat, rewarm the affected part with your own body heat (hands should be placed in the armpits; feet on another person's abdomen). Cover other exposed areas with loose, layered material. Never blow on your hands, since the resultant moisture will cause the skin to freeze or refreeze. Deep frostbite causes your skin to take on a white appearance, lose feeling, and become extremely hard. Should you sustain a deep frostbite injury, don't attempt to rewarm it. Rewarming it will be extremely painful, and if the frostbitten area is a limb, it will be rendered useless (you can walk on a frostbitten limb). Be sure to prevent any further freezing and injury from occurring by wearing proper clothing and avoiding further exposure to the elements.

IMMERSION INJURIES (TRENCH FOOT)
Trench feet are a direct result of long-term exposure to cold, wet socks. It usually takes several days to weeks of this exposure before the damage occurs. Signs and symptoms include painful, swollen feet or hands that have a dishpan appearance. Since immersion injuries can be so debilitating, it's best to avoid them all together by changing wet socks quickly, not wearing tight clothing, and increasing foot circulation with regular massages. If trench foot develops, treat it by keeping the feet dry and elevated. Since rubbing may result in further tissue damage, pat wet feet dry.

SNOW AND SUN BLINDNESS
Snow and sun blindness is a result of exposing your eyes to the sun's ultraviolet rays. It's most often seen in areas where the sun's reflected off snow, water, or light-colored rocks. The resultant burn to the eyes' surface can be quite debilitating. Signs and symptoms include bloodshot and tearing eyes, painful and gritty sensation in eyes, light sensitivity, and headaches. Prevention by wearing 100 percent UV sunglasses is a must, but if snow blindness does occur, treat it by avoiding further exposure, applying a cool wet compress to the eyes, and treating the pain with aspirin as needed. If symptoms are severe, apply an eye patch for twenty-four to forty-eight hours.

ALTITUDE ILLNESS
As your elevation increases, so does your risk of developing a form of altitude illness. As a general rule, most mountaineers use the following three levels of altitude to determine their potential for medical problems: high altitude, 8,000 to 14,000 feet; very high altitude, 14,000 to 18,000 feet; extreme high altitude, 18,000 feet and above. Since most travelers seldom venture to heights greater than 14,000 feet, the majority of altitude illnesses are seen in the high altitude, 8,000- to 14,000-foot range.

As your altitude increases, your body goes through a compensatory change, which is noted by an increased respiratory and heart rate, increased red blood cell and capillary production, and changes in the body's oxygen delivery capacity. Most of these changes occur within several days to weeks of exposure at high altitudes. To diminish the impact of altitude, ascend gradually, avoid heavy exertion for several days after rapidly ascending to high altitudes, ingest only small amounts of salt, and if you have a history of pulmonary edema or worse, consider taking Diamox (Acetaxolamide). Diamox is a prescription medication contraindicated for individuals with kidney, eye, or liver disease. The usual dose is 250 mg taken two to four times a day. It's started twenty-four to forty-eight hours prior to ascent and continued, while at high altitude, for forty-eight hours or as long as needed.

High altitude illnesses are a direct result of a reduction in the body's oxygen supply. This reduction occurs in response to the decreased atmospheric pressure that's associated with higher elevations. The three illnesses of high altitude are acute mountain sickness, high altitude pulmonary edema, and high altitude cerebral edema.

Acute mountain sickness
Acute mountain sickness is a group of unpleasant symptoms that usually occur as a result of decreased oxygen supply to the brain at altitudes greater than 8,000 feet. Signs and symptoms include headache, fatigue, dizziness, shortness of breath, decreased appetite, nausea and vomiting, feeling of uneasiness, cyanosis (bluing around lips and fingers), fluid retention in the face and hands, and in severe cases, evidence of some impaired mental function (forgetfulness, memory loss, decreased coordination, hallucinations, and psychotic behavior). To treat, allow time to acclimatize by keeping activity to a minimum for the first two to three days after arriving at elevations greater than 8,000 feet, avoid alcohol and tobacco, eat a small, high carbohydrate diet, and drink plenty of fluids. If symptoms are severe and oxygen is available, give 2 liters per minute through a face mask for a minimum of fifteen minutes. If symptoms persist or worsen, then descend at least 2,000 to 3,000 feet (this is usually enough to relieve symptoms).

High altitude pulmonary edema (HAPE)
This is an extremely common and dangerous type of altitude illness that results from abnormal accumulation of fluid in the lungs. It most often occurs when a climber rapidly ascends above 8,000 feet and immediately

begins performing strenuous activities. Signs and symptoms of high altitude pulmonary edema include shortness of breath with exertion (may
progress to shortness of breath at rest), shortness of breath when lying
down (making it hard to sleep), and a dry cough that progresses to a wet
productive and persistent cough. If symptoms progress, the climber may
develop impaired mental function similar to those seen in acute mountain
sickness. If the climber becomes unconscious, death will occur within
several hours unless quick descent and oxygen treatment is started. An
early diagnosis is the key to successfully treating pulmonary edema. If
you think someone has HAPE, immediately descend a minimum of 2,000
to 3,000 feet or until symptoms begin to improve. Once down, rest for two
to three days, and allow the fluid that has accumulated in the lung to be
reabsorbed by the body. If oxygen is available, administer it using a tight-
fitting face mask at a flow rate of 4 to 6 liters per minute for fifteen minutes, and then decrease its flow rate to 2 liters per minute. Continue using
the oxygen for an additional twelve hours if possible. If the victim has
moderate to severe HAPE, he should be evacuated to the nearest hospital
as soon as possible. If prone to HAPE, it may be worth trying Diamox
prior to the climb. As discussed earlier, this is a prescription medication
and needs to be discussed with your primary care provider prior to its use.

High altitude cerebral edema (HACE)

High altitude cerebral edema is swelling or edema of the brain, and it
most often occurs at altitudes greater than 12,000 feet. Edema forms as a
consequence of the body's decreased supply of oxygen, known as hypoxia.
Symptoms specific to HACE include those seen with acute mountain sickness, severe headache, abnormal mental function (confusion, loss of memory, poor judgment, and hallucinations), ataxia (poor coordination), coma,
and death. Early recognition is of the utmost importance in saving someone who develops HACE. If someone has a severe chronic headache with
confusion or ataxia, he must be treated for high altitude cerebral edema—
a true emergency. To treat, descend immediately. If the victim is ataxic or
confused, he will need help. If oxygen is available, administer it—via a
tight-fitting face mask—at 4 to 6 liters per minute for fifteen minutes, and
then decrease its flow rate to 2 liters per minute. Continue using the oxygen for an additional twelve hours if possible. Even if the victim recovers,
he shouldn't return to the climb. If he's unconscious or has severe symp-

toms, all efforts should be made for an air evacuation to the nearest hospital.

BOWEL DISTURBANCES

Bowel disturbances in the wilderness are common and include diarrhea and constipation. Diarrhea is a very common occurrence in a survival situation. In the desert, diarrhea can predispose you to dehydration and hyponatremia. Some common causes are change in water and food consumption, drinking contaminated water, eating spoiled food or eating off dirty dishes, and fatigue or stress. Diarrhea is almost always self-limiting, and unless you have anti-diarrhea medications, treatment should consist of supportive care. To treat, consume clear liquids for twenty-four hours, and then follow with another twenty-four hours of clear liquids plus bland foods. Constipation is also common in a survival setting. The treatment is to drink fluids and exercise. Laxatives are contraindicated and rarely needed.

SNAKE, LIZARD, AND ANIMAL BITES

Snakebites

Although snakebites are seldom poisonous, you should treat all as if they are unless you can positively identify the snake as nonpoisonous. Of those that are poisonous, however, few are ever fatal or debilitating. Poisonous snakebites are often categorized as hemotoxic (damaging blood vessels and causing hemorrhage) or neurotoxic (paralyzing nerve centers that control respiration and heart action). Common signs that envenomation has occurred include some of the following.

Hemotoxic envenomation (rattlesnake, puff adder, sidewinder, sand viper, horned viper)

Immediate: One or more fang marks and bite-site burning.

5 to 10 minutes: Mild to severe swelling at the bite site.

30 to 60 minutes: Numbness and tingling of the lips, face, fingers, toes, and scalp occurs. If these symptoms occur immediately following a bite, they are likely due to anxiety and hyperventilation.

30 to 90 minutes: Twitching of the mouth, face, neck, eye, and bitten extremity occur. In addition, the victim may develop a metallic or rubbery taste in the mouth.

1 to 2 hours: Sweating, weakness, nausea, vomiting, chest tightness, rapid breathing, increased heart rate, palpitations, headache, chills, confusion, and fainting often occur.

2 to 3 hours: The area begins to appear bruised and often develops large blood blisters within 6 to 10 hours.

6 to 12 hours: Difficulty breathing, increased internal bleeding, and collapse.

Neurotoxic envenomation (coral snake, cobra, kraits, mambas)

Immediate: Bite-site burning may or may not occur and only a small amount of localized bruising and swelling is often noted.

Within 90 minutes: Numbness and weakness of the bitten extremity.

1 to 3 hours: Twitching, nervousness, drowsiness, giddiness, increased salivation, and drooling often occur.

5 to 10 hours: Slurred speech, double vision, difficulty talking and swallowing, and impaired breathing.

10 hours or more: Death is often the end result without medical intervention.

Snakebite treatment centers on getting the victim to a medical facility as fast as you safely can. In doing so, follow these basic treatment guidelines to increase survivability.

1. Stop, lie down, and stay still. Physical activity will actually increase the spread of venom.
2. Move out of the snake's range, and if you can, try to identify what type it is (safely). If you can kill the snake, do so, and bring it along for identification purposes. Be sure to protect yourself from accidental poisoning by cutting the head off and burying it. For details on how to kill a snake, refer to chapter 9.
3. Remove the toxin as soon as possible using a mechanical suction device (in accordance with the manufacturer's instructions) or by squeezing for 30 minutes.
4. Remove all jewelry and restrictive clothing.
5. Clean the wound, and apply a dressing and bandage to the site. If the bite is on an extremity and you are more than two hours from a medical

facility, use a pressure dressing over the wound or constrictive band (not a tourniquet) placed 2 inches above the site (between it and the heart). This will help restrict the spread of the poison.

Pressure dressing: Place a clean dressing over the bite, and cover it with an elastic wrap that encircles the extremity. The wrap should be about 10 inches wide and placed so that it is centered firmly on top of the bite site. Although it should be snug, make sure it isn't so tight that it cuts off the circulation to the fingers and toes. Nail bed capillary refill should return within 2 to 3 seconds, and the victim should have normal feeling beyond the dressing site.

Constrictive band: A constrictive band is not a tourniquet. It merely slows down the flow in the superficial veins and lymph system. Use any material that allows you to create a 4-inch band and wrap it around the extremity so that it is between the bite and the heart. If limb swelling makes the band too tight, it can be advanced up the extremity.

6. Splint the extremity, and keep it positioned below the level of the heart.
7. Drink small amounts of water.
8. Transport the victim to the nearest hospital.

Things you shouldn't do when treating a snake bite

Don't cut and suck. This will hasten the spread of the poison and expose the small blood vessels under the aid-giver's tongue to the venom.

Do not apply ice to the wound. Circulation to the site is already an issue, and applying ice may cause symptoms similar to severe frostbite.

Do not pour alcoholic beverages on the site.

The best treatment for snakebite is not to get one! Avoid known habitats like rocky ledges and woodpiles, and if you see a snake, leave it alone unless you intend to kill it for food (read chapter 9 for guidance on how to procure a snake safely). Carry a walking stick that can be used for protection, and wear boots and appropriate full-length pants.

Lizard bites

The Gila monster and its venomous cousin, the Mexican bearded lizard, are the only two known species of venomous lizards. Both are similar in appearance and habits, but the Mexican bearded lizard is slightly larger and darker. The Gila monster averages 18 inches in length and has a large head, stout body, short legs, strong claws, and a thick tail that acts as a food reservoir. Its skin is course and beadlike with a marbled coloring that combines brown or black with orange, pink, yellow, or dull white. Most of the lizard's teeth have two grooves that guide the venom, a nerve toxin, from glands in the lower jaw. The venom enters the wound as the lizard chews on its victim. Although it can be fatal to humans, it usually isn't. Treatment for lizard bites is the same as that for a snake.

Animal bites

Thoroughly clean the site and treat it as any other open wound.

INSECTS, CENTIPEDES, SPIDERS, AND SCORPIONS

Any sting or bite that cannot be identified should be cleaned and antihistamines used when appropriate. If a stinger is present, it should be removed using whatever means are suitable. Monitor for secondary infection, and treat with antibiotics if infection occurs. Several specific concerns are covered below.

Bees or wasps

If stung, immediately remove the stinger by scraping the skin at a 90-degree angle with a knife or your fingernail. This will decrease the amount of venom that is absorbed into the skin. Applying cold compresses or a cool paste made of mud or ashes will help relieve the itching. To avoid infection, don't scratch the stinger site. If carrying a bee sting kit, review the procedures of its use prior to departing for the wilderness. If someone has an allergic anaphylactic reaction, it will be necessary to act fast. Using the medications in the bee sting kit and following basic first-aid principles will, in most cases, reverse the symptoms associated with this type of reaction.

Ants

Ants, especially fire ants, can produce a very painful bite that often leaves small, clear blisters on the skin. The biggest concern outside of pain is avoidance of secondary infection. Clean the bite with soap and water, and use antihistamines if needed. If an infection occurs, treat as any other infection. If allergic, use a bee sting kit, and seek immediate medical attention.

Ticks
Remove the tick by grasping it at the base of its body (where its mouth attaches to the skin) and applying gentle backward pressure until it releases its hold. If its head isn't removed, apply antibiotic ointment, bandage, and treat as any other open wound.

Mosquitoes and flies
Use insect repellant, and cover the body's exposed parts with clothing or mud to decrease the number of bites you'll experience from these pesky insects.

Centipedes and millipedes
Centipedes inject venom using fanglike front legs; millipedes have toxins on their bodies that, when touched, are highly irritating. Both can cause redness, swelling, and pain to the bite site. If bitten, clean the area with soap and water and use pain medications if needed.

Spiders
The greatest spider risk for North American travelers comes from the black widow and brown recluse.

Black widow
The black widow's venom is fifteen times as toxic as the venom of the prairie rattlesnake, and it is considered the most venomous spider in North America. However, black widow spiders only inject a relatively small amount of venom and are not usually deadly to adults. Only the female spider is venomous. The black widow is shiny black and often has a reddish hourglass shape on the underside of her spherical abdomen. Her body is about 1½ inches long. Adult males are harmless, about half the female's size, with smaller bodies, longer legs, and usually yellow and red bands and spots over the back. The black widow's bite may be painless and go unnoticed. Symptoms may include muscle cramps (to include

The female black widow has a reddish hourglass on its abdomen.

abdomen), sweating, swollen eyelids, nausea, vomiting, headache, and hypertension. Persons younger than 16 and older than 60, especially those with heart conditions, may require hospital stays. Healthy people recover rapidly in two to five days. To treat, clean the site well with soap and water. Apply a cool compress over the bite location, and keep the affected limb elevated to about heart level.

Brown recluse
The brown recluse spider is ¼ to ½ inch long, has a yellowish to brown color, and sports a distinct violin-shaped patch on its head and midregion. Its bite causes a long-lasting sore that involves tissue death and takes months to heal. In some instances, its bite can become life threatening. The bite initially causes mild stinging or burning and is quickly followed by ulcerative necrosis that develops within several hours to weeks. The initial sore is often red, edematous, or blanched, and often it develops a blue-gray halo around the puncture. As time passes, the lesion may evolve into ashen pustules or fluid-filled lesions surrounded by red patchy skin. After several days the tissue begins to die. Other symptoms include fever, weakness, rash, muscle and joint pain, vomiting, and diarrhea. To treat, clean the site with soap and water, immobilize the site, apply a local com-

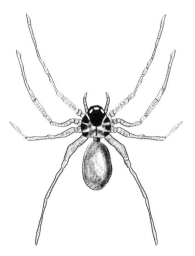

The brown recluse has a violin-shaped patch on its head and midregion.

press, and provide for pain control. The bite site ultimately needs rapid debridement, and transport to a medical facility should be done soon.

Scorpions

Scorpions are among the best-adapted creatures to the desert climates. They have a flat, narrow body, two lobsterlike claws, eight legs, and a segmented abdominal tail. Their upward- and forward-curved tail has a venomous stinger that is supplied by a pair of poison glands. Most scorpions are tan to brown in color and can range from 1 to 8 inches in length. Most scorpion stings are painful but not fatal to humans. Besides pain, other symptoms may include swelling at the site of the sting, numbness, muscle twitching, difficulties in breathing, and convulsions. Death is rare. There are a few species (approximately twenty worldwide) that can be potentially fatal, but survival rates are generally high. A scorpion's poison is neurotoxic, and treatment should follow that of a neurotoxic snakebite.

COLD OR FLU

Treating a cold or flu in the wilderness is no different than treating it at home. The problem arises in trying to ensure that you get adequate fluids, rest, and warmth. Be sure to protect yourself from the elements.

SURVIVAL STRESS

The effects of stress upon a survival situation cannot be understated. To decrease its magnitude, you must not only understand it but also prevail over it. The most important key to overcoming these survival stresses is the survivor's will. The will or drive to survive is not something that can be taught. However, your will is directly affected by the amount of stress associated with a survival situation.

SURVIVAL STRESSORS

The environment, your condition, and the availability of materials will either raise or decrease the amount of stress you'll experience.

Environmental influences

Three environmental conditions directly affect your survival: climate (temperature, moisture, and wind); terrain (mountainous, desert, jungle, or arctic); and life forms (plants and animals). Sadly, many people have perished when these influences have been unfavorable. In other situations, however, survivors have been successful in either adapting to the given conditions or traveling to another location that better meets their needs. Understanding how the environment might affect you is the first step to overcoming the unpredictable hardships of nature.

Your physical and mental condition

Both the physical and psychological stresses of survival will directly affect your outlook and may even dictate the order in which you meet your needs. To prioritize your needs properly, it is important to make decisions based on logic and not emotion. Recognizing the physical and psychological stresses of survival is the first step to ensuring that this is done.

Physical stresses

These stresses are brought about by the physical hardships of survival. Overcoming them requires proper preparation. A good rule for all wilderness travelers is the six Ps of survival: Proper prior preparation prevents poor performance. Properly preparing involves ensuring that your immunizations are up-to-date, staying well hydrated both before and during any outback adventure, and being physically fit prior to traveling into the wilderness.

Psychological stresses
The amount of time a survivor goes without rescue will have a significant impact upon his will or drive to survive. As time passes, the survivor's hopes of being found ultimately begin to diminish. With decreased hope comes increased psychological stress. The basic stresses that affect the survivor psychologically are pain, hunger and thirst, heat or cold, fatigue, loneliness, and fear.

Availability of materials
The materials available to meet your needs include both what you have with you and what you can find in the surrounding environment. It's unlikely that a lone survivor will have all the necessary tools and equipment to meet all of his survival needs.

Overcoming survival stress
The most important key to surviving is the survivor's will. The will or drive to survive is not something that can be taught. However, your will is directly affected by the amount of stress associated with a survival situation. Prior preparation and using the three-step approach to survival (stop, identify your needs and prioritize them, and improvise) will help alleviate some of this stress.

Prior preparation
Take the time to prepare for each outing. Leave a detailed trip outline along with return times with someone you can trust. Carry gear specific to the trip, and make sure your survival kit is adequate. Be fit for the adventure. Failing to prepare is preparing to fail. Keep the odds in your favor by taking a little extra time to think the trip through and develop contingencies should things go wrong.

Stop
Stop what you're doing, clear your thoughts, and focus on the problem. Are you lost? Do you have a physical problem that prevents further move-

ment? No matter what the problem is, stop, clear your thoughts, and begin looking at possible solutions.

Identify and Prioritize Your Needs

Recall the five basic elements of survival: personal protection, signaling, sustenance, travel, and health. Recognizing and prioritizing these essentials

During training to become a USAF SERE (survival instructor), Greg Davenport underwent extreme physical and psychological stress.

will help alleviate many of the fears you may have. The exact order in which they're met will depend upon the effects of the surrounding environment. In addition, your conditions, availability of materials, the expected duration of stay, and the given situation all affect how you meet your needs. For example, shelter is of higher priority in an arctic environment than in a mild climate; in the desert, search for water takes on an especially high priority. Take the time to logically plan how to meet your needs, allowing for adjustments as necessary. Through this process, you can greatly diminish the potentially harmful effects of Mother Nature.

Improvise
Improvising is a method of constructing equipment that can be used to meet your needs. With creativity and imagination, you should be able to improvise the basic survival necessities. This will increase your chances of survival and decrease the amount of stress. For more details on the five-step improvising process refer to chapter 12.

SURVIVAL TIPS
If you take care of your five survival essentials, health needs should not be an issue. For example, properly meeting your personal protection needs will decrease the odds of environmental injuries (cold and hot injuries). In addition, using the three-step approach to survival will decrease the effects of psychological stress and make you feel more confident about your outcome.

Faith (perhaps the greatest motivator), fear, and pride are three examples of what people have used to overcome what appeared to be insurmountable. Several years back I met a man who told me that his sole motivation for rescue was that his wife had the checkbook. Although I can't verify the validity of his story, I did find it amusing. What motivates you? Whatever it is, you'll need to learn to harness it and allow it to produce the energy needed to overcome your preconceived limits.

8

Personal Protection

Personal protection consists of three distinct categories: clothing, shelter, and fire. Each plays a vital role in protecting us from the harsh realities that can be dealt by nature. Clothing is your first line of defense against the environment, shelter your second, and fire your third. They should be met in this order. Don't spend all day trying to build a bow and drill fire and end up sleeping in a substandard shelter.

CLOTHING

As heat is lost or gained through radiation, conduction, convection, evaporation, and respiration, you'll need to adjust your clothing to help maintain your body's core temperature.

HOW HEAT IS GAINED OR LOST

The body loses or gains heat through radiation, conduction, convection, evaporation, and respiration. Understanding how each occurs is key to prevention.

Radiation

Heat transfers from the environment to your body or vice versa through the process of radiation. The greatest causes of radiant heat gain are the ambient air (sunlight) and heat reflection (sun's rays bouncing off of the ground). The head, neck, and hands pose the greatest threat for heat loss due to radiation. Adding layered clothing will slow the process of heat loss but doesn't stop it from occurring.

Conduction

Body heat is gained when you contact any item that is hotter than you are. If the item is cooler, then the opposite occurs—you lose body heat. The

Your body absorbs heat from sunlight and the sun's rays bouncing off the ground.

greatest cause of conduction heat gain is a result of contact with sand and rock. During the day, this exposure should be minimized. On cold nights, however, a rock may harbor enough heat to use as an added means of staying warm. Heat loss from conduction is often a result of getting wet. Don't get wet, but if this does occur, change into dry clothing. If you don't have a change of clothing, wring out as much moisture as possible and, if able, dry yourself and your clothing by a fire.

Convection
Convection is a process of heat loss from the body to the surrounding colder air. But unlike radiation, heat loss due to convection would not occur if you were standing completely still and there was absolutely no

wind. The wind and your movements cause you to lose heat from convection. Wearing clothes in a loose and layered fashion will help trap the warm air next to your body, which in turn decreases the heat lost from convection and also insulates you from the environment.

Evaporation

Heat is lost through the evaporative process that occurs with perspiration. Since heat loss equates to calorie loss, it should be avoided as much as possible. Monitoring your activity to ensure you avoid sweating will help. If you are inactive, light layered clothing will trap dead air that will decrease the amount of heat lost through evaporation and keep you warmer on cold days (warm air will stay close to the body) and cooler on hot days (the layers decrease the amount of UV penetration).

Respiration

Heat is lost through the normal process of breathing. One method of decreasing this type of heat loss is to cover or encircle your mouth with a

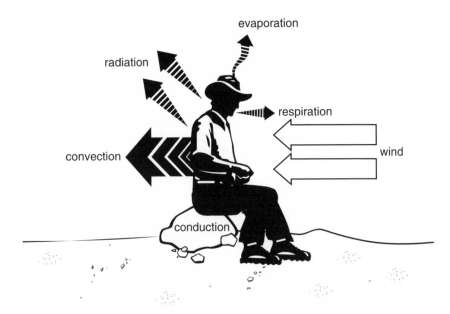

How heat is lost

loose cloth. By doing this, you will trap dead air and allow it to warm up slightly prior to breathing it in.

UNDERSTANDING YOUR CLOTHES

The body is constantly regulating itself in an attempt to keep its thermostat between approximately 97 and 99 degrees F. Your clothes are the first line of protection that keeps you in this fine temperature balance. In hot climates, your clothes decreases the risk of sunburn, help keep you cool by trapping dead air, and when light-colored, reflect heat away from the body. In cold climates, your clothes protect you from cold and wet conditions. I normally wear three loose-fitting layers, which allow for better insulation from cold and heat: one that wicks moisture away, an insulating layer, and an outer shell. The ability to take a layer off or add it back when needed is like having a thermostat that can be adjusted for the changing weather and conditions around you.

Wicking layer

Perspiration and moisture wick through this layer, keeping you dry. This is a very important layer since wet clothes next to the skin cause twenty-five times more heat loss than dry ones. Polyester and polypropylene are best for this layer. Cotton is not recommended.

Insulating layer

This layer traps air next to the body. Multiple layers may work better than one due to their ability to trap additional air between them. The best fabrics for this layer are wool, polyester pile, compressed polyester fleece, Hollofil, Quallofil, Polarguard, Thinsulate, Microloft, and Primaloft. Down can be used in dry climates or when you know it won't get wet. In cold climates I often wear two middle layers, creating another dead air space and providing a finer ability to adjust my layers.

Outer shell

This layer protects you from wind and precipitation. The ideal shell will protect you from getting wet when exposed to rain or snow and have enough ventilation for body moisture to escape. Best for this layer are waterproof coatings that breathe or laminated waterproof membranes that breathe (Gore-Tex). Headgear and gloves are a must—one-third to one-half of body heat loss occurs from the head and hands.

Clothes are made from both natural and synthetic fabrics. Natural fabrics include cotton, down, and wool. Examples of synthetic materials are polyester, polypropylene, and nylon.

Natural fabrics

Cotton

Cotton is commonly referred to as "death cloth" since it loses almost all of its insulating quality when wet. Cotton has extremely poor wicking qualities, takes forever to dry, and when wet it absorbs many times its weight. Although cotton may work well during a hot desert day, it doesn't under almost all other circumstances. Do not wear cotton.

Down

Down is a very good lightweight and natural insulating material. However, like cotton, down becomes virtually worthless when wet. Once wet, the feathers clump together and no longer trap dead air. The material is best used in dry climates or when you can guarantee it won't get wet.

Wool

Wool retains most of its insulating quality when wet. It also retains a lot of the moisture, however, making it extremely heavy when wet. Wool is fairly effective at protecting you from the wind, making it a good choice for an outer layer. Its main drawbacks are its weight and bulkiness.

Synthetic fabrics

Polyester and polypropylene

As a wicking layer, these work well, maintain their insulating quality when wet, and dry quickly. As an insulating layer, they are lightweight and compressible. However, unlike wool, these materials are not very effective at protecting you from the wind and are best accompanied by an outer shell. Common examples of polyester that are used for the insulating layer are polyester pile and fleece.

Polarguard, Hollofil, Quallofil, etc.

Although these synthetic fibers are most often used in sleeping bags, they can also be found in heavy parkas. Polarguard is composed of sheets, Hollofil of hollow sheets, and Quallofil of hollow sheets that have holes running through the fibers. Basically Hollofil and Quallofil took Polarguard one step further by creating more insulating dead air space. As with all synthetic fabrics, these materials will dry quickly and retain most of their insulation quality when wet.

Thinsulate, Microloft, Primaloft, etc.

These thin synthetic fibers make an outstanding lightweight insulating material by creating more layers. Thinsulate is the heaviest of the three and is most often used in clothing. Microloft and Primaloft are extremely light and are an outstanding alternative to the lightweight down sleeping bag since they retain their insulation quality when wet.

Nylon

In recent years, nylon has been used in the construction of lightweight breathable short- and long-sleeved shirts. In the past, nylon was used primarily as an outer layer in parkas, rain and wind garments, and mittens. Since nylon is not waterproof, most manufacturers will use either special fabrication techniques or treatments to add the feature (the following refers to parkas, rain and wind garments, and mittens).

Polyurethane coatings

These are inexpensive lightweight coatings that protect from outside moisture, but since they are nonbreathable, they don't allow inside moisture to escape. I'd advise you to only use outer garments with polyurethane coatings when physical exertion is at a minimum.

Waterproof coatings that breathe

When applied to the inside of a nylon shell, these coatings leave billions of microscopic pores (per square inch) that are large enough for inside vapors to escape yet small enough to keep raindrops out. These coats cost more than those with polyurethane but less than garments made using a laminated waterproof membrane that breathes.

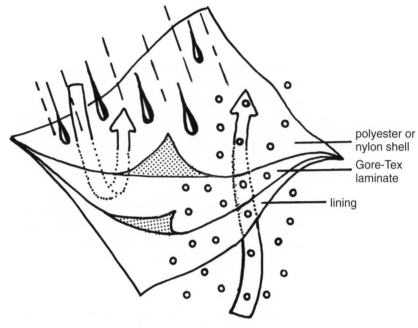

Waterproof breathable nylon

Laminated waterproof membrane that breathes

Instead of an inner coating, these garments have a separate waterproof and breathable membrane laminated to the inside of the nylon. The membrane is perforated with millions of microscopic pores that work under the same principle as the waterproof coating above. Gore-Tex is the most common example.

In order for the breathable fabrics to be effective, you'll need to keep the pores free of dirt and sweat. In addition, only wash and dry them according to the tag instructions, as some will be ruined if cleaned wrong. Finally, don't expect these breathable garments to be perfect. If your heat output is high and you begin to sweat, this moisture cannot escape anymore than the rain can get in. To prevent this, you'll need to wear your clothing in a loose and layered fashion. An acronym I use to help me remember how to care and wear my clothing is COLDER.

COLDER Acronym

C: Clean

Clothes are made of intertwined fibers that, when clean, trap dead air. As the body loses heat, it is trapped inside the dead air space, and that is how clothes keep you cool or warm. The trapped air keeps you cooler when your body's radiant heat is lower than the surrounding air and keeps you warmer when it is higher. If clothes are dirty, they lose their ability to insulate you since they can no longer trap air in a space that is occupied by dirt.

O: Avoid overheating

Clothes absorb sweat (in most cases vapor will pass through). Once they absorb sweat, they lose their insulating quality. In addition, valuable body heat is lost through evaporation when you become overheated.

L: Loose and layered

Clothing that is too tight will constrict circulation and predispose you to frostbite. Multiple layers increase the amount of dead air space surrounding the body. They also allow you to add or remove a layer as necessary for the weather conditions or workload. I normally wear three layers: one that wicks moisture away, an insulating layer, and an outer shell that protects me from wind and moisture.

D: Dry

Wet clothes lose their insulating quality. To keep the inner layer dry, avoid sweating. Protect your outer layer from moisture either by avoiding exposure to rain or snow or by wearing proper clothing as listed above. If your clothes do become wet, dry them by a fire or in the sun. If it's below 32 degrees F and you can't build a fire, let the clothes freeze; once they are frozen, break the ice out of the clothing. If snow is on your clothes, shake it off; don't brush it off, as this will force the moisture into the fibers.

E: Examine

Examine clothes daily for tears, dirt, etc.

Greg Davenport using the COLDER acronym during a trip to northern Montana

R: Repair

Repair any rips and tears as soon as they occur. This may require a needle and thread, so make sure you've packed them.

OUTDOORS CLOTHES

When deciding on what to wear into the outdoors, keep in mind the loose and layered concept. Choose clothes that wick moisture away, insulate, and protect you from the wind and precipitation. A few basics about outdoor clothes are outlined here. This list is not all-inclusive. Take the time to see what's available and meets the needs of your activity before departing on a trip. Remember, your clothes are your first line of personal protection.

Parka and rain pants

A lightweight parka and rain pants provide protection from moisture and wind. They are normally made from nylon that has a polyurethane coating, a waterproof coating that breathes, or a laminated waterproof membrane that breathes (Gore-Tex). In some cases a parka comes with an insulating garment that can be zipped inside. The parka weight you choose depends on the area you are traveling in. Regardless of which material is used or how heavy the parka is, it should meet the following criteria.

Size

Find one big enough for you to comfortably add wicking and insulating layers underneath without compromising your movement. In addition, the parka's lower end should extend beyond your hips to keep wind and moisture away from the top of your pants.

Zippers

The last thing you want is a zipper that doesn't work. Under mild conditions this may not present a great problem. In a wet and cold weather climate, however, a lot of heat is lost when a garment is left unzipped. Buy clothes made with zippers that have polyester teeth that won't rust or freeze, a dual separating system that separates at both ends, and a baffle or backing that has a waterproof coating (both help waterproof the seam).

Ventilation adjustment

For parkas, the openings should be located in front, at your waist, under your arms, and at your wrist. For pants, the openings should be located in the front and along the outside of the lower legs (extending to about mid-calf, making it easier to add or remove your boots). For females, some pants have a zipper that extends down and around the crotch. These openings can be adjusted with zippers, Velcro, or drawstrings.

Sealed seams

Seams that are not taped or well bonded will allow moisture to penetrate through the clothing.

Accessible pockets
What good is a pocket if you can't get to it? In addition, make sure the opening has a protective rain baffle.

Brimmed hood
The brim will help protect you from the sun, and if it rains, it will channel moisture away from the eyes and face.

Shoes and Boots
Boots are a very important part of your clothing, and you should always wear the ones that fit your needs and break them in before your trip. In addition, wear clean, dry socks and immediately apply moleskin to any hot spots that you develop (before they become blisters). When selecting boots, consider the type of travel you intend to do. I have three styles, each of which serves a different purpose. They are leather, lightweight leather/fabric, and rubber.

Leather boots
Leather boots are the ideal all-purpose boot. Under extreme conditions, you'll need to treat them with a waterproofing material (read the manufacturer's directions on how this should be done) and wear a comfortable protective wool-blend sock. Some leather boots come with Thinsulate and a Gore-Tex liner that help protect your feet from the cold and most conditions. If you elect to use Thinsulate or Gore-Tex, be sure you follow the manufacturer's directions on how to care for and treat the boots. If oils soak through the leather and into the lining, they will nullify their insulating qualities.

Lightweight leather and fabric boots
In mild to hot climates I'll often wear a lightweight leather and fabric boot. These boots are lighter and dry faster than leather boots. However, moisture easily soaks through the fabric, and it provides less stability for your ankle. I prefer a lightweight boot that has a ⅛-inch upper made from leather and denier Cordura (which provides great ankle support and circulation), a wicking liner that promotes rapid drying, and a Vibram outsole (for stability on varying terrain).

Rubber boots

The rubber boot is most often used for nontechnical extreme cold weather conditions. They normally have nylon uppers with a molded rubber bottom and a removable felt inner boot.

Like all clothing, boots provide better protection when kept clean. For leather and lightweight leather and fabric boots, wash off dirt and debris using a mild soap that doesn't damage leather. For rubber boots, wash and dry the liners and clean all dirt and debris from the outer boot. If you decide to waterproof the leather boot, make sure to check with the manufacturer on its recommendations regarding what you should use.

Socks

Socks need to provide adequate insulation, reduce friction, and wick and absorb moisture away from the skin. Socks often consist of materials like wool, polyester, nylon, or an acrylic material. As mentioned before, cotton should be avoided since it collapses when wet, losing its insulation qualities. For best results wear two pairs of socks. The inner sock (often made of polyester or silk) wicks the moisture away from the foot; the outer sock provides the insulation that protects your feet (often a wool or synthetic-blend material). Regardless of what sock you decide to wear, make sure you keep your feet dry and change your socks at least once a day.

Gloves and Mittens

Since a fair amount of heat is lost from the hands, it is best to keep them covered. Gloves encase each individual finger, leaving you the dexterity to perform many of your daily tasks. On the flip side, mittens encase the fingers, decreasing your dexterity but increasing hand warmth from the captured radiant hear. The type you wear will depend on the climate and your activity. In mild to moderate weather, I often bring a pair of lightweight fingerless fleece or wool gloves and a larger pair of leather gloves. The fleece gloves protect me during most activity and the leather during times when I am dealing with materials that are sharp or abrasive to my hands. To get the best of both worlds, I often wear gloves when working with my hands and carry mittens. When not working, I insert the gloved hand inside a mitten. My gloves are made from a polyester fleece or a wool/synthetic blend. My mittens are made from a waterproof yet breathable fabric like Gore-Tex.

Headgear

Since over 50 percent of your body heat is lost through the head, you'll need to keep it covered. There are many types of headgear. The climate and your activity will dictate which you choose. As a general rule there are three basic types.

Rain hat

A rain hat is often made from nylon or an insulating material with an outer nylon covering (often Gore-Tex). Adding insulated earflaps makes this hat a good choice for wet and cold conditions.

Insulating hats for cold weather

These insulating hats are made from wool, polypropylene, or polyester fleece. The most common styles of these types of hats are the watch cap and the balaclava. The balaclava is a great option since it can cover the head, ears, and neck (front and back), yet leaves an opening for your face.

Insulating hats for warm weather

These insulating hats are made from a lightweight nylon. The most common styles of these kinds of hats are the neck-draping Sahara and the wide-brimmed bush hats. During the day these hats protect your head, face, and neck from harmful UV rays, and at night they reduce the amount of radiant heat lost from the head.

Since so much heat is lost through the head, removing your hat should always be the last adjustment made when overheating. Mild adjustments—such as opening the zipper to your coat—will create the gradual changes needed to cool you down.

Gaiters

Gaiters protect your legs from moisture, insects, and from getting scratched by low underbrush. They also keep boots free from moisture and dirt. Most gaiters are made of Gore-Tex or similar waterproof materials held together with Velcro, snaps, or a zipper. If a zipper is used, make sure it is strong and that there is a covering protective flap. A full-length gaiter covers your lower leg from the boot's lowest lace to just above the calf muscle.

Eye Protection
Goggles or sunglasses with side shields that filter out UV wavelengths are a must for travel in most environments. It doesn't take long to burn the eyes, and once it happens you will have several days of eye pain along with light sensitivity, tearing, and a foreign-body sensation. Since the symptoms of the burn usually don't show up for four to six hours after the exposure, you can get burned and not even realize it is happening. Once a burn occurs, you'll need to get out of the light, remove contacts if you're wearing them, and cover both eyes with a sterile dressing until the light sensitivity subsides. If pain medication is available, you'll probably need to use it. Once healed, make sure to protect the eyes to prevent another burn. If no goggles or sunglasses are available, improvise by using either a man-made or natural material that covers the eyes and provides a narrow horizontal slit for each eye.

IMPROVISED CLOTHING
In some circumstances you will need to improvise to meet your clothing needs. Provided you can think outside the box, this shouldn't pose much of a problem. A few examples of improvised clothes are listed here.

Improvised layers
Hopefully you'll always have the needed clothing to keep you warm in cold climates. If you don't, consider increasing the middle and outer layers using both man-made and natural resources.

Insulating middle layer
One method of increasing the insulating quality of your clothes can be accomplished by adding dry lichen, moss, or grass between layers. For example, if you have a T-shirt and outer shirt tuck them in and loosely pack the space between them with Mother Nature's insulation material. The new layer traps additional dead air that helps keep you warm.

Outer shell
If you have a garbage bag or space blanket, wrap it around you. This layer will keep you dry and increase the dead air space surrounding your body.

If using the blanket next to a fire at a safe distance, open the front so the fire's heat can get to you.

Immediate-action shoe

During moments of inactivity, cold feet can consume your thoughts. If this is a problem, remove your boots, dry them by a fire, and put on clean, dry socks. If a fire is out of the question, take your boots off, and put on an immediate-action shoe while the boots air-dry. This improvised shoe uses a layered technique. Clean, dry socks are the inner layer; feathers, dry grass, or man-made cushion padding is the middle layer, held in place by a second pair of socks; nylon or a rubber material is used as the outer layer and held in place by cords wrapped around the feet and ankles. If socks are in short supply, cut any appropriate material into a triangle and use it instead of the socks (next to the skin and over the insulation layer). The immediate-action shoe keeps the feet warm so you can focus your thoughts on meeting other survival needs.

Gaiters

The gaiter is a good item to bring. If you didn't, however, there might be a time when you wish you had them, and an improvised gaiter is easy to create. Simply wrap canvas, poncho material, or nylon around the lower leg—from the top of the calf to below the ankle—and hold it in place with cords.

Snowshoes

In the odd circumstance you may find yourself in a snow-laden terrain where your shoes aren't enough to keep you on top of the snow. If you have snowshoes, this isn't a problem. Snowshoes (even improvised ones) help distribute your body weight over a greater surface area, making snow travel much easier. In a crisis, snowshoes can be improvised from boughs. Use boughs from a tree where the smaller branches and needles are thick and abundant, such as fir. Cut five to ten boughs that are each four to five feet long, lash the base of all the branches together, and loosely tie them around their midpoint. Secure the bough snowshoe to your foot by tying a line around the toe of your boot and the forward third of the boughs. If you have more time on your hands, an elaborate trail snowshoe can be improvised using saplings and cords.

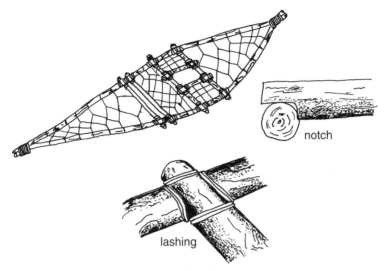

Improvised trail snowshoe

1. Gather two saplings 5 feet long (1 inch in diameter), lay them side by side, and lash them together at each end.
2. Spread the saplings 18 inches back from the front of the snowshoe, and lash a 12-inch stick perpendicular to them. Lash another stick, of similar size, 8 inches beyond the first. (For best results, notch the ends of each stick before lashing.)
3. Lash two more sticks between and perpendicular to the 12-inch ones. Place them approximately 2 inches from each sapling, and don't forget to notch the ends. (The middle space provides an opening for the toe of your boot.)
4. Lash two 10-inch-long sticks to the snowshoe where the heel of your boot rests when the toe is centered in the forward opening. (Once again, notch the sticks for better results.)
5. Incorporate parachute line, nylon line, or other durable material in all other spaces between the two saplings. This will increase the amount of surface area contacting the snow.
6. Using one piece of line, attach the boot to the snowshoe so that it can pivot while you walk. This is done by securing a line to the second stick (from the front) and then wrapping it over the top of the boot and around the heel. Finish by tying the two free ends together.

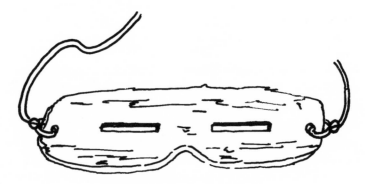

Improvised sun/snow goggles

Sun/Snow Goggles

A good pair of UV protective sunglasses should always be on hand. Sun and snow blindness is debilitating. In the unforeseen circumstance where this threat is high and you don't have sunglasses, improvised goggles can provide needed eye protection. These goggles are made from any shielding material, such as bark, webbing, or leather, cut as long and wide as necessary to cover both eyes. Cut a small horizontal slit at the point where the material is directly over each eye and attach line to both sides of the goggles long enough to tie together when the goggles are worn.

SHELTER

A shelter is your second line of personal protection—an extension of your clothing. Shelters use dead air to insulate you from the climate, keeping you cool in hot weather and warm in cold weather. In addition, a properly built shelter should protect you from the wind and rain. Your circumstances, available materials, and the climate will determine the type of shelter you use.

CAMPSITE SELECTION

The best shelter site location will allow you to easily meet your other survival needs. The ideal site will meet the following conditions:

Location and size
Your site should be level and big enough for both you and your equipment. If close to shore, make sure it is above high-tide mark and at least one dune shoreward beyond the sea.

Optimize the sun's warmth
Position the shelter so that it has a southern exposure if it's north of the equator or a northern exposure if south of it. This allows for optimal light and heat from the sun throughout the day. Try to position the door so that it faces east, since an east side opening will allow for best early-morning sun exposure.

Avoid wind problems
Since wind can wrap over the top of a tent and through its opening, do not place the door in the path of or on the opposite side of the wind's travel. Instead, position the door 90 degrees to the prevailing wind. Avoid building shelters on ridge tops and open areas. When setting up your tent, secure it in place by staking it down. It doesn't take much wind to move or destroy your shelter.

Use the snow's insulation
If in snow, dig down to bare ground whenever possible. The ground's radiant heat and the surrounding snow will help keep you warmer at night.

Water source
To protect your water source, build your shelter and bathroom at least 100 feet or so from a stream or lake.

Safety first
Avoid sites with potential environmental hazards that can wipe out all your hard work in just a matter of seconds. Examples include avalanche slopes; drainage and dry riverbeds with a potential for flash floods; rock formations that might collapse; dead trees that might blow down; overhanging dead limbs; and large animal trails. If near bodies of water, stay above the high-tide mark.

Survival

During an emergency, make sure your camp is located next to a signal and recovery site.

TENT OR BIVOUAC BAG

A tent or bivouac bag provides you with shade, protects you from pesky night creatures that think your sleeping bag is a nice home, and takes little time to put up. If you have a tent or bivouac bag, use it. If not, take the time to build an emergency tarp or natural shelter. For information on tents and bivouac bags refer to chapter 3.

THE BASICS OF SHELTER DESIGN

The environment, materials on hand, and the amount of time available will determine the type of shelter you choose. Regardless of type, you should construct your shelter so that it is safe and durable.

Framework

Ridge and other supporting poles need to be sturdy, wrist diameter, de-stubbed (surface made smooth), and long enough to create the desired

Commercial tent

shelter size. The ridgepole is the main beam—it supports all other structures. Supporting poles often rest on the ridgepole (at a 90-degree angle). Support poles need to be cut so they don't extend beyond the ridgepole. In addition, these poles should be capped using tarp, bark, or other roofing material. Poles that extend beyond the ridgepole allow moisture to track down into the shelter. If using a tarp, support poles may or may not be needed. For nontarp shelters, you can increase the strength of the overall structure by weaving sapling-sized branches between the supporting poles (at 90 degrees).

Roof
In order to withstand the elements (wind, rain, heat, and cold) make sure the shelter's roof and walls have a 45- to 60-degree pitch. Tarps, boughs, bark, sod, or ground covering is used to create the roof.

Lashings
When building your shelter, various lashings may be needed to hold the structure together. Two are listed below.

Shear lash
This lash is best used when making a bipod or tripod structure. Lay the poles side by side, attach the line to one of the poles (a clove hitch will work), run the line around all the poles three times (called a wrap). Next, run the line two times between each of the parallel poles (called a frap). It should go around and over the wrap. Make sure to pull it snug each time. Finish by tying another clove hitch. For details on specific knots refer to chapter 12.

Square lash
The square lash is used to join poles at right angles. As with the shear lash, start with a clove hitch. Wrap the line, in a box pattern, over and under the poles, alternating between each pole. After you have done this three times, tightly run several fraps between the two poles and over the preceding wrap. Pull it snug, and finish with a clove hitch. For details on specific knots refer to chapter 12.

Drainage

The ideal solution to drainage problems is to build your shelter so that it sits slightly higher than the surrounding ground. However, if this is not possible, it will only take you a few minutes to dig a trench around your shelter and the benefit will make it a worthwhile process. The small trench should fall directly below the roof's ends and follow the ground's natural pitch until the water is directed far away from your home. This design works similar to the gutters on a modern home. The trench collects the water, and via a small slope that extends from one end to another, it directs the water away from the house.

Bedding

A bed is necessary to protect you from the cold, hard ground. If a commercial sleeping pad is unavailable, bedding may be prepared using natural materials such as dry leaves, grasses, ferns, boughs, dry moss, or cattail down. For optimal insulation from the ground, the bed should have a loft of at least 18 inches.

EMERGENCY TARP SHELTERS

An emergency shelter can be made using a tarp, poncho, blanket, or other similar item. The exact type of shelter you build will depend on the environment, available materials, and time. Whatever you choose, it must meet basic camp and design criteria already outlined. Tarp layers, line attachments, and how to safely pound an improvised stake into the ground are a few items unique to building a tarp shelter.

Tarp layers

If you have two tarps, adding a rain fly (second tarp) over the first increases insulation and decreases potential misting during hard rains.

Attaching line

If you use line, attach it to the tarp's grommet or a makeshift button created from rock, grass, or other malleable substance that will not tear or cut the tarp. To create a makeshift button, ball up the material inside a corner of the tarp and secure it with a slipknot. You can fasten the shelter piece to the ground by tying the free end of the line to vegetation, rocks, big logs, or an improvised stake.

Improvised stake

If using an improvised stake, make sure to pound it into the ground so it is leaning away from the tarp at a 90-degree angle to the wrinkles in the material. To avoid breaking your hand when pounding the stake into the ground, hold the stake so that your palm is facing up. Holding it this way allows a missed strike to hit the forgiving palm verses the unforgiving back of the hand.

Various options for building an emergency tarp shelter are outlined here. Don't limit yourself to these options. Each situation is different. There might be a time when combining a tarp and natural material is the best choice. As long as you meet the basics of shelter design, you should be okay.

A-tent

The A-tent is most often used in the warm temperate and snow environments. To construct, tightly secure a ridgeline or ridgepole 3 to 4 feet above the ground and between two trees approximately 7 feet apart. When using a ridgepole, secure it in place using a square lash so that it spans at least 6 inches beyond each tree. Drape the tarp over the stretched line (or pole) and use trees, boulders, tent poles, twigs, or stakes to tightly secure its sides at a 45- to 60-degree angle to the ground.

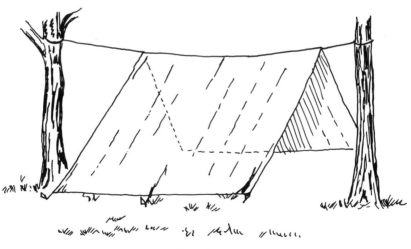

Tarp A-tent

Tarp A-frame

A-frame

An A-frame is most often used in the warm temperate and snow environments. Find a tree with a forked branch about 3 to 4 feet high on the trunk of a tree. Break away any other branches that pose a safety threat or interfere with the construction of your A-frame. Place your ridgepole into the forked branch, forming a 30-degree angle between the pole and the ground. The ridgepole should be 12 to 15 feet long and the diameter of your wrist. If you are unable to find a tree with a forked branch, lash the ridgepole to the tree. Other options include finding a fallen tree that forms an appropriate 30-degree angle between the tree and the ground or laying a strong ridgepole against a 3- to 4-foot-high stump. Drape the tarp over the pole and using trees, boulders, tent poles, or twigs tightly secure both sides of the tarp at a 45- to 60-degree angle to the ground. For best results you'll most likely need to use line and attach it to the tarp with a makeshift button.

Lean-to

Like the A-tent and A-frame, a lean-to is most often used in the warm temperate and snow environments. To construct, find two trees about 7 feet apart with forked branches 4 to 5 feet high on the trunk. Break away any other branches that pose a safety threat or interfere with the construction of your lean-to. Place a ridgepole (a fallen tree that is approximately

10 feet long and the diameter of your wrist) into the forked branches. If unable to find two trees with forked branches, lash the ridgepole to the trees. Another option is to tie a line tightly between the two trees and use it in the same fashion as you would the pole. Lay three or more support poles across the ridgepole at a 45- to 60-degree angle to the ground. Support poles need to be about 10 feet long and placed 1 to 2 feet apart. (If using a line instead of the ridgepole, you may elect not to use support poles.) Drape the tarp over the support poles, and attach the top to the ridgepole. Tightly secure the tarp over the support poles and to the ground using lines, rocks, logs, or another stabilizing method. You may elect to draw the excess tarp underneath the shelter, providing a ground cloth in which to sleep on.

If you have a life raft and a tarp, you can make a quick and easy lean-to on a sandy shore beyond the reach of high tide. To construct, bury approximately one-fifth of the raft while it is perpendicular to the ground, attach a tarp to the top of the raft, and secure the tarp to the ground forming a 45- to 60-degree angle between the tarp and the ground.

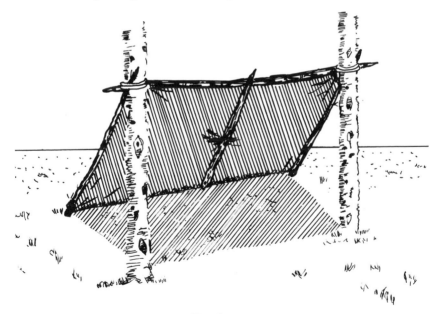

Tarp lean-to

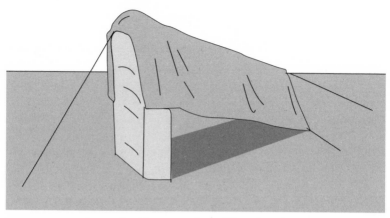

Improvised lean-to using a life raft and tarp

Desert/shade shelter

A desert/shade shelter is most often used in dry environments. Ideally, you'll need to locate an area with an 18- to 24-inch depression between rocks or dunes. Another option is to dig an 18- to 24-inch-deep trench large enough for you to comfortably lie down in. If you dig a trench, pile the removed sand around three of the four sides. Provide an adequate entryway by removing additional sand from the remaining open area. Cover the trench with your tarp or poncho and secure it in place by weighing down its edges with sand or rocks. If you have a second tarp or poncho, place it 12 to 18 inches above the first. (Layering the material reduces the inside temperature even more.) If you have a raft and paddle or solid branch, propping the raft up with the paddle can make a shade shelter.

A desert/shade shelter will reduce midday heat by as much as 30 to 40 degrees. To avoid sweating or dehydrating, build this shelter during the morning or evening hours. Until then, get out of the heat by attaching a tarp to your raft (see above), elevated rock, or sand dune and stretching it out so that a 45- to 60-degree angle is formed between the tarp and the ground.

EMERGENCY NATURAL SHELTERS

A natural shelter is composed of materials that are procured from the wilderness. The exact type of shelter you build will depend on the envi-

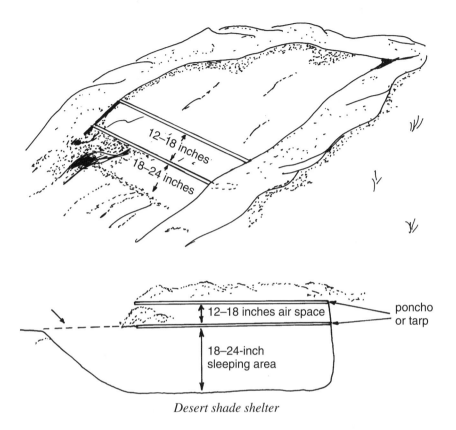

Desert shade shelter

ronment, available materials, and time. Whatever you choose, it must meet basic camp and design criteria already outlined. A natural shelter must have a well-designed and well-crafted roof and walls.

Framework

The framework must be strong enough to support the roof and wall weight (which is often substantial). Without a tarp, the wall angle is one of the keys to a shelter that repels moisture. Make sure it has a 45- to 60-degree pitch. Make sure to cut the support poles so they don't extend beyond the ridgepole, and cap them using bark or other roofing material. Uncut and uncapped poles allow moisture to track down into the shelter. For non-tarp shelters, you can increase the strength of the overall structure by weaving sapling-sized branches between the supporting poles (at 90 degrees).

Roofs and walls

Roofs created using boughs, bark, or sodlike material need to be layered, from bottom to top, so that the upper piece overlaps the bottom. Overlapping the material creates a shingle-type roof that prevents moisture from entering the shelter. If you have enough ground covering or snow is available, throw about 18 inches on top of the existing roof. This added material greatly increases the insulating quality of your shelter. Using snow, however, should only be done in a climate with temperatures below freezing. Make sure to ventilate any shelter that is completely enclosed.

Various options for building an emergency natural shelter are outlined here. As with a tarp shelter, don't limit yourself to these options. Each situation is different. There might be a time when combining a tarp and natural material is the best choice. As long as you meet the basics of shelter design, you should be okay.

Tree pit

A tree pit shelter is a quick immediate-action shelter used in most forested environments. The optimal tree will have multiple lower branches—like a Douglas or grand fir—that protect its base from the snow, rain, and sun. Pine and deciduous trees provide little protection and are not a good choice. In snow environments, the snow level rises around the tree, creating an excellent source of insulation for your shelter. To make a tree pit, remove any lower dead branches and snow from the tree's base, making an area big enough for you and your equipment. If snow is present, dig until you reach bare ground, and remove obstructive branches, which can be used for added overhead cover to protect you from the elements.

Wickiup

The wickiup shelter is common in areas where building materials are scarce. However, this shelter can be used anywhere that poles, brush, leaves, grass, boughs, etc. can be found. The wickiup is not the ideal shelter for areas where prolonged rains prevail, but if the insulation material is heaped on thick, it will provide adequate protection from most elements.

Tree pit

To make a wickiup, gather three strong 10- to 15-foot poles and use a
shear lash to connect them together at the top. If one or more of the poles
has a fork at its top, it may not be necessary to lash them together. Spread
the poles out until they can stand without support to form a tripod at
approximately a 60-degree angle. Using additional poles, fill in all the sides
by leaning them against the top of the tripod. Don't discard shorter poles;
they can be used in the final stages of this process. Make sure you leave a
small entrance that can later be covered with your backpack or other appropriate material. Create the roof by layering (from bottom to top) boughs,

Wickiup framework

grass, or plant stalks covered with mulch and dirt. Finally, to hold the roof material in place, lay poles on top and around the wickiup. Be sure to leave a vent hole at the top if you plan on having fires inside the shelter.

A-frame

An A-frame is most often used in the warm temperate and snow environments. The A-frame's basic design is covered under tarp shelters. Unlike the tarp shelter, however, the A-frame built using only natural materials requires support poles and roofing material. Lay support poles across the ridgepole, on both sides, at a 60-degree angle to the ground. Support poles need to be long enough to extend above the ridgepole slightly, and they should be placed approximately 1 to 1½ feet apart. Crisscross small branches into the support poles. Cover the framework with any available grass, moss, boughs, and so forth. The material is placed in a layered fashion, starting at the bottom. If snow is available, throw at least 8 inches (you may add more but this is the minimum) over the top of the shelter. Cover the door opening with your pack or similar item. When using snow,

Natural A-frame

Snow-covered A-frame

don't allow the temperature inside your shelter to rise above 32 degrees or the snow will start to melt.

Lean-to

A lean-to is most often used in the warm temperate and snow environments. The lean-to's basic design is covered under tarp shelters. Unlike the tarp shelter, however, the lean-to built using only natural materials requires additional support poles and roofing material. Lay several support poles across the ridgepole at a 45- to 60-degree angle to the ground. Support poles need to be long enough to provide this angle and yet barely extend beyond the top of the ridgepole. Weave small saplings into and perpendicular to the support poles. Cover the entire shelter with 12 to 18 inches of boughs, bark, duff, and snow in that order (depending on availability of resources). The material should be placed in a layered fashion starting at the bottom. If snow is available, throw a minimum of 8 inches on top of the shelter. The lean-to allows you to build a fire in front of the shelter as long as the fire is safely spaced away from you and your gear. To help heat your shelter, build a fire reflector behind the fire. In cold climates create an opposing lean-to by making a front wall in the same fashion as the back wall. Be sure to incorporate the sides into the framework

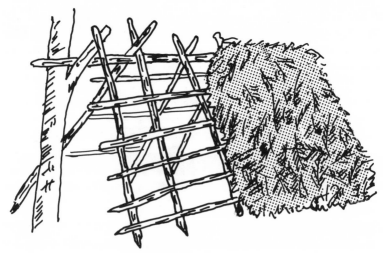

Opposing lean-to

and leave enough room for a small doorway on either side. The doorway can be covered with your pack or a snow block when needed. For an opposing lean-to make a vent hole in top if you plan to have a small fire inside. As always, when using snow, don't let the temperature inside your shelter go above 32 degrees Fahrenheit or the snow will start to melt.

Snow cave

Used most often in winter and snow environments, a snow cave is a quick and easily constructed one- to two-man shelter. When using this type of shelter, the outside temperature must be well below freezing to ensure that the walls of the cave will stay firm and the snow will not melt. Once the snow shelter is built, never let the inside temperature go above freezing. If this happens, the snow cave will lose its insulation quality, and you will get wet from the subsequent moisture. Therefore, these shelters are not designed for large groups, since the radiant heat of many people will raise the temperature above freezing, making this shelter a dangerous environment. As a general rule of thumb, if you cannot see your breath, the shelter is too warm. When constructing the cave, use the COLDER principle (explained earlier in the chapter), and take care not to get wet or overheated.

To construct a snow cave, find an area with firm snow at least 6 feet deep. A steep slope such as a snowdrift will work, as long as there is no risk of an avalanche. Dig an entryway into the slope deep enough to start a tunnel and wide enough for you to fit into. Since cold air sinks, you must construct a snow platform 2 to 3 feet above the entryway. The platform should be flat, level, and large enough for you to comfortably lie down on. Use the entryway as a starting point, and hollow out a domed area large enough for you and your equipment. To keep the ceiling from settling or falling in, create a high domed roof. To prevent asphyxiation, make a ventilation hole in the roof. For best results, the hole should be at a 45-degree angle to your sleeping platform, creating a triangle between the platform, the door, and the hole. If available, insert a stick or pole through the hole so that it can be cleared periodically. To further protect the shelter from the elements, place a block of snow or your pack in the entryway. Since you will be oblivious to the conditions outside you should check the entrance periodically to make sure it is clear of snow.

Snow cave

Snow A-frame

A snow A-frame is most often used in warm temperate winter, snow, and ice environments where the snow has been windblown and firmly packed. To make a snow A-frame, find an 8- by 4-foot flat area that is clear of trees and underbrush. (The snow must be at least 3 to 4 feet deep.) Stomp out a rectangular platform wide and long enough to accommodate your body, and let it harden for at least thirty minutes. Dig a 3-foot-deep entryway just in front of the rectangular area. Evacuate the compacted snow by cutting multiple 3-foot-square blocks that are 8 to 10 inches wide. You will need an instrument like a snow saw, large machete, stick, or ski. Once the blocks have been removed, place them one against the other forming an A-frame above the trench. For best results, cut one of the first opposing blocks in half lengthwise. This makes it easier to place the additional blocks one at a time instead of trying to continually lay two against one another. Fill in any gaps with surrounding snow and cover the doorway.

Snow A-frame

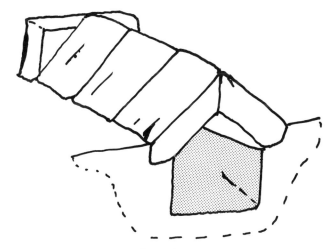

Snow A-frame

A variation of the snow A-frame shelter can be made when the snow is not wind-packed and a snow cave is not an option. Simply dig a trench (as described above but making one side higher than the other), cover it with a framework of branches or similar material (in a lean-to design), and then add a thick layer of snow roofing for a quick and easy alternative. Again, make sure you can see your breath and the temperature stays below freezing.

Molded dome

The molded dome, a variation of the snow cave and snow A-frame, is used where the snow is not wind-packed and a snow cave is not an option. Using your gear, boughs, or similar material, create a cone to serve as the foundation to your shelter. You could build this shelter without doing this step, but it would require more work. Pile snow on top of the cone until you have a dome that is approximately 5 feet high and has at least 3 feet of snow covering the inner core. Smooth the outer surface, and let the snow sit for one to two hours, depending on weather conditions, so that it can

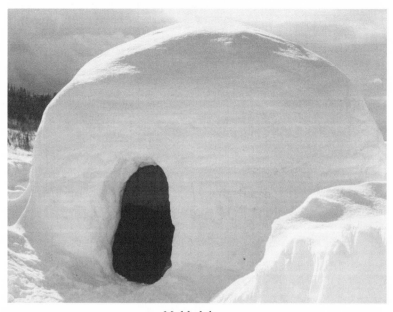

Molded dome

settle. Since 18 inches is an ideal insulating depth for a molded dome, gather multiple 2-foot-long branches and insert them into the dome, toward its center, leaving approximately 6 inches exposed. Decide where you'd like your entryway, and dig a 3-foot-deep entry tunnel. Keep the height of the tunnel equal to the bottom of the inner core, and dig approximately a third of the way toward the center of the molded dome or until you reach the core material. Now remove the gear and boughs from the core, and hollow out the inside using the sticks as your guide for how thick to make the inner wall. Make sure you can see your breath inside this shelter, too.

Tropical hut

These huts are used in tropical regions, swamps, or areas that have excessive amounts of rain. The elevated bed and floor provide protection from the moist or water-covered ground while the overhead roof keeps you dry. To construct a small tropical hut, pound four poles (8 to 12 feet long) 8 to 12 inches into the ground at each of the shelter's four corners. Tap dirt around them to make them more secure. Create the floor by lashing a strong pole 2 feet off the ground on each side of the shelter so that the poles connect to form a square or rectangle. Next, create a solid platform by laying additional poles on top of and perpendicular to the side poles. Make sure that all the poles are strong enough to support your weight. Finish the floor by using moss, grass, leaves, or branches.

The create the roof, use the same support poles that you used to build the floor. A lean-to roof is quick and easy. Attach two support poles to the front and back of the shelter so that they are horizontal to the ground and perpendicular to the shelter's sides. The front support pole should be higher than the back support pole so that a 45- to 60-degree downward angle forms when the roof poles are placed. Lay roof poles on top of and perpendicular to the roof's support poles and lash them in place. Cover the roof with tarp, large overlapping leaves (placed shingle-style), or other appropriate shingling material.

If time or materials are an issue, building a triangular platform is another option. This can be done by pounding poles in the ground (as above) or by using three trees that form a triangle. In both scenarios, the triangle sides need to be at least 7 feet long.

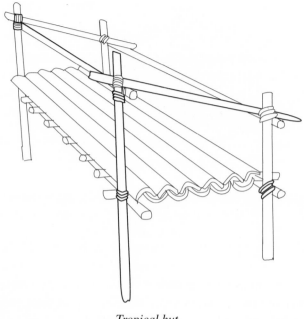

Tropical hut

Hobo shelter

A hobo shelter is used in the temperate oceanic environments, where a more stable long-term shelter is necessary. To construct one, you will need to find several pieces of driftwood or boards that have washed ashore. Next locate a sand dune beyond the reach of high tide, and on the land side of the dune, dig a rectangular space big enough for you and your equipment. Place the removed sand close by so that you can use it later. Gather as much driftwood and boards as you can find, and using any available line, build a strong frame inside the rectangular dugout. Create a roof and walls by attaching driftwood and boards to the frame, leaving a doorway. If your wood supply is limited, don't place support walls at the back or on the two sides of the structure. Some sand may fall into the shelter, but the design will still meet your needs. If you have a poncho or tarp that's not necessary for meeting your other needs, consider placing it over the roof. Insulate the shelter by covering the roof with 6 to 8 inches of sand.

Hobo shelter

Cave

A cave is the ultimate natural shelter. With very little effort it can provide protection from the various elements. However, caves are not without risk. Some of these risks include, but are not limited to, animals, rodents, reptiles, and insects; bad air; slippery slopes, rocks, and crevasses; floods or high-water issues; and combustible gases (most common in caves with excessive bat droppings). When using a cave as a shelter, follow some basic rules:

1. Never light a fire inside a small cave. It may use up oxygen or cause an explosion if there are enough bat droppings present. Fires should be lit near the entrance to the cave, where adequate ventilation is available.
2. To avoid slipping into crevasses, getting lost, or breathing bad gases, never venture too far into the cave.
3. Make sure the entrance is above high tide.
4. Be constantly aware of water movement within a cave. If the cave appears to be prone to flooding, look for another shelter.
5. Never enter or use old mines as a shelter. The risk is not worth it. Collapsing passages and vertical mine shafts are just a few of the potential dangers.
6. If possible, use a cave where the entrance is facing the sun (a south entrance if north of the equator; north entrance if south of the equator).

If you take shelter in a cave, build a wall at the cave entrance by leaning support poles against it and covering them with natural materials. Be sure to leave an area large enough to build a fire and provide adequate ventilation within the shelter.

FIRE

Fire is the third line of personal protection and in most cases will not be necessary if you've adequately met your clothing and shelter needs. In extreme conditions, however, fire is very beneficial for warding off hypothermia and other exposure injuries. Fire serves many other functions as well: providing light, warmth, and comfort; a source of heat for cooking, purifying water, and drying clothes; and a means of signaling. In addition, a fire is relaxing and helps reduce stress. For some of these purposes, building a fire is not always necessary. You might instead use a backpacking stove, Sterno stove, or solid compressed fuel tablets.

MAN-MADE HEAT SOURCES

A man-made heat source can be used in any shelter, provided there is proper ventilation. If you are in a tent, however, limit its use to the vestibule area to avoid fuel spills or burning the tent.

Backpacking stove

The two basic styles of backpacking stoves are canister and liquid fuel. Canister designs use butane, propane, or isobutane cartridges as their fuel source. The most common types of liquid fuels used are white gas and kerosene. (For more details on the various styles of backpacking stoves, see chapter 3).

Sterno

Sterno has been around for a long time and still has a place for many backcountry explorers. The fuel is a jellied alcohol that comes in a 7-ounce can. Under normal conditions, it has a two-hour burn time. Although far inferior to a good backpacking stove for cooking, it is very effective at warming water and a shelter in an emergency. An inexpensive folding stove is made for use with Sterno, but with a little imagination, you can create the same thing.

Solid Compressed Fuel Tablets

Esbit, Trioxane, and Hexamine are the three basic compressed fuel tablets on the market. Esbit is the newest of the three, and unlike its predecessors, it is nontoxic. This nonexplosive, virtually odorless and smokeless tablet can generate up to 1,400 degrees F of intense heat, providing twelve to fifteen minutes of usable burn time per cube. When combined with a commercial or improvised stove, it can sometimes boil a pint of water in less than eight minutes. These tablets easily light from a spark and can also be used as a tinder to start your fire.

BUILDING A FIRE

When man-made heat sources are not available or don't meet your needs, you may elect to build a fire. Always use a safe site, and put the fire completely out, so that it is cold to the touch, before you leave. Locate the fire in close proximity to fire materials and your shelter. It should be built on flat, level ground and have adequate protection from the elements. Before starting the fire, prepare the site by clearing a 3-foot fire circle, scraping

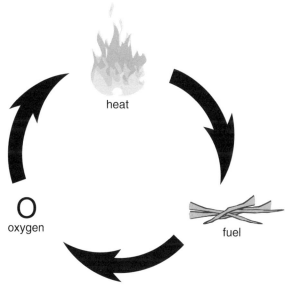

Fire triangle

away all leaves, brush, and debris down to bare ground, if possible. To successfully build a fire, you need to have all three elements of the fire triad present—oxygen, fuel, and heat.

Oxygen

Oxygen is necessary for the fuel to burn, and it needs to be present at all stages of a fire. To ensure this, you'll need a platform and brace. Gather or create a platform and brace before you start breaking your fuel down, and use it to keep the smaller stages off the wet moist ground.

Platform

A platform can be any dry material that protects your fuel from the ground, such as dry tree bark or dry nonporous rock. Waterlogged rocks may explode when wet; don't use them. In snow-covered areas, a snow platform may be necessary. To build this platform, use green wrist-size logs, and break or cut them into workable lengths (approximately 3 feet long). Construct a 3-foot-square platform by using two rows of the green logs. Place the top row perpendicular to the bottom row.

Brace

A brace is vital. It ensures that the fire will get the oxygen it needs to exist. A 6-foot-long wrist-thick branch or a dry, nonporous rock 2 to 3 inches high will suffice. (Caution: Waterlogged rocks may explode when

A platform and brace keep tinder dry and help ensure adequate oxygen flow to your fuel.

heated. Don't use them.) Lay the brace on or next to the platform. Leaning the kindling against the brace, and over the tinder, allows oxygen to circulate within the fire.

Fuel

Fuel can be separated into three categories: tinder, kindling, and fuel. Each builds upon the previous one. Before gathering the fuel, make sure to prepare your site and position the platform and brace in the center. Next, gather enough fuel to build three fires. This allows you to step back to a smaller fuel if your fire has problems igniting a larger stage. When breaking the fuel down, lay the smaller stages of kindling against the brace, keeping it off the ground, and within reach of the fire you intend to build. The exact type of fuel used will vary depending on your location.

Tinder

Tinder is any material that will light from a spark. It's extremely valuable in getting the larger stages of fuel lit. Tinder can be man-made or natural.

Man-made tinder

When venturing into the wilderness, always carry man-made tinder in your survival kit. If you should become stranded during harsh weather conditions, it may prove to be the key in having or not having a fire that first night. Since it is a one-time-use item, immediately start gathering natural tinder so that it can be dried out and prepared for use once your man-made tinder is used up. For natural tinder to work it needs to be dry, have exposed edges, and allow oxygen to circulate within it. For man-made tinder, this is not always the case; it may just need to be scraped or fluffed so it can catch a spark. The most common man-made forms of tinder are petroleum-based, compressed tinder tabs, and solid compressed fuel tablets.

Petroleum-based tinder: This is very effective, even under harsh, wet, windy conditions. Many kinds are available, but perhaps the most common is the Tinder-Quik tab. It is waterproof, odorless, and made from a light compressible fiber that is impregnated with beeswax, petroleum, and silicones. To use it, simply fluff the fiber so that it has edges exposed to catch a spark. The tinder will burn for approximately two minutes.

Cotton balls and Vaseline make an excellent inexpensive tinder.

Although Tinder-Quik was designed for use with the spark-lite flint system (see heat sources) it can be used with any heat source. Less expensive petroleum-based tinder can be made by saturating 100 percent cotton balls with petroleum jelly and carrying them in a 35-millimeter film canister.

Compressed tinder tabs: WetFire tinder tablets are perhaps the most common compressed tinder tablets. Each tablet is waterproof, nontoxic, odorless, smokeless, and burns around 1,300 degrees F for two to three minutes. Unlike the Tinder-Quik Fire Tabs, they are not compressible. To use, prepare the tinder by making a few small shavings to catch the sparks from your metal match (see heat sources).

Solid compressed fuel tablets: Besides serving as a heat source, these tablets easily light from a spark and can also be used as tinder to start a fire. More details can be found under man-made heat sources.

Natural tinder
For natural tinder to work, it generally needs to be dry, have exposed edges, and allow oxygen to circulate within it. Gather natural materials for tinder before you need it so that you have time to dry it in the sun,

between your clothing, or by a fire. Remove any wet bark or pith before breaking the tinder down, and keep it off the damp ground during and after preparation. Some tinder will collect moisture from the air, so prepare it last and keep it dry until you're ready to use it. Natural tinder falls into three basic categories: bark; scrapings; and grass, ferns, and lichen. If you are uncertain if something will work for tinder, try it.

Bark: Prepare layered forms of tinder by working pieces of bark between your hands and fingers until they're light and airy. To do this, start by holding a long section of the bark with both hands, thumb to thumb. Use a back-and-forth twisting action, working the bark until it becomes fibrous. Next, place the fibrous bark between the palms of your hands and role your hands back and forth until the bark becomes thin, light, and airy. At this point, you should be able to light it from a spark. Prepare this tinder until you have enough to form a small bird's nest. Place any loose dust created from the process in the center of the nest. Many barks will work as tinder, but birch is best as it will light even when wet due to a highly flammable resin it contains.

Breaking down birch bark

Wood scrapings provide a good tinder.

Wood scrapings: Wood scrapings are created by repeatedly running your knife blade, at a 90-degree angle, across a flat section of pitch wood or heartwood. To be effective, you'll need enough scrapings to fill the palm of your hand. Like birch bark, pitch wood will light even when wet. The high concentration of pitch in the wood's fibers makes it highly flammable.

Grass, ferns, leaves, and lichen: As with bark, fashion a bird's nest with these materials. You may need to break them down further, depending on the materials at hand. This form of tinder needs to be completely dry to work successfully.

Kindling
Kindling is usually comprised of twigs or wood shavings that range in diameter from pencil lead to pencil thickness. It should easily light when placed on a small flame. Sources include small dead twigs found on the dead branches at the bottom of many trees; shavings from larger pieces of dry dead wood; small bundles of grass; dry sagebrush or cactus; heavy cardboard; and gasoline- or oil-soaked wood.

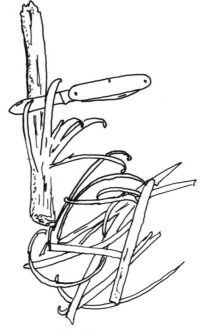

Wood shavings

Fuel

Fuel is any material that is thumb-size or bigger that will burn slowly and steadily once it is lit. Kinds of fuel include dry dead branches at the bottom of trees; heartwood (the dry inside portion of a dead standing tree, fallen tree, tree trunk, or large branch); green wood that is finely split; dry grasses twisted into bunches; dry cacti or sagebrush; and dry animal dung.

Dry, dead branches at the bottom of trees

This material is great during dry or very cold weather. It provides all of the various stages of fuel when broken down properly. To decrease injury, wear gloves to protect your hands, and protect your eyes by looking away when snapping the branch off the tree. If the branches are wet, you'll need to prepare them by scraping off all of the wet bark and lichen. Run your knife across the wood's surface at a 90-degree angle. If it is still too wet, split the wood to expose its inner dry material.

Fuel acquired from the dead lower tree branches

Heartwood

Heartwood requires a lot more energy and time when used to build a fire. However, it is ideal during wet conditions when you need a dry surface that will easily ignite. The best source is a stump that has a sharp pointed top—in other words, a stump that wasn't created with a chainsaw. Stumps that have a flat surface can absorb massive amounts of moisture, especially when capped with snow. In addition, certain coniferous trees that die from natural causes will contain large amounts of pitch. This wood is commonly called pitch wood and is a great find when you are cold and in need of a quick fire, since it easily lights even under the worst conditions. To gather heartwood, pull, kick, or rip the pieces off of the stump. If unable to separate the wood from the stump, wedge a sturdy pole between the stump and a loose piece of wood, or use your ax or large fixed blade knife to help it along. A small-diameter standing dead tree can be knocked over and broken into workable sections by running it between two trees (a foot or so apart) and pulling one end back until the pole snaps in half. Once gathered, break the wood down from large to small. If using an ax or knife, follow basic safety rules.

Fuel acquired from heartwood

Green wood
If you have a hot fire, green wood that is finely split will burn. However, it should not be used in the early stages of your fire. To increase your odds of success, remove the outer bark and cambium layer.

Dry grass twisted into bunches
Dry grass is not only great tinder, but also provides an excellent fuel when tied into bundles. If this is your only source of fuel, tie the grass into bundles that are 12 to 24 inches long with varying diameters, so you can stage your fire up from small to big.

Dead cacti and sagebrush
Once cacti are devoid of moisture, the material provides an excellent fuel source, and can quickly be broken down into the various stages of fuel. Cacti may be standing or lying on the desert floor. Sagebrush often has dead lower portions similar to the dead lower branches found on many trees. Breaking these branches away and then preparing them into the various stages of fuel is an easy process.

Dead sagebrush and shrubs provide an excellent fuel source for building fires.

Animal dung
Because herbivores eat grass and other plants, their dried dung makes excellent fuel. Break the dung into various sizes to create tinder, kindling, and fuel. I consider them Mother Nature's Pres-to-Logs.

Heat

Heat is required to start a fire. Before applying heat to your fuel, however, make sure you have enough of each stage to light three fires. This allows you to step back to a smaller fuel when your fire has problems igniting a larger stage. Since matches and lighters often fail and will eventually run out, you must consider alternative sources of heat to start your fire. Options include both man-made (often spark-based) and primitive (friction-based) heat sources, and several are covered here.

Man-made and sparked-based heat sources
Man-made heat sources include matches, lighters, artificial flint, flint and steel, pyrotechnics, battery and steel wool, and convex glass. Most man-

made heat sources are easy to use, and at least one should be part of your emergency survival kit.

Matches

Matches run out, get wet, and seem to never work in a time of crisis. However, if you are dead set on using matches, I'd recommend NATO-issue survival matches, which have hand-dipped and varnished heads that are supposed to light even when wet and exposed to strong wind or rain. These matches will burn around twelve seconds—enough time to light most fires. In order to protect the match from going out, light it between cupped hands while positioning your body to block the flame from the wind and rain. Regardless of the type you carry, store them in a water-proof container until ready for use.

Lighters

Lighters are a form of flint and steel with an added fuel source that keeps the flame going. Like matches, they have a tendency to fail when used during inclement weather, and once the fuel runs out, they become dead weight. If you understand a lighter's shortcoming and still elect to use one, I recommend a Colibri Quantum. These high-end lighters are water resistant, shockproof, ignite at high altitudes, and are marketed as wind-resistant. To use, simply place the flame directly onto the tinder.

Metal match (artificial flint)

A metal match is similar to the flints used in a cigarette lighter but much bigger. When stroked with an object, the friction creates a long spark that can be used to light tinder. Most metal matches are made from a mixture of metals and rare earth elements. The mixture is alloyed at high temperature and then shaped into rods of various diameters.

To use a metal match, place it in the center of your tinder, and while holding it firmly in place with one hand, use the opposite hand to strike it with your knife blade, using a firm yet controlled downward stroke, at 45 to 90 degrees. The resulting spark should provide enough heat to ignite the tinder. This may take several attempts. If after five tries it has not lit, the tinder should be reworked to ensure that adequate edges are exposed and oxygen is able to flow within it. The S.O.S. Strike Force is the most popular commercial metal match available. There also are two one-hand-use metal matches on the market: the Spark-Lite and the BlastMatch.

S.O.S. Strike Force: The S.O.S Strike Force has a half-inch round alloy flint attached to a hollow, hard plastic handle that houses emergency tinder. It also has a flint cover with a hardened steel striker attached, making this system completely self-sufficient. Although the system is a little bulky, it weighs slightly less than 4 ounces.

Spark-Lite: The Spark-Lite is small and light, measuring approximately 2¼ by ⁹⁄₃₂ by ⁹⁄₃₂ inches. Its spark is also smaller than that of the larger metal matches. It has a serrated wheel, similar to that of a cigarette lighter, that strikes a small flint when stroked. In order to make this a one-hand-use item, the flint is spring-loaded, maintaining contact with the wheel at all times. The small flint is supposed to allow for approximately 1,000 strokes before it runs out. To use, stroke the sparking wheel with your thumb while holding the Spark-Lite's body with your fingers from the same hand.

Unlike matches and lighters, an artificial flint virtually never runs out.

BlastMatch: The BlastMatch is larger and weighs more than the Spark-Lite, measuring 4 by 1⅜ by ⅞ inches. It has a much larger molded plastic body that holds a 2½-inch-long by ½-inch-diameter rod of flint. The flint is spring-loaded, and when the cap is released the flint is propelled out. To use it, place the flint tip in the center of your tinder, apply pressure to the side catch with your thumb, and push the body downward. This action will force the scraper, located inside the catch, down the flint, creating a large spark.

Flint and steel
Flint and steel are effective for starting fires, but the necessary materials may be hard to find. Some flint options are quartzite, iron pyrite, agate, or jasper. Any steel can be used with the flint, but most people use an old file. By striking the iron particles, heat is created when they are crushed and torn away. To use the flint and steel, hold the flint in one hand as close to the tinder as possible. With the steel in your other hand, strike downward onto the flint. Direct the resulting spark into the center of the tinder. The best tinder to use is charred cloth, which can be created in advance by placing several 2-inch squares of cotton cloth inside a tin can with ventila-

Flint and steel and charred cloth

tion holes in its top. Place this in a fire's coals for fifteen to thirty minutes. Turn the can every couple of minutes, and remove from the fire when smoke stops coming out of the holes.

Pyrotechnics

Flares should be used only as a last resort to start fires. It's best to save these signaling devices for their intended use. However, if you are unable to start a fire and the risk of hypothermia is present, a flare is a very effective heat source. Using it is simple: After preparing the tinder, safely ignite it by lighting the flare and directing its flames onto the tinder. Time will be of the essence, so prepare your firelay in advance, leaving an opening large enough to direct the flare's flame onto the underlying tinder.

Battery and steel wool

Stretching a fine grade 0000 steel wool between the positive and negative posts of a battery will ignite the steel wool. Lit steel wool can be used to ignite tinder, using the same technique discussed under friction-based heat sources. This method works best with a 9-volt battery.

Burning glass

A convex-shape piece of glass, such as that from binoculars, a broken bottle, or a telescope, can be used to ignite tinder by focusing the sun's rays into a concentrated source of heat.

Natural Friction-Based Heat Sources

Friction-based heat works through a process of pulverizing and heating appropriate woods until an ember is created. This ember can be used to ignite awaiting tinder. The biggest problems associated with these techniques are muscle fatigue, poor wood selection, and moisture that prevents the material from reaching a hot enough temperature. Once you have an ember, relax and take your time. Don't blow on it; the moisture from your mouth may put it out. If you feel it needs more oxygen, gently fan it with your hand. In most cases, however, simply waiting a few seconds will allow the ember to achieve its pleasant glow. Two circular methods covered here are the bow and drill and hand drill.

Bow and drill

The bow and drill is often used when the spindle and baseboard materials are not good enough to create a char using a hand drill technique. The bow helps establish the friction that is needed in order to use materials that would otherwise be inferior or when bad weather adversely affects your ability to create an ember with the hand drill. The bow and drill is composed of four separate parts.

Bow: The bow is a 3- to 4-foot branch of hardwood that is seasoned, stout, slightly curved, about ¾ inch in diameter, and with a small fork at one end. If the bow doesn't have a fork, create one by carving a notch at the appropriate place. Add a strong line, attached to the bow to create enough tension to turn the spindle once it is inserted. You can use a strip of leather, parachute line, shoelace, or improvised cordage (details on how to make cordage are covered in chapter 12). Securely attach the line to one end of the bow by carefully drilling a hole through the bow with a pump drill or knife, tying a knot in the line, and then running the line through the hole. The knot ensures that the line will not slip or slide forward, and since the line's tension will inevitably loosen, it allows you to make quick adjustments. Use a fixed loop to attach the line's free end to the fork on the other side.

Cup: Made from hardwoods, antlers, rocks, or pitch wood, the cup has a socket for the top of the spindle. The cup's purpose is to hold the spindle in place while it is turned by the bow. When using deadwood, you must lubricate the cup's socket to decrease the friction between the cup and the spindle. You can use body oils, animal fat, or soap shavings to accomplish this.

Spindle: The spindle is a smooth, straight cylinder made from a dry, soft wood or other plant material that is approximately ¾ inch in diameter and 8 to 12 inches long. The ideal spindle is made from yucca, sotol (a variation of yucca), cottonwood, aspen, willow, sage, or cactus. Dead smaller branches of cedar, locust, and ash may also be used for a spindle. The best way to evaluate the material is to press on it with a fingernail; if it makes an indention, the material should work. To prepare the spindle for use, carve both ends so that one is cone-shaped and smooth and the other is round with rough edges.

Fireboard: Fireboard should be made from a material similar in hardness to the spindle. The ideal fireboard is 15 to 18 inches long, ¾ inch thick, and 2 to 3 inches wide. The fireboard needs to be prepared for use using the following steps.

1. Carve a circular socket three-quarters the diameter of the spindle, at least 4 inches from one end, close to the long side (but not right on the side), and about one-quarter the thickness of the board. If the socket is too close to the side, there will not be enough material to prevent the spindle from kicking out of the hole.

2. Prime the hole by twisting the bowline around the spindle so that the coned end is up and the rounded blunt end is down. If it doesn't feel like it wants to twist out, then the bow's line needs to be tightened. While holding the bow and spindle together, kneel on your right knee and place your left foot on the fireboard. Insert the cone end of the spindle inside the cup, and place the round, blunt end into the fireboard socket that you created with your knife. Holding the bow in the right hand (at the closest end) and the cup in the left, apply gentle downward pressure on the spindle, keeping the spindle perpendicular to the ground. For added support and stability, rest the left arm and elbow around and on the left knee and shin. (If left-handed, do the reverse.) With a straightened arm, begin moving the bow back and forth with a slow, even, steady stroke. Once the friction between the spindle and the fireboard begins to create smoke, gradually increase the downward pressure and continue until a smooth, round indentation is made in the fireboard.

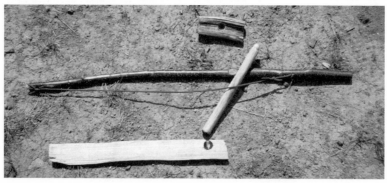

The various parts of the bow and drill

3. Using your knife or saw, cut a pie-shape notch through the entire thickness of the fireboard so that its point stops slightly short of the hole's center. Place a piece of bark, leather, or other appropriate material under your fireboard for the ember to sit on. This will protect it from the moist ground and help you move it to your tinder.

Once the separate parts of the bow and drill are prepared, it is then ready. Simply apply the same technique used for priming the hole when preparing the fireboard. Once the smoke is bellowing out and you can't go any longer, check within or below the fireboard's notch for an ember created by the friction.

The bow and drill in use

Hand drill

The hand drill is similar to the bow and drill, except you use your hands to turn the spindle. This method is used when conditions are ideal; no moisture is in the air, and you have excellent materials. The hand drill is composed of two parts:

Spindle: The spindle is a smooth, straight cylinder made from a dry, soft wood or other plant material that is approximately ½ to ¾ inch in diameter and 2 to 3 feet long. The ideal spindle is made from yucca or sotol. I have heard reports of people using cattail and mullein, but these materials can be finicky. To prepare the spindle for use, carve the fatter end so that it is round with rough edges. If you can find a straight spindle, you might use a piece of cattail, bamboo, or other available reed as the shaft. Create a plug from a short piece of sotol or other material to fit inside the end, leaving 2 to 3 inches of the plug extending out of the shaft. To help protect the end of the shaft from splitting, wrap it with a thin strand of cord. You could also use this technique to drill holes by replacing the friction plug with a stone bit.

Fireboard: The fireboard is created from a soft wood or plant material of similar but not quite the same hardness as the spindle. Yucca and sagebrush are my favorites. The optimal size is 15 to 18 inches long, 2 to 3 inches wide, and ½ to ¾ inch thick. Prepare a notch as described above for the bow and drill.

When using a hand drill, some people sit and others kneel. The key is to be comfortable while still being able to turn the spindle and apply appropriate downward pressure. To use, while sitting or kneeling, rub the spindle between your hands. In order to optimize the number of revolutions the spindle makes, start at the top and use as much of the hands, from heel to fingertip, as you can. Apply downward pressure, as your hands move down the spindle, until you reach bottom, and then quickly move both hands up while ensuring that the spindle and fireboard maintain contact at all times. Since the spindle will cool rapidly, this step is very crucial to your success. When you begin to see smoke, increase your speed and downward pressure until you can't do it anymore. Just before you finish, push the top of the spindle slightly away from the fireboard's notch to help push the coal out. At times, it may be necessary to create additional downward pressure on your spindle. Two methods that are commonly used are:

Mouthpiece: A mouthpiece is created similarly to the cup of a bow and drill, but instead of using your hands to hold it on the spindle you use your teeth. When using this technique, shorten the spindle to 18 to 24 inches in length.

Thumb thong: To make a thumb thong, tie a thumb loop at each end of a thong, and attach its center to the top of the spindle. By sliding your thumbs into the loops you are able to provide a nonstop spin with increased downward pressure. As with the mouthpiece, this technique will require you to use a shorter spindle.

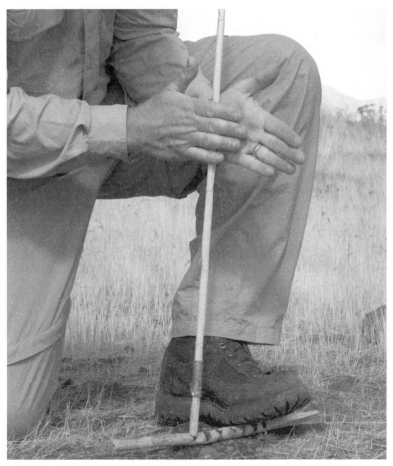

Creating a coal using a hand drill

Lighting a tinder using a coal from a friction-based heat source

Bark and grass are the most common tinder used with a friction heat source such as the bow and drill and hand drill. Form a bird's nest, and put it in a dry place where it is protected from the elements. Once you have created an ember, gently move it into the center of the bird's nest, and loosely fold the outer nest around it. Holding it all above your head, lightly blow on the ember, increasing in intensity until the tinder ignites. To avoid burning your fingers, it may be necessary to hold the tinder between two sticks. Once the tinder ignites, place it on your platform next to the brace, and begin building your fire.

Steps to Building a Fire

When building a fire, it is important to gather enough fuel to build three knee-high fires. This allows you to go back to a previous stage if the fire starts to die and to keep the fire going while you get more material. Once the wood or other fuel is gathered, break it down from big to small, always preparing the smallest stages last. This will help decrease the amount of moisture your tinder and kindling collect during the preparation process. If conditions are wet, you'll need to strip off all lichen and bark, and for best results, split the branches in half to expose the inner dry wood. Construct a platform and brace (described under oxygen above), and use the brace to keep the various stages of fuel off the ground while breaking it down.

Once all the stages are prepared, either light or place the lit tinder on the platform next to the brace. Use the brace to place your smaller kindling directly over the flame. Spread a handful of kindling over the flame all at once, instead of one stick at a time. Once the flames lick up through the kindling, place another handful perpendicularly across the first. When this stage is burning well, advance to the next size. Continue crisscrossing your fuel until the largest size is burning and the fire is self-supporting. If you have leftover material, set it aside in a dry place so that it can be used to start another fire later. If you have a problem building your fire, reevaluate your heat, oxygen, and fuel to determine which one is not present or is inadequate for success.

FIRE REFLECTOR
Consider building a firewall to reflect the fire's heat in the direction you want. Secure two 3-foot-long poles into the ground 1 foot behind the fire circle. In order to pound the poles into the ground, you'll need to sharpen the ends and use a rock or another sturdy pole to safely drive them in.

Fire reflector

Next, place two poles of similar size 4 to 6 inches in front of the first ones. Gather green logs of wrist diameter, and place them between the poles to form a 3-foot-high wall. You can angle the wall slightly to reflect the heat down or up.

MAINTAINING A HEAT SOURCE
Several methods are commonly used to maintain a heat source for ongoing or later use.

Keeping a flame
The best way to keep a flame is to provide an ongoing fuel source. The type of wood you use will directly impact this process. Soft woods such as cedar, pine, or fir provide an excellent light and heat source, but they burn up rather fast. Hardwoods, such as maple, ash, oak, or hickory, will burn longer and produce less smoke. These woods are ideal for use at night.

Keeping a coal
Either banking the fire or storing it inside a fire bundle can maintain a coal.

Banking the fire
If you are staying in one place, bank the fire to preserve its embers for use at a later time. Once you have a good bed of coals, cover them with ashes and/or dry dirt. If done properly, the fire's embers will still be smoldering in the morning. To rekindle the fire, remove the dry dirt, lay tinder on the coals, and gently fan it until the tinder ignites.

Fire bundle
If you plan on traveling, use a fire bundle to transport the coal. A fire bundle can keep a coal for six to twelve hours. To construct it, surround the live coal with dry punk wood or fibrous bark, such as cedar or juniper, and wrap this with damp grass, leaves, or humus. Around this, wrap a heavy bark such as birch. The key to success is to ensure that there is enough oxygen to keep the ember burning but not enough to promote its ignition. If the bundle begins to burn through, it may be necessary to stop and build another fire from which to create another coal for transport.

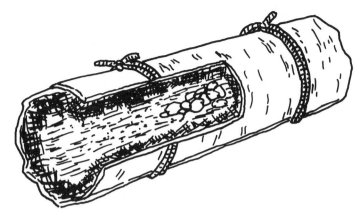

Fire bundle

FIRE BED

In extremely cold temperate or desert environments, a fire bed will help keep you warm during the night. It takes about two hours to prepare. Used in large shelters or when none is available, the heat generated from these beds has been known to last as long as two days.

Dig a 4- to 6-inch-deep rectangle that is big enough for you to lie in. Since the heat will radiate outward, you may make the area smaller if digging is hard. If available, line the bottom with flat rocks (avoid rocks that contain moisture). Build a long fire inside the large rectangular hole. As the fire grows, spread out the wood until it evenly covers the whole area and let it burn for one to two hours before you stop feeding it new fuel. Once only coals remain, spread them out so they cover the bottom of the hole evenly. Next, place dirt over the coals, stamping it down as you go, until there is approximately 4 inches of it covering the bed. To make sure the dirt covering is enough, push your whole index finger into the dirt that is over the coals. If your fingertip can't handle the heat, add more dirt. Finally, cover the fire bed with an insulating material like duff, boughs, or leaves. Make sure there aren't any loose embers that may ignite your insulation bed. Sleeping on this soft, warm fire bed will take the bite out of most cold nights. Once a bed has been created, this process can be repeated as needed. Subsequent fire beds will be easier to make since the dirt will require less energy to remove.

SURVIVAL TIPS

Although deserts are known for hot days, don't be fooled into thinking the nights are the same. Temperature extremes are common in deserts. Knowing how to build a fire may help take the chill off that evening air. Once you have finished building a shelter, take the time to collect fire-building materials. You'll be happy you did.

In hot environments, protect your skin from the elements. Wearing a wide-brimmed hat that also covers the neck will cool you significantly. Sunglasses will help decrease eyestrain and damage from the glaring sun, and loose-layered clothes covering skin work better than sunscreen. In addition, it is strongly advisable to avoid the harmful midday sun whenever you can.

To avoid the dreaded morning ritual of putting on frozen stiff boots, before bed place your boots inside a stuff sack that is turned inside out and sleep with them behind the bend in your knees.

Remove all damp or wet clothes prior to going to bed. Those that are slightly damp can be placed inside your bag behind the bend in your knees to be dried by your radiant heat. Since bags work by trapping dead air, make sure to fluff them prior to getting inside. Exercising and eating a protein snack before bed will help your body to produce the needed heat to keep you warm once inside your bag. To avoid inner bag condensation, make sure to keep your mouth and nose uncovered. If conditions are extreme, cover your face with a T-shirt or other porous material.

9

Sustenance

Sustenance includes both food and water. Although food is important to replenish the body's nutrients, it's not essential in most survival situations. Water is far more important than food. You can live anywhere from three weeks to two months without food but only days without water. Both are covered here.

WATER

Our bodies are composed of approximately 60 percent water, and it plays a vital role in our ability to get through a day. About 70 percent of our brains, 82 percent of our blood, and 90 percent of our lungs are composed of water. In our bloodstream, water helps to metabolize and transport vital elements, carbohydrates, and proteins that are necessary to fuel our bodies. Water also helps us dispose of our bodily waste.

WATER REQUIREMENTS

During a normal, nonstrenuous day, a healthy individual will need 2 to 3 quarts of water. When physically active or in extreme hot or cold environments, that same person would need at least 4 to 6 quarts of water a day. Being properly hydrated is one of the various necessities that wards off dehydration and environmental injuries. A person who's mildly dehydrated will develop excessive thirst and become irritable, weak, and nauseated. As the dehydration worsens, individuals will show a decrease in their mental capacity and coordination. At this point it will become difficult to accomplish even the simplest of tasks. The ideal situation would dictate that you don't ration your water. Instead you should ration sweat. If water is not available, don't eat.

DISPELLING MYTHS ABOUT WATER

Never drink urine!

By the time you think about drinking your urine, you are very dehydrated, and your urine would be full of salts and other waste products. For a hydrated person, urine is 95 percent water and 5 percent waste products like urea, uric acid, and salts. As you become dehydrated, the concentration of water decreases and the concentration of salts increases substantially. When you drink these salts, the body will draw upon its water reserves to help eliminate them, and you will actually lose more water than you might gain from your urine.

Never drink salt water!

The concentrations of salts in salt water are often higher than those found in urine. When you drink these salts, the body will draw upon its water reserves to help eliminate them, and you will actually lose more water than you might gain from salt water.

Never drink blood!

Blood is composed of plasma, red blood cells, white blood cells, and platelets. Plasma, which composes about 55 percent of the blood's volume, is predominately water and salts, but it also carries a large number of important proteins (albumin, gamma globulin, and clotting factors) and small molecules (vitamins, minerals, nutrients, and waste products). Waste products produced during metabolism, such as urea and uric acid, are carried by the blood to the kidneys, where they are transferred from the blood into urine and eliminated from the body. The kidneys carefully maintain the salt concentration in plasma. When you drink blood, you are basically ingesting salts and proteins, and the body will draw upon its water reserves to help eliminate them. You will actually lose more water than you might gain from drinking blood.

WATER INDICATORS

Insects, frogs, birds, mammals, and land features are helpful when trying to find water.

Insects
If bees are present, water is usually within several miles of your location. Ants require water and will often place their nest close to a source. Swarms of mosquitoes and flies are a good predictor that water is close.

Birds
Birds frequently fly toward water at dawn and dusk in a direct, low flight path. This is especially true of birds that feed on grain, such as pigeons and finches. Flesh-eating birds can also be seen exhibiting this flight pattern, but their need for water isn't as great; they don't require as many trips to the water source. Birds seen circling during the day are often doing it over water as well.

Frogs
Most frogs require water and are usually a good indicator that water is near.

Mammals
Like birds, mammals will frequently visit watering holes at dawn and dusk. This is especially true of mammals that eat a grain or grassy diet. Watching their travel patterns or evaluating mammal trails may help you find a water source. Trails that merge into one are usually a good pointer, and following the merged trail often leads to water.

Land features that indicate water
Drainages and valleys are a good water indicator, as are winding trails of deciduous trees. Green plush vegetation found at the base of a cliff or mountain may indicate a natural spring or underground source of water.

WATER SOURCES AND PROCUREMENT
Since your body needs a constant supply of water, you will eventually need to procure water from Mother Nature. Various sources include surface water, ground water, precipitation, condensation, plant sources, and man-made options that transform unusable sources.

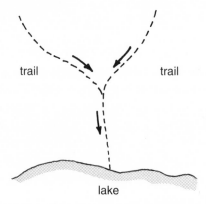

Two trails that merge together often point toward water.

Surface water

Surface water may be obtained from rivers, ponds, lakes, or streams. It is usually easy to find and access, but because it is prone to contamination from protozoan, viruses, and bacteria, it should always be treated. If the water is difficult to access or has an unappealing flavor, consider using a seepage basin to filter the water. The filtering process is similar to what happens as ground water moves toward an aquifer. To create a seepage basin well, dig a 3-foot-wide hole about 10 feet from your water source. Dig it down until water begins to seep in, and then dig about another foot. Line the sides of your hole with wood or rocks so that no more mud will fall in, and let it sit overnight so the dirt and sand will settle.

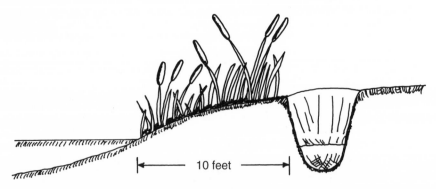

Seepage basin well

Ground water

Ground water is found under the earth's surface. This water is naturally filtered as it moves through the ground and into underground reservoirs called aquifers. Although treating this water may not be necessary, you should always err on the side of caution. Locating ground water is probably the most difficult part of accessing it. Look for things that seem out of place, such as a small area of green plush vegetation at the base of a hill or a bend in a dry riverbed that is surrounded by vegetation. A marshy area with a fair amount of cattail or hemlock growth may provide a clue that groundwater is available. Using these same clues, I have found natural springs in desert areas and running water less than 6 feet below the

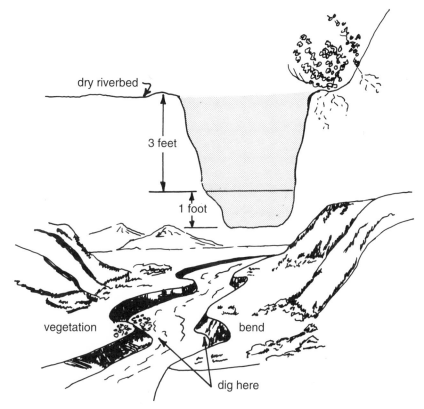

Dry riverbed water source

earth's surface. To easily access the water, dig a small well at the source (see direction for seepage basin above), line the well with wood or rocks, and let it sit overnight before using the water. When close to shore, you can procure fresh water by digging a similar well one dune inland beyond the beach.

Precipitation
The four forms of precipitation are rain, snow, sea ice, and dew.

Rain
When it rains, you should sit out containers or dig a small hole and line it with plastic or any other nonporous material to catch the rainwater. After the rain has stopped, you may find water in crevasses, fissures, or low-lying areas.

Snow
Snow provides an excellent source of water, but it should not be eaten. The energy lost eating snow outweighs the benefit. Instead, melt it by suspending it over a fire or adding it to a partially full canteen and then shaking the container or placing it between the layers of your clothing and allowing your body's radiant heat to melt the snow. If you are with a large group, a snow-to-water generator can be created from a tripod and porous material. Create a large pouch by attaching the porous material to the tripod. Fill the pouch with snow, and place the tripod just close enough to the fire to start melting the snow. Use a container to collect the melted snow. Although the water will taste a little like smoke, this method provides an ongoing large and quick supply of water. If the sun is out, you could melt the snow by digging a cone-shaped hole, lining it with a tarp or similar nonporous material, and placing snow on the material at the top of the cone. As the snow melts, water will collect at the bottom of the cone.

Sea ice
If using sea ice, you will want to make sure the ice is virtually free of any salts in the sea water. Sea ice that has rounded corners, shatters easily, and is bluish or black is usually safe to use. When in doubt, however, do a taste test. If it tastes salty, don't use it. As with snow, ice should be melted prior

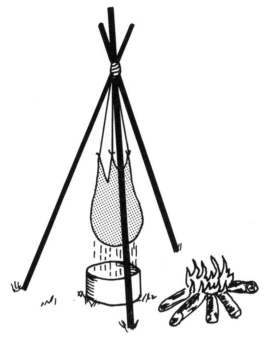

Snow water generators produce large volumes of water from snow.

to consumption. Melt sea ice next to a fire or add it to a partially full container of water and either shake the container or place it between the layers of your clothing and allow your body's radiant heat to melt the snow.

Dew

Although dew does not provide a large volume of water, it should not be overlooked as a source of water. Dew accumulates on grass, leaves, rocks, and equipment at dawn and dusk and should be collected at those times before it freezes or evaporates. Any porous material will absorb the dew, and the moisture can be consumed by wringing it out of the cloth and into your mouth.

Condensation

Solar stills are a great water procurement option in hot climates. The vegetation bag and transpiration bag are great land options.

Vegetation bag

To construct a vegetation bag, you will need a clear plastic bag and an ample supply of healthy, nonpoisonous vegetation. A 4- to 6-foot section of surgical tubing is also helpful. To use, open the plastic bag and fill it with air to make it easier to place vegetation inside. Next fill the bag one-half to three-quarters full of lush green vegetation. Be careful not to puncture the bag. Place a small rock or similar item into the bag, and if you have surgical tubing, slide one end inside and toward the bottom of the bag. Tie the other end in an overhand knot. Close the bag, and tie it off as close to the opening as possible. Place the bag on a sunny slope so that the opening is on the downhill side slightly higher than the bag's lowest point. Position the rock and surgical tubing at the lowest point in the bag. For best results, change the vegetation every two to three days. If using surgical tubing, simply untie the knot and drink the water that has condensed in the bag. If no tubing is used, loosen the tie and drain off the available liquid. Be sure to drain off all liquid prior to sunset each day, or it will be reabsorbed into the vegetation.

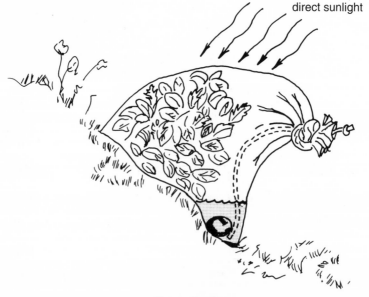

Vegetation bag

Transpiration bag

Because the same vegetation can be reused after allowing enough time for it to rejuvenate, a transpiration bag is better than a vegetation bag. To construct a transpiration bag, you will need a clear plastic bag and an accessible, nonpoisonous brush or tree. A 4- to 6-foot section of surgical tubing is also helpful. Open the plastic bag and fill it with air to make it easier to place the bag over the brush or tree. Next place the bag over the lush leafy vegetation of a tree or brush, being careful not to puncture the bag. Be sure

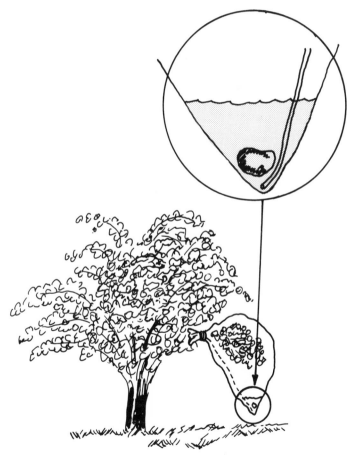

Transpiration bag

the bag is on the side of the tree or brush with the greatest exposure to the sun. Place a small rock or similar item into the bag's lowest point, and if you have surgical tubing, place one end at the bottom of the bag next to the rock. Tie the other end in an overhand knot. Close the bag, and tie it off as close to the opening as possible. Change the bag's location every two to three days to ensure optimal outcome and to allow the previous site to rejuvenate so it might be used again later. If using surgical tubing, simply untie the knot and drink the water that has condensed in the bag. If no tubing is used, loosen the tie, and drain off the available liquid. Be sure to drain off all liquid prior to sunset each day, or it will be reabsorbed into the tree or brush.

Vegetation

Depending on your location, you may find an abundant source of water from vegetation. Plants and trees with hollow portions or leaves that overlap, such as air plants and bamboo, often collect rainwater in these natural receptacles. Other options include cacti, water vines, banana trees, and coconuts.

Cacti

Cacti are prominent in the deserts of the Southwest and can provide a limited supply of liquid. To procure it, cut off the top of a cactus (this will be difficult without a large knife because the cactus has a tough outer rind), remove the inner pulp, and place it inside a porous material, such as a cotton T-shirt. The pulp's moisture can now be easily wrung out directly into your mouth or an awaiting container. Since the amount of fluid obtained will be minimal, don't eat the pulp. It will require more energy and body fluids to digest the pulp than can be gained from it.

Banana trees

Banana trees are common in the tropical rain forests and can be made into an almost unending water source by cutting them in half with a knife or machete, starting about 3 inches from the ground. Next, carve a bowl into the top surface of the trunk. Water will almost immediately fill the bowl, but do not drink it; the initial water will be bitter and upsetting to your stomach. Scoop the water completely out of the bowl three times before consuming.

The initial water from a banana tree will be very bitter and should be avoided.

Water Vines

Water vines average from 1 to 6 inches in diameter, are relatively long, and usually grow along the ground and up the sides of trees. Not all water vines provide drinkable water. Avoid water vines that have a white sap when nicked, provide cloudy milklike liquid when cut, or produce liquids that taste sour or bitter. Nonpoisonous vines will provide a clear fluid that often has a woody or sweet taste. To collect the water, cut the top of the vine first and then cut the bottom, letting the liquid drain into an awaiting container. If you plan to drink it directly from the vine, avoid direct contact between your lips and the outer vine as an irritation sometimes results.

Coconuts
Green unripe coconuts about the size of grapefruits provide an excellent source of water. Once coconuts mature, however, they contain an oil, which, if consumed in large quantities, can cause an upset stomach and diarrhea. If you do not have a knife, accessing the liquid in coconuts presents the greatest challenge.

Saltwater conversion methods
Never drink salt water without first converting it to a drinkable source using desalting tablets, solar stills, or a reverse osmosis water maker.

Desalting tablets
One desalting tablet will desalt 1 pint of salt water. Desalting tablets come alone or in a kit. Kits have a plastic bag that holds about 1 pint. These containers have a filter that will keep you from drinking the tablet's sludge by-product. To use, add sea water to the bag (and tablet), and wait one hour (agitating periodically) before drinking the water through the valve attached to the bag. If you don't have a kit, follow the same process using whatever container you have available, and make sure not to drink the sludge left at the bottom. Water treated this way will taste like water obtained from a water hose that has set out in the sun all day.

Solar stills
A solar still creates drinkable water through condensation. These devices use sea water and the sun to make this happen. Most stills are an inflatable ball that allows you to pour sea water into a cup on top of the balloon. The balloon has a donut-shaped ballast ring that keeps it afloat and upright. It takes about half a gallon of sea water to fill the ballast. Note that the ballast ring has a fabric-covered center that must be wet in order for the balloon to be inflated. Additional sea water is required to fill the cup on top of the balloon, and this water provides a constant drip onto multiple cloth wicks located inside the balloon. As the outside heat warms the balloon, condensation forms on the inner wall and runs down into a plastic container. The use of a solar still is limited to calm seas, and results will depend on temperatures. When seas are calm, stills should be put out as soon as possible, even if clouds obscure the sun. For complete details on how to use these devices, read their accompanying directions.

Solar still

Reverse Osmosis Water Maker

Standard freshwater filters and purifiers will not desalinate sea water and should not be used for this process. Instead a reverse osmosis water maker should be part of your survival gear. These hand-powered devices turn sea water into drinkable water. Reverse osmosis water makers range in weight from 2 to 7 pounds and can roughly produce 6 gallons of water a day, depending on the model you have. To use, simply place the device's hose into sea water and pull the handle. To achieve the maximum amount of water output requires a pump rate of thirty to forty times a minute. Be sure to follow the manufacturer's maintenance and use instructions and have the system serviced accordingly.

WATER FILTERS

Filtering water does not purify it. Filtering is done to reduce sediment and make the water taste better. There are several methods of filtering water.

Seepage basin

This system is used for stagnant or swamp water. For best results, dig a hole approximately 3 feet from the swamp to a depth that allows water to begin seeping in. Line the sides with rocks or wood to prevent dirt or sand from falling back into the hole. Allow the water to sit overnight so that all the sediment can settle to the bottom.

Three-tiered tripod filter

This system should be used for filtering sediment from the water. To construct it, you'll need three 7- to 8-foot-long wrist-diameter poles, line, three 3-foot-square sections of porous cloth, grass, sand, and charcoal.

1. Build a tripod with the poles and line by laying the poles down, side by side, and lashing them together 6 inches to 1 foot from the top. For details on lashing see chapter 12.
2. With the lashed end up, spread the legs of the poles out to form a stable tripod.
3. Tie the three sections of cloth to the tripod in a tiered fashion with a 6-inch to 1-foot space between each section.
4. Place grass on the top cloth, sand on the middle cloth, and charcoal on the bottom cloth.
5. To use, simply pour the water into the top section of cloth and collect it as it filters through the bottom section.

Cloth filter

Any porous material can be used to filter out sediment by simply pouring your liquid through it and into a container.

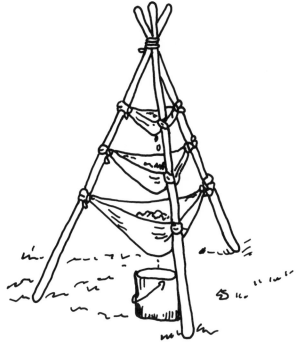

Three-tiered tripod

WATER PURIFICATION

According to the Centers for Disease Control (CDC), water contaminated with microorganisms will cause over 1 million illnesses and 1,000 deaths in the United States each year. The primary pathogens (disease-causing organisms) fall into three categories: protozoan (including cysts), bacteria, and viruses. Other potential risks that can be found in water include disinfectants and their by-products, inorganic chemicals, organic chemicals, and radionuclides. There are three basic methods for treating your water: boiling, chemical treatments, and commercial filtration systems.

Boiling

To kill any disease-causing microorganisms that might be in your water, the Environmental Protection Agency's (EPA) Office of Water advocates using a vigorous boil for one minute. My rational mind tells me that this must be based on science and should work. After seeing a friend lose about 40 pounds from a severe case of giardiasis, however, I tend to over-boil my water. As a general rule, I almost always boil it longer. I'll let you decide what is right for you. Boiling is far superior to chemical treatments and should be done whenever possible.

Chemical Treatments
When unable to boil your water, you may elect to use chlorine or iodine. These chemicals are effective against bacteria, viruses, and *Giardia,* but according to the EPA, there is some question about their ability to protect you against *Cryptosporidium.* In fact, the EPA advises against using chemicals to purify surface water. Once again, I'll let you decide. Chlorine is preferred over iodine since it seems to offer better protection against *Giardia.* Both chlorine and iodine tend to be less effective in cold water.

Chlorine
The amount of chlorine to use for purifying water will depend upon the amount of available chlorine in the solution. This can usually be found on the label.

Available Chlorine	Drops per Quart of Clear Water
1%	10 drops
4–6%	2 drops
7–10%	1 drop
unknown	10 drops

If the water is cloudy or colored, double the normal amount of chlorine required for the percentage used. Once the chlorine is added, wait three minutes, and then vigorously shake the water with the cap slightly loose (allowing some water to seep out through the seams). Then seal the cap on the container, and wait another twenty-five to thirty minutes before loosening the cap and shaking it again. At this point consider the water safe to consume, provided there is no *Cryptosporidium* in the water.

Iodine
There are two types of iodine that are commonly used to treat water: tincture and tablets. The tincture is nothing more than the common house-

hold iodine that you may have in your medical kit. This product is usually a 2 percent iodine solution, and you'll need to add five drops to each quart of water. For cloudy water, double the amount. The treated water should be mixed and allowed to stand for thirty minutes before used. If using iodine tablets, you should place one tablet in each quart of water when it is warm and two tablets per quart when the water is cold or cloudy. Each bottle of iodine tablets should have instructions for how it should be mixed and how long you should wait before drinking the water. If no directions are available, wait three minutes, and then vigorously shake the water with the cap slightly loose (allowing some water to seep out through the seams). Then seal the cap on the container, and wait another twenty-five to thirty minutes before loosening the cap and shaking it again. At this point consider the water safe to consume, provided the water does not contain *Cryptosporidium.*

Commercial purifying systems
A filter is not a purifying system. In general, filters remove protozoan; microfilters remove protozoan and bacteria; and purifiers remove protozoan, bacteria, and viruses. Purifiers are simply a microfilter with an iodine and carbon element added. The iodine kills viruses, and the carbon element removes the iodine taste and reduces organic chemical contaminants like pesticides, herbicides, and chlorine, as well as heavy metals. Unlike filters, purifiers must be registered with the EPA to demonstrate effectiveness against waterborne pathogens, protozoan, bacteria, and viruses. A purifier costs more than a filter. You'll need to decide what level of risk you are willing to take, as waterborne viruses are becoming more and more prominent. One downside is that a purifier tends to clog more quickly than most filters. To increase the longevity of your system, you should carefully read and follow the manufacturer's guidelines on how to use and clean the system you have. Purifiers come in a pump style or a ready-to-drink bottle design.

Pump purifiers
There are many pump filters on the market, and new ones arrive each year. As a purifying system, they protect against protozoan, bacteria, and viruses. I advise choosing a system that is lightweight, easy to use, has a high output, and is self-cleaning.

Bottle purifiers

Probably the best-known bottle filter is the 34-ounce Exstream Mackenzie, an ideal system for the wilderness traveler. As a purifying system, it protects against protozoan, bacteria, and viruses. The benefit of a bottle purifier is its ease of use—simply fill the bottle with water and start drinking (according to the manufacturer's directions). It requires no assembly or extra space in your pack. On the downside, it only filters about 26 gallons (100 liters) before you'll need to replace the cartridge, and unless you carry several, you will need to be in an area with multiple water sources throughout your travel.

WATER STORAGE

An ideal water container will hold a minimum of 1 quart. It should have a wide mouth, which allows for easier filling. The best storage container, of course, is the survivor.

Improvised water containers

It sometimes becomes necessary to improvise containers in which to store water. You can use such things as plastic bags, cooking pots or pans, hollowed-out pieces of wood, ponchos (must use ingenuity to create a pouch), or nonlubricated and nonspermicidal condoms (these will work provided they are placed in a scarf or other forming structure). Don't limit yourself. Anything that doesn't leak can hold water.

Night storage in cold environments

There is nothing worse than waking up with a frozen water bottle. Make sure you store your water in a way that keeps it liquid and allows you to remove the cap and continue using the container. If this can't be done and there is a replacement supply of water available, empty the container each night and leave the cap off. If water is scarce, store it in a sealed container between the layers of your bedding (make sure it doesn't leak), or place it in a snow refrigerator. A snow refrigerator can be made by digging a 2-foot-square section 3 feet into the side of a snow bank, placing the water container inside, and then covering the outside opening with a foot-wide piece of snow. Make sure to loosen the water container caps, and place them inside the hole in an upright position.

WATER CONSERVATION
If water is in short supply, ration your sweat, not the water. In addition, don't eat unless you have water, limit your daytime physical activity, and try to work or travel at dawn and dusk.

FOOD

In a survival situation, food should be deemphasized. Water is far more important. When water is available, however, eating food will help sustain your energy level. The ideal diet has foods that can be grouped into five basic groups:

1. Carbohydrates: Easily digested food that provides rapid energy. Most often found in fruits, vegetables, and whole grains.
2. Protein: Helps with the building of body cells. Most often found in fish, meat, poultry, and blood.
3. Fats: Slowly digested food that provides long-lasting energy that is normally utilized once the carbohydrates are gone. Most often found in butter, cheese, oils, nuts, eggs, and animal fats.
4. Vitamins: Provide no calories but aid in the body's daily function and growth. Vitamins occur in most foods, and when you maintain a well-balanced diet, you will rarely become depleted.
5. Minerals: Provide no calories but aid with building and repairing the skeletal system and regulating the body's normal growth. Like vitamins these needs are met when a well-balanced diet is followed. In addition to food, minerals are often present in water.

Even during harsh conditions, the ideal daily diet will consist of approximately 50 to 70 percent carbohydrates, 20 to 30 percent proteins, and 20 to 30 percent fats. The time required to convert carbohydrates, proteins, and fats into simple sugars increases—in that order—due to the complexity of the molecule.

FOODS TO TAKE
If you are backpacking, weight will be an issue. Take dry foods like cereal, pasta, rice, wheat, and oatmeal, or purchase freeze-dried meals, which are a great option but tend to be expensive. If you prefer to carry enough water to drink but not enough to reconstitute food, then consider using the military MRE (meal ready to eat), which doesn't require reconstitution.

As long as you planned the food for your trip properly and nothing goes wrong, you'll never need to look for food elsewhere. Should you find yourself short, however, or perhaps in a survival situation, you may need to look to Mother Nature to replenish your supply.

PLANTS

It has been said that over 300,000 species of plants can be found on the earth's surface. With this in mind, it seems logical that plants can provide a major source of your diet. The best way to learn if a plant is edible is from those who are indigenous to the area, along with a good plant reference book. Still, be careful and always positively identify a plant before eating it. If you don't have any references and need to establish the edibility of a plant, then I'd suggest using the universal edibility test. However, this test should only be used under the most extreme conditions when survival doesn't seem eminent.

Universal edibility test

General rules

1. Ensure there's an abundant supply of the plant.
2. Use only fresh vegetation.
3. Always wash your plants with treated water.
4. Perform the test on only one plant and plant part at a time.
5. During the test, don't consume anything else other than purified water.
6. Don't eat eight hours prior to starting the test.

Avoid plants with these characteristics
(these are general guidelines; there are exceptions)

1. Mushrooms or mushroomlike appearance.
2. Umbrella-shaped flower clusters (resembling Queen Anne's lace or dill).
3. Sap that is milky or turns black when exposed to the air.
4. Bulbs (resembling onion or garlic).
5. Carrotlike leaves, roots, or tubers.
6. Bean- and pealike appearance.
7. Fungal infection (common in spoiled plants procured off the ground).
8. Shiny leaves or fine hairs.

Avoid plants with these characteristics.

To test a plant

1. Break the plant into its basic components: leaves, stems, roots, buds, and flowers.
2. Test only one part of the potential food source at a time.
3. Smell the plant for strong or acid odors. If present, it may be best to select another plant.
4. Prepare the plant part in the fashion in which you intend to consume it (raw, boiled, or baked).
5. Place a piece of the plant part being tested on the inside of your wrist for 15 minutes. Monitor for burning, stinging, or irritation. If any of these occur, discontinue the test, select another plant or another component of the plant, and start over.

6. If you experienced no reaction, hold a small portion, about a teaspoonful, to your lips and monitor for five minutes. If any burning or irritation occurs, discontinue the test, select another plant or another component of the plant, and start over.

7. Place the plant on your tongue, holding it there for fifteen minutes. Do not swallow any of the plant juices. If any burning or irritation occurs, discontinue the test, select another plant or another component of the plant, and start over.

8. Thoroughly chew the teaspoon portion of the plant part for fifteen minutes. Do not swallow any of the plant or its juices. If you experience a reaction, discontinue the test, select another plant or another component of the plant, and start over. If there is no burning, stinging, or irritation, swallow the plant.

9. Wait eight hours. Monitor for cramps, nausea, vomiting, or other abdominal irritations. If any occur, induce vomiting, and drink plenty of water. If you do experience a reaction, discontinue the test, select another plant or another component of the plant, and start over.

10. If no problems are experienced, eat ½ cup of the plant, prepared in the same fashion as before. Wait another eight hours. If no ill effects occur, the plant part is edible when prepared in the same fashion as tested.

11. Test all parts of the plant you intend to use. Some plants have both edible and poisonous sections. Do not assume that a part that is edible when cooked is edible when raw, or vice versa. Always eat the plant in the same fashion in which the edibility test was performed.

12. After the plant is determined to be edible, eat it in moderation. Although considered safe, large amounts may cause cramps and diarrhea.

The berry rule

In general, the edibility of berries can be classified according to their color and composition. The following are approximate guidelines to help you determine if a berry is poisonous. In no way should the berry rule replace the edibility test. Use it as a general guide to determine whether the edibility test needs to be performed upon the berry. The only berries that should be eaten without testing are those that you can positively identify as nonpoisonous.

Aggregate berries are 99 percent edible.

1. Green, yellow, and white berries are 10 percent edible.
2. Red berries are 50 percent edible.
3. Purple, blue, and black berries are 90 percent edible.
4. Aggregate berries such as thimbleberries, raspberries, and blackberries are considered 99 percent edible.

Edible parts of a plant
Some plants are completely edible, whereas others have both edible and poisonous parts. Unless you have performed the edibility test on the whole plant, eat only the parts that you know are edible. Plants can be broken down into several distinct components: underground, stems and leaves, flowers, fruits, nuts, and seeds and grains, gums, resins, and saps.

Underground (tubers, roots and rootstalks, and bulbs)
Found underground, these plant parts have a high degree of starch and are best served baked or boiled. Some examples of these are potatoes (tuber), cattail (root and rootstalk), and wild onion (bulbs).

Stems and Leaves (shoots/stems, leaves, pith, and cambium)
Plants that produce stems and leaves are probably the most abundant source of edible vegetation in the world. Their high vitamin content makes them a valuable component to our daily diet. Shoots grow like asparagus and are best when parboiled (boiled five minutes, drained off, and boiled again until done). Some examples of these are bracken fern (only to be eaten in moderation), young bamboo, and cattail. Leaves may be eaten raw or cooked,

but to achieve the highest nutritional value, they are best eaten raw. Dock, plantain, amaranth, and sorrel are a few examples of edible leaves. Pith, found inside the stem of some plants, is often very high in its food value. Some examples are sago, rattan, coconut, and sugar. Cambium is the inner bark found between the bark and the wood of a tree. It can be eaten raw, cooked, or dried and then pulverized into flour.

Flowers (flowers, buds, and pollens)
Flowers, buds, and pollens are high in food value and are served best when eaten raw or in a salad. Some examples include hibiscus (flower), rosehips (buds), and cattail (pollen).

Fruits (sweet and nonsweet)
Fruits are the seed-bearing part of a plant and can be found in all areas of the world. Best when eaten raw (when it retains all of its nutritional value) but may also be cooked. Examples of sweet fruits are apples, prickly pear, huckleberries, and wild strawberries. Examples of nonsweet fruits include tomatoes, cucumber, plantain, and horseradish.

Nuts
Nuts are high in fat and protein and can be found around the world. Most can be eaten raw but some, like acorns, require leaching with several changes of water to remove their tannic acid.

Seeds and Grains
The seeds and grains of many fruits are a valuable food resource and should not be overlooked. Some examples are grasses and millet and are best eaten when ground into flour or roasted. Purple or black grass seeds should not be eaten; they often contain a fungal contamination, which can make you very sick.

Gums and Resins
Gums and resins are sap that collects on the outside of trees and plants. Their high nutritional value makes them a great augment to any meal. Examples can be found on pine and maple trees.

BUGS

Many cultures around the world eat bugs as part of their routine diet. Pan-fried locusts are considered a delicacy in Algeria and several Mexican states. In Malaysia bee larvae are considered a special treat. Our phobia about eating bugs is unfortunate, as they provide ample amounts of protein, fats, carbohydrates, calcium, and iron. Compared with cattle, sheep, pigs, and chickens, bugs are far more cost effective to raise and have far fewer harmful effects related to their rearing. Although bugs are not harvested for food in the United States, those of us who purchase our foods at the store are eating them every day. The FDA allows certain levels of bugs to be present in various foods. The accepted standards are for up to 60 aphids in 3½ ounces of broccoli, two to three fruit fly maggots in 200 grams of tomato juice, 100 insect fragments in 25 grams of curry powder, 74 mites in 100 grams of canned mushrooms, 13 insect heads in 100 grams of fig paste, and 34 fruit fly eggs in every cup of raisins.

A study done by Jared Ostrem and John VanDyk for the entomology department of Iowa State University comparing the nutritional value of various bugs to that of lean ground beef and fish showed the following results per 100 grams:

	protein (g)	fats (g)	carbohydrates (g)	calcium (mg)	iron (mg)
crickets	12.9	5.5	5.1	75.8	9.5
small grasshoppers	20.6	6.1	3.9	35.2	5.0
giant water beetles	19.8	8.3	2.1	43.5	13.6
red ants	13.9	3.5	2.9	47.8	5.7
silkworm pupae	9.6	5.6	2.3	41.7	1.8
termites	14.2	n/a	n/a	0.050	35.5
weevils	6.7	n/a	n/a	0.186	13.1
lean ground beef (baked)	24.0	18.3	0	9.0	2.09
fish (broiled cod)	22.95	0.86	0	0.031	1.0

Bugs are a great source of food.

Bugs can be found throughout the world, and they are easy to procure. In addition, the larvae and grubs of many are edible and easily found in rotten logs, underground, or under the bark of dead trees. Although a fair number of bugs can be eaten raw, it is best to cook them in order to avoid ingesting unwanted parasites. As a general rule, avoid bugs that carry disease (flies, mosquitoes, and ticks), poisonous insects (centipedes and spiders), and bugs that have fine hair, bright colors, and eight or more legs.

CRUSTACEANS
Freshwater and saltwater crabs, crayfish, lobster, shrimp, and prawns are all forms of crustaceans. Although all are edible, it is important to cook freshwater crustaceans, as many carry parasites.

Freshwater Shrimp
Freshwater shrimp are abundant in most tropical streams, especially where the water is sluggish. They can be seen swimming or clinging to branches and are easily procured by using either a scoop net or your hand.

Saltwater Shrimp
Saltwater shrimp live on or near the sea bottom. Since these shrimp are attracted to light, it's best to hunt them during a full moon or to lure them to the water's surface with a flashlight. Once spotted, simply scoop them up with a net or pluck from the water with your hand.

Freshwater Crabs and Crayfish
Freshwater crabs and crayfish are found on moss beds and under rocks and brush at the bottom of streams or swimming in a stream's shallow

water. Since they are nocturnal, they are easier to spot at night and then catch by hand or with a scoop net. To catch during the day, use a lobster trap or baited hook. An improvised lobster trap can be made by securely placing bait on the inside bottom of a container (improvised or not) the size of a large coffee can. If using a can, be sure to puncture small holes into the bottom so that water can pass through it. Punch the holes from outside to inside to decrease the chance of cutting yourself on the sharp points. Attach enough line to the trap's sides so that it can be lowered and raised from the stream bottom. Once the trap is placed, it won't take long before the crab or crayfish crawls inside to eat the bait. Thus, it should be checked often. When pulling the container from the water, do it swiftly but with enough control to avoid pouring your dinner out.

Saltwater Crayfish and Lobster
Saltwater crayfish and lobster are found on the ocean bottom in 10 to 30 feet of water. These crustaceans behave similarly to the freshwater crabs and crayfish and can be procured using the same techniques. If you find yourself on land next to a tropical reef, avoid saltwater crabs. Many there are poisonous.

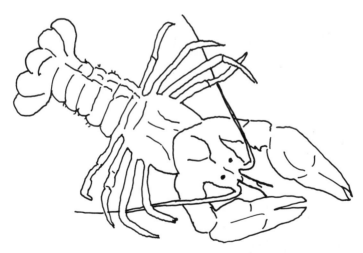

Crustaceans are a great source of food but in some instances may be poisonous.

Avoid mollusks that are not covered at high tide.

MOLLUSKS

Mollusks can provide an almost never-ending food source. However, they should be avoided from the warm months of April to October. During this time, they accumulate certain poisons that can be harmful to humans. Also avoid marine shellfish that are not covered by water at high tide. The most common types of mollusks are freshwater and saltwater shellfish: bivalves (those with two shells, such as clams, oysters, scallops, and mussels), river and sea snails, freshwater periwinkles, limpets, and chitons. All can be boiled, steamed, or baked.

Freshwater Mollusks

Freshwater mollusks include some bivalves, river snails, and periwinkles and are easily procured. Bivalves are found worldwide under all water conditions. River snails and freshwater periwinkles are most plentiful in the rivers, streams, and lakes of the northern coniferous forests.

Saltwater Mollusks

Mussels, chitons, sea snails, and limpets are all sea water mollusks and are easily procured at low tide. All can be found in dense colonies on rocks and logs above the surf line.

SNAKES

All poisonous and nonpoisonous freshwater and land snakes are edible and can be located almost anywhere there is cover. For best results, hunt them in the early morning or evening hours. To catch or kill a snake, first stun it with a thrown rock or stick, and then use the forked end of a long stick to pin its head to the ground. Kill it with a rock, knife, or another

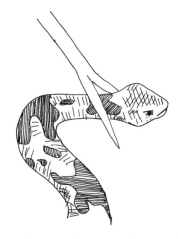

Procuring a snake using a forked stick

stick. Be careful throughout this procedure, especially when dealing with poisonous snakes. Snakes can be cooked in any fashion, but all should be skinned and gutted. To skin a snake, severe its head (avoid accidental poisoning by burying the head), and peel back its skin until you can grab it and pull it down, inside out, the length of the snake. If you can't pull it free, make a cut down the length of the snake to help you free the skin. The entrails will usually come out during this process; if not, grab them at the top and pull them down to remove them.

FISH

There are no poisonous freshwater fish. There are, however, certain species of saltwater fish that have a poisonous flesh (seasonal or permanent). Avoid any fish that fit within the following criteria.

1. Fish with poisonous flesh commonly have bodies with a boxed or round appearance, hard shell-like skin, and bony plates or spines. In addition, they often have small parrotlike mouths, small gills, and small or absent belly fins.

2. Barracuda and red snapper have been known to carry ciguatera (usually not fatal). Ciguatera is poisonous to humans and is caused by eating fish that accumulated these toxins through their diet. The greatest risk is from those that live around shallow waters or lagoons. The tox-

ins originate from several dinoflagellate (algae) species that are known to cause red tides. Avoid fish during or around red tide.

3. Avoid fish that have slimy bodies, bad odor, suspicious color (gills should be pink and scales pronounced), and flesh that remains indented after being pressed on.

4. Do not eat fish organs, as many are poisonous.

When and where to fish

The best times to fish are just before dawn or just after dusk, at night when the moon is full, and when bad weather is imminent. Freshwater fish tend to be close to banks and shallow water in the morning and evening hours. In addition, fish can be found in calm, deep pools (especially where they transition from ripples to calm or calm to ripples); under outcroppings and overhanging undercuts, brush, or logs; in eddies below rocks or logs; and at the mouth of an intersection with another stream. Ocean fish can often be procured in tidal channels using fishing line and a hook or in shallow water and low tides with a hook and line, spear, or by chop fishing (see below). To decrease the odds of catching a poisonous saltwater fish, use the following guidelines.

1. Avoid fishing in saltwater lagoons sheltered from the wind or those with sandy or broken coral bottoms. These locations tend to house reef-feeding fish, some of which may be poisonous.

2. Avoid fishing in ocean water that is an unnatural color, indicating a red tide. Fish or shellfish in red tides contain a poison that is harmful to humans.

Procuring fish

The world is covered with water, and fish should not be overlooked as a food source. Various methods of procuring fish include using fishing tackle, bare hands, chop fishing, spearing, and using a net.

Fishing tackle

If you have fishing tackle, use it. If you don't, you'll need to improvise. Crude tackle isn't very useful for catching small fish like trout but has proven somewhat effective with larger fish like carp, catfish, and whitefish.

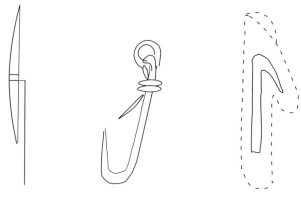

Improvised fish hooks

Hooks

Some commonly used hooks are skewer and shank hooks (made from bone, wood, or plastic) and safety pin hooks.

1. Skewer hook: A skewer hook is a sliver of wood or plastic that is notched and tied at the middle. When baited, this hook is turned parallel to the line making it easier for the fish to swallow. Once the fish takes the bait, a simple tug on the line will turn the skewer sideways, lodging it in the fish's mouth.

2. Shank hook: A shank hook is made by carving a piece of wood or plastic until it takes on the shape of a hook that is notched and tied at the top. When the fish swallows the hook, a gentle tug on the line will set it by causing the hook end to lodge in the fish's throat.

3. Safety pin hook: A safety pin can be manipulated to create a hook. Depending on the size of the safety pin, this system can catch fish of various sizes and is a good option.

Lines

If you don't have fishing line, use a 10-foot section of improvised cordage (see chapter 12). Although you could attach your line to a single pole, I'd advise setting out multiple lines tied to the end of one or several long, straight branches. Sticking these poles into the ground allows you to catch fish while attending to other chores. The goal is to return and find a fish attached to the end of your line. To attach a standard hook, safety pin, or

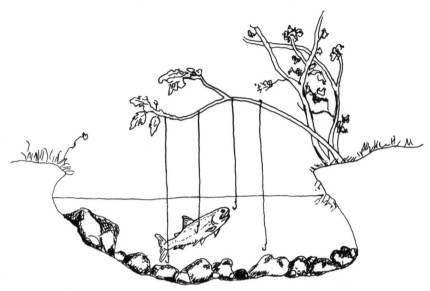

Fishing with multiple lines increases your chances of success.

fixed loop to your line, use an improved clinch knot. All other improvised hooks can be attached to line using any knot. Following are the steps to attach a hook with a clinch knot.

1. Run the free end of the line through the hook eye and fold it back onto itself.
2. Wrap the free end up and around the line six or seven times.
3. Run the line's free end down and through the newly formed loop just above the hook eye.
4. Finally, run the line through the loop formed between the two lines twisted together and the free end that just went through the loop next to the hook eye.
5. Moisten the knot, and pull it tight. Cut the excess line.

Barehanded

Catching fish barehanded is best done in small streams with undercut banks. Place your hand into the water and slowly reach under the bank, moving it as close to the bottom as possible. Let your arm become one with the stream, moving it slightly with the current. Once contact with a

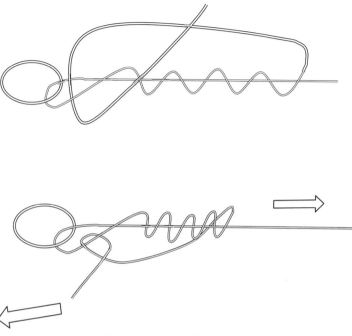

Improved clinch knot

fish is made, gently work the palm of your hand up its belly until you reach its gills. Grasp the fish firmly behind the gills, and scoop it out of the water.

Chop fishing

Chop fishing is most often used to procure ocean fish at night and during low tide. Fish in shallow water are struck and stunned with the back of a machete or other solid handheld object. The stunned fish are then easily removed from the water. Fish are attracted to light, and shiny or reflecting objects may be used to lure them into shallower water.

Spears

A spear can be used to procure both fish and small mammals. To make a straight spear, sharpen one end of a long, straight sapling to a barbed point. If practical, fire harden the tip to make it more durable by holding it

Fire hardening the tip of the spear will make it far more durable.

a few inches above a hot bed of coals until it's brown. To make a forked spear, fire harden the tip of a long, straight sapling. Snuggly lash a line around the stick 6 to 8 inches down from one end. Using a knife, split the wood down the center to the lash. To keep the two halves apart, lash a small wedge between them. (For best results, secure the wedge as far down the shaft as possible.) Sharpen the two prongs into inward pointing barbs. Using a spear to procure fish is a time-consuming challenge, but under the right circumstances, it can yield a tasty supper. You'll need to compensate for light refraction below the water's surface. To obtain proper alignment, place the spear tip into the water before aiming. Moving the spear tip slowly will allow the fish to get accustomed to it until you are ready. Once the fish has been speared, hold it down against the bottom of the stream until you can get your hand between it and the tip of the spear.

Forked spear

Gill net

If you have the time and materials to construct a gill net, it is worth doing. It is a very effective method of procuring fish, requiring limited work once the construction is complete, and it will work for you while you attend to other needs. If you have parachute cord or similar material, its inner core provides an ideal material for making a net. Other options are braided cordage (details on improvised cordage appear in chapter 12). In order for the net to stay clear of debris, it should be placed at a slight angle to the current using stones to anchor the bottom and wood to help the top float. Follow these steps to make a gill net:

1. Tie a piece of line between two trees at eye height. The bigger the net you want, the further apart the trees should be.

2. Using a girth hitch, tie the center of your inner core line or other material to the upper cord. Use an even number of lines. Space the lines apart at the width you desire for your net's mesh. For creeks and small rivers, 1 inch is about right.

3. Starting at either end, skipping the line closest to the tree, tie the second and third lines together with an overhand knot. Continue on down the line, tying the fourth and fifth, sixth and seventh, and so on. When you reach the end, there should be one line left. If you are concerned about the mesh size, first tie a guideline between the two trees. For a 1-inch mesh, tie this line 1 inch below the top line, and use it to deter-

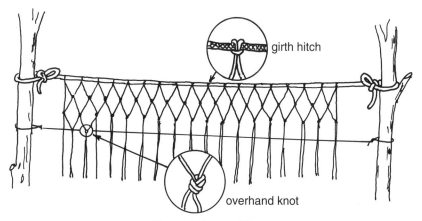

girth hitch

overhand knot

Constructing a gill net

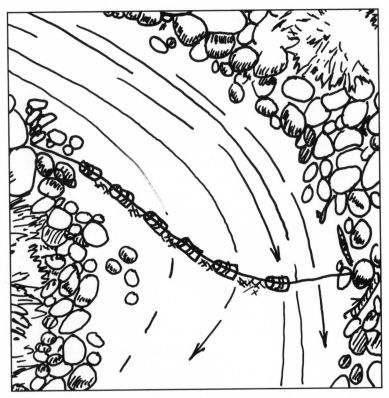

Gill net placement

mine where the overhand knots should be placed. Once a row of knots is completed, move this guideline down another inch.

4. Moving in the opposite direction, tie the first line to the second, third to the fourth, and so on. When you reach the end there shouldn't be any lines left.

5. Repeat the last two steps until done.

6. When done, run parachute line or other material along the net's sides and bottom to help stabilize it.

Scoop net

A scoop net can help secure a line-caught fish or can be used alone to scoop a fish out of the water. To make a scope net, procure a 6-foot sapling or similar material and bend the two ends together to form a circle, allowing some extra length for a handle. You can also use a forked branch by forming a circle with the forked ends. Lash the ends together. The net's mesh can be made in the same method as described for building a gill net, tying the initial girth hitch to the sapling. Once the net is the appropriate size, tie all the lines together with an overhand knot and trim off any excess. A net should be used in shallow water or other area where fish are visible. Because you'll need to compensate for light refraction below the water, first place the net into the water to obtain proper alignment. Next, slowly move the net as close to the fish as possible, and allow the fish to become accustomed to it. When ready, scoop the fish up and out of the water.

Fish traps

Fish traps would perhaps be better called corrals since the idea is to herd the fish into the fenced enclosure. The opening is designed like a funnel with the narrow end emptying into a cage. When building these traps in ocean water, select your location during high tide and construct the trap during low tide. On rocky shores use natural rock pools, on coral islands use the natural pools that form on the reefs, and on sandy shores create a dam on the lee side of the offshore sandbar. If able, block all the openings before the tide recedes. Once the tide goes back out, you can use either a scoop net or spear to bring your dinner ashore. As always, the potential for

Fish trap in a creek

poisonous fish must be considered. In creeks and small rivers, use saplings to create the trap and its funnel. The opening should be on the upstream side so the current will aid in the funneling process. To herd the fish into your trap, start upstream and wade down toward your corral. Once there, close its opening and scoop net or spear the fish out.

Preparing Fish to Eat
To prevent spoilage, prepare the fish as soon as possible. Gut the fish by cutting up its abdomen and then removing the intestines and large blood vessels (kidney) that lie next to the backbone. Remove the gills and when applicable, scale or skin the fish. On bigger fish you may want to filet the meat off of the bone. Be sure to prepare the fish well away from your shelter. Smoke, sun-dry, or cook in any fashion desirable.

BIRDS
Almost all birds are edible. If nests are near, eggs may also be available for consumption. Birds are commonly found at the edge of the woods where clearings end and forests begin, on the banks of rivers and streams, and on lakeshores and seashores.

Almost all birds are edible

Methods of procuring birds

Eggs are available for taking and young birds are easy to procure with a baited hook, snares, or on occasion clubbed.

Baited hook

Using a baited hook (meat works best) on fishing line is probably the best method for procuring birds. A secured fishing line is preferable to a hand-held one; it allows a survivor to attend to other tasks while waiting for a bird to take the bait.

Ojibwa bird snare

The Ojibwa snare is an effective snaring device, yet it requires time and materials to create. If you have both, it may be worthwhile to set one out. Find a sapling that is 1 to 2 inches in diameter, and cut the top off so it's approximately 4 to 5 feet high. To prevent birds from landing on the top, carve it into a point. The bait can also be attached here. Make a hole slightly larger than ½ inch in diameter near the top of the sapling. The perch will eventually be placed into this hole. Cut a stick 6 to 8 inches long and about ½ inch in diameter. If you prefer, you can sharpen one end of the stick and attach the bait there. Using a piece of 3- to 4-foot line, make a slip knot or noose at one end. The noose should be 6 to 8 inches in diameter. One to 2 inches beyond the noose, tie an overhand knot. (This knot is instrumental in securing the perch to the sapling until a bird lands on it.) Pull the free end of the snare line through the hole in the sapling until the knot reaches the opening. Insert the perch into the hole, and use the knot to lightly secure it in place. If using the perch to hold the bait, be sure to bait it first. Tie a rock or heavy stick to the free end of the line. It must be heavy enough to pull the noose tight once the bird dislodges the perch from the sapling. Lay the noose on top of the perch. It may be easier to tie the rock to the line before inserting the perch into the hole. An alternative to the rock is to cut a sapling about 3 feet long with its upper and midsection to the backside of the upright (its top end should be below the perch's hole). Carve a small notch on the downside of the twig so that knot in the free end of your line can be attached. Finally, adjust the line length so that when the snare is armed, there is enough tension created to quickly tighten the noose when the bird dislodges the perch from the sapling.

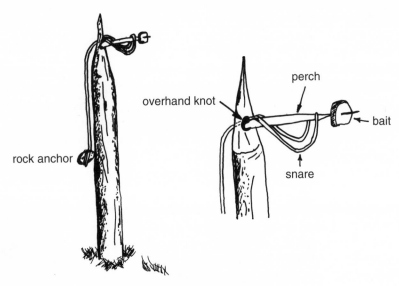

An Ojibwa bird snare using a rock

An Ojibwa bird snare using a sapling

Clubbing or catching
Other options include clubbing or catching, but these methods are extremely difficult and often unsuccessful.

How to prepare birds for consumption
Pluck all birds unless they are scavengers or seabirds, which should be skinned. Leaving the skin on other kinds of birds will retain more of their nutrients when cooked. Cut the neck off close to the body. Cut open the chest and abdominal cavity and remove the insides. Save the neck, liver, heart, and gizzard, which are all edible when cooked. Before eating the gizzard, split it open and remove the stones and partially digested food. Although all birds should be cooked, seabirds can be eaten raw. Don't, however, eat the intestines of seabirds. Instead save them for bait. Cook scavenger birds a minimum of 20 minutes to kill parasites.

MAMMALS
Mammals provide a great source of meat and should not be overlooked as a viable food source. Signs that indicate the presence of mammals are well-traveled trails (which usually lead to feeding, watering, and bedding areas); fresh tracks and droppings; and fresh bedding signs (nests, burrows, trampled-down field grass). The odds of procuring a big game animal without a rifle are small, and the risk of injury from trying to snare one is too high. Procuring small game can be done using handheld devices or by setting out snares.

Small game is easier than large game to procure without a rifle.

Methods of procuring mammals

Handheld weapons
Handheld weapons include rocks, throwing sticks, spears, bolas, weighted clubs, slingshots, and rodent skewers. Skill and precise aim is the key to success when using these devices. It will require practice to acquire the talents to use them.

Rocks
Hand-size stones can be used to stun an animal long enough for you to approach and kill it. Aiming toward the animal's head and shoulders, throw the rock as you would a baseball.

Throwing sticks
The ideal throwing stick is 2 to 3 feet long and larger or weighted on one end. Holding the thin or lighter end of the stick, throw it in either an overhand or sidearm fashion. For best results, aim for the animal's head and shoulders.

Spears
For the details on how to construct a spear, refer to the preceding section on fish procurement. A throwing spear should be between 5 and 6 feet long. To throw a spear, hold it in your right hand, and raise it above your shoulder so that the spear is parallel to the ground. Be sure to position your hand at the spear's center point of balance. (If left-handed, reverse these instructions.) Place your body so that your left foot is forward and your trunk is perpendicular to the target. In addition, point your left arm and hand toward the animal to help guide you when throwing the spear. Once positioned, thrust your right arm forward, releasing the spear at the moment that will best enable you to strike the animal in the chest or heart.

Bola
A bola is a throwing device that immobilizes small game long enough for you to approach and kill it. To construct a bola, use an overhand knot, tie three 2-foot-long lines together about 3 to 6 inches from one end. Securely

Bola

attach rocks (each about ½ pound) to the other end of the three lines. To use a bola, hold the knot in your hand, and twirl the line and rocks above your head or sidearm until adequate control and speed are obtained. Once this is accomplished, release the knot when the bola is directed toward the intended target.

Weighted club

A weighted club is a device that can not only be used to kill an animal at close range but is also a valuable tool for meeting other survival needs. To construct a weighted club, find a rock that is 6 to 8 inches long, 3 to 4 inches wide, and approximately 1 inch thick. Cut a 2- to 3-foot branch of straight-grained wood that is approximately 1 to 2 inches in diameter. Hardwood is best, but softwood also works. Six to 8 inches down from one end of the stick, snugly lash a line around the wood. Split the wood down the center and to the lash with a knife. (You can also use a strong forked branch, and secure the rock between the two forked branches.) Insert the stone between the wood and as close to the lashing as possible. Finally, secure the rock to the stick with a tight lashing above, below, and across the rock. The weighted club can be used in the same fashion as a throwing stick.

Weighted club

Improvised slingshot

The improvised slingshot is a fairly effective tool for killing small animals. Elastic cord, bungee cord, or surgical tubing is required for its construction. In addition, it's necessary to have webbing or leather to make a pouch. To construction a slingshot, cut a strong forked branch with a base 6 to 8 inches long and a 3- to 5-inch forked side. Carve a notch around the top of each forked side, ½ inch down from the top. Cut two 10- to 12-inch pieces of elastic cord or line, and secure them to the branches by wrapping the end of each cord around the carved notches and then tightly lashing them together. Cut a piece of webbing or leather 3 inches long and 1 to 2 inches wide. Make a small hole and center it ½ inch in from each side. Using the free end of the elastic cord, run ½ inch through the hole in the webbing or leather. Secure the cord to the webbing or leather by lashing it to each side. To use a slingshot, hold a small marble-size rock in the slingshot's pouch with the thumb and pointer finger of your right hand. Place your body so that your left foot is forward and your trunk is perpendicular to the target. Holding the slingshot with a straightened left arm, draw the pouch back toward your right eye. Position the animal between the forked branches, and aim for the head and shoulder region. Release the rock.

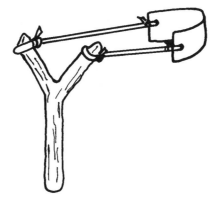

Improvised slingshot

Rodent skewer

A forked spear made from a long sapling can also be used as a rodent skewer. To use it, thrust the pointed end into an animal hole until you feel the animal. Twist the stick so that it gets tightly snagged in the animal's fur. At this point, pull the animal out of the hole. Remember that the rodent will try to bite and scratch you if you let it, so keep it at a distance. Use a club or rock to kill it.

Snares and traps

You can also procure small game with snares or traps. Once placed, they continue to work while you tend to other needs. It shouldn't take much to find the indigenous animals' superhighways. These trails are located in heavy cover or undergrowth or parallel to roads and open areas, and most critters routinely use the same pathway. Although several snares are covered in this section, for squirrel- and rabbit-size game, a simple loop snare is the best method of procurement in all climates.

Rodent skewer

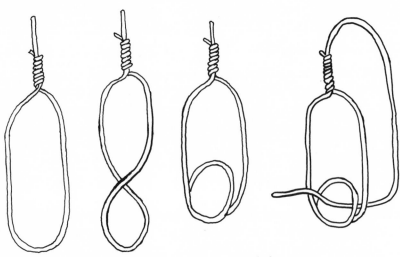

Four steps for constructing a simple loop snare

Simple loop snare

An animal caught in this type of snare will either strangle itself or be held secure until your arrival. To construct a simple loop snare, use either snare wire or improvised line that's strong enough to hold the mammal you intend to catch (details on how to make cordage appear in chapter 12). If using snare wire, start by making a fixed loop at one end. To do this, bend the wire 2 inches from the end, fold it back on itself, and twist or wrap the end of the wire and its body together, being sure to leave a small loop. Twist the fixed loop at its midpoint until it forms a figure eight. Fold the top half of the figure eight down onto the lower half. Run the free end of the wire through the fixed loop. The size of the snare will determine the

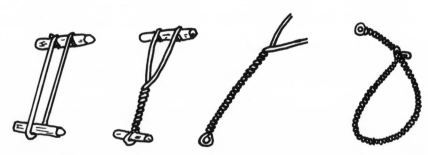

Doubling the line will increase its strength

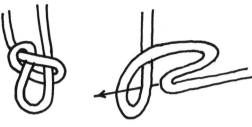

Slipknot

resultant circle's diameter. It should be slightly larger than the head of the animal you intend to catch. In extremely cold weather, it's best to double the wire in order to prevent the snare from breaking.

If using improvised line, make a slipknot that tightens down when the animal puts its head through it and lunges forward.

Avoid removing the bark from any natural material used in the snare's construction. If the bark is removed, camouflage the exposed wood by rubbing dirt on it. Since animals avoid humans, it's important to remove your scent from the snare. One method of hiding your scent is to hold the snaring material over smoke or under water for several minutes prior to its final placement. Place multiple simple loop snares, at least fifteen for every one animal you want to catch, at den openings or well-traveled trails

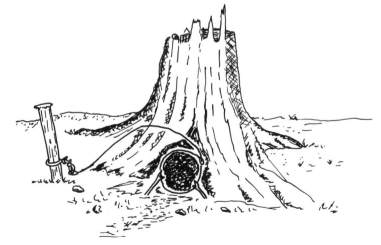

Simple loop snare

Funneling

so that the loop is equal in height to the animal's head. When placing a snare, avoid disturbing the area as much as possible. If establishing a snare on a well-traveled trail, try to utilize the natural funneling of any surrounding vegetation. If natural funneling isn't available, create your own with strategically placed sticks. (Again, hide your scent.) Attach the free end to a branch, rock, or drag stick. A drag stick is a big stick that either is too heavy for the animal to drag or gets stuck in the surrounding debris when the animal tries moving it. Check your snares at dawn and dusk. Always make sure any caught game is dead before getting too close.

Squirrel pole

A squirrel pole is an efficient means to catch multiple squirrels with minimal time, effort, or materials. Attach several simple loop snares (see above) to a pole approximately 6 feet long, and then lean the pole onto an area with multiple squirrel feeding signs; look for mounds of pinecone scales, usually on a stump or fallen tree. The squirrel will inevitably use the pole to try getting to his favorite feeding site.

Squirrel pole

Twitch-up strangle snare

An animal caught in this type of snare will either strangle itself or be held securely until your arrival. The advantage of the twitch-up snare over the simple loop snare is that it will hold your catch beyond the reach of other predatory animals that might wander by. To construct a twitch-up strangle snare, begin by making a simple loop snare out of either snare wire or strong improvised line. Find a sapling that, when bent to 90 degrees, is directly over the snare site you have selected.

You'll need to construct a two-pin toggle trigger to attach the sapling to the snare while holding its tension. Procure two small forked or hooked branches that ideally fit together when the hooks are placed in opposing positions. If you are unable to find such branches, construct them by carving notches into two small pieces of wood until they fit together.

To assemble the twitch-up snare, firmly secure one branch of the trigger into the ground so that the fork is pointing down. Attach the snare to the second forked branch, which is also tied to the sapling at the location that places it directly over the snare when bent 90 degrees. To arm the snare, bend the twig, and attach the two-pin toggle together. The resultant tension will hold it in place. Adjust the snare height to the approximate position of the animal's head. When an animal places its head through the

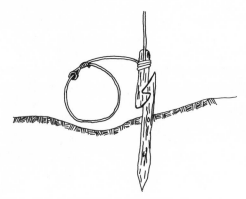

Two-pin toggle trigger

snare and trips the trigger, it will be snapped upward and strangled by the snare. If you are using improvised snare line, it may be necessary to place two small sticks into the ground to hold the snare open and in a proper place on the trail.

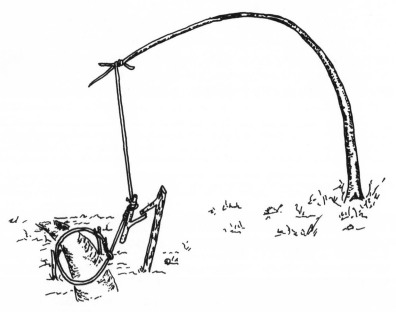

Twitch-up strangle snare using a two-pin toggle trigger

Figure-four mangle snare

The figure-four mangle snare is often used to procure small rodents like mice, squirrels, and marmots. An animal caught in this snare will be mangled and killed. To construct a figure four, procure two sticks that are 12 to 18 inches long and approximately ¾ to 1 inch in diameter (the upright and diagonal) and one stick that is the same diameter but 3 to 6 inches longer (the trigger).

The upright stick is prepared by cutting a 45-degree angle at its top end and creating a squared notch 3 to 4 inches up from the bottom. For best results, cut a diagonal taper from the bottom of the squared notch to the stick's bottom. This will aid in the trigger's release from the upright. In addition to being at opposite ends, the squared notch and the 45-degree angle must be perpendicular to one another.

To create the diagonal piece, cut a diagonal notch 2 inches from one end and a 45-degree angle on the opposite end. In addition to being at opposite ends, the diagonal notch and 45-degree angle must be on the same sides of the stick.

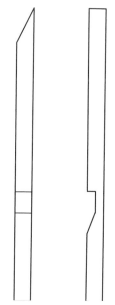

Upright piece of a figure-four mangle snare

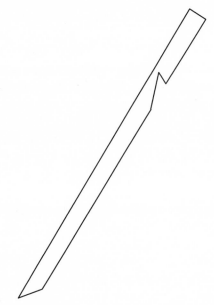

Diagonal piece of a figure-four mangle snare

The trigger piece needs to have a diagonal notch cut 1 to 2 inches from one end and a squared notch at the spot where this piece crosses the upright when the three sticks are put together. To determine this location, place the upright perpendicular to the ground and insert its diagonal cut into the notch of the diagonal piece. Put the angled cut of the diagonal stick into the trigger's notch, and hold it so that the shape of the number four is created between the three sticks when the trigger passes the

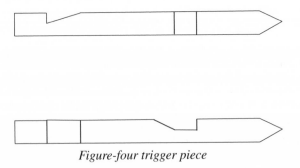

Figure-four trigger piece

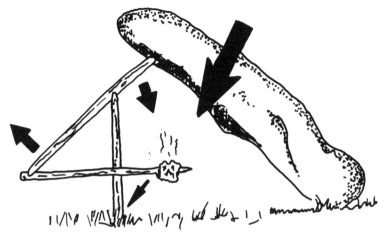

Figure-four mangle snare

upright's square notch. Mark the trigger stick, and make a squared notch
that has a slight diagonal taper from its bottom toward its other notched
end. If you intend to bait the trigger, then make sure you sharpen its free
end to a point.

To use a figure four, put the three pieces together and lean a large rock
or other weight against the diagonal at an approximate 45-degree angle to
the upright. The entire structure is held in place by the tension between
the weight and the sticks. This object will fall and mangle an animal that
trips the trigger.

Paiute deadfall mangle snare

Another option for procuring small mammals is the Paiute deadfall mangle snare. Its touchy trigger system is a unique part of its design. To construct a Paiute snare, gather four slender branches and a short piece of
line. The trap has five parts: upright, diagonal, trigger, bait stick, and line.

The upright, the only piece in contact with the ground, needs to have a
flat bottom and beveled top. It should be long enough to create a 45-degree
angle between the mangle device (most often a rock) and the ground.

The diagonal piece is approximately ⅔ the length of the upright. Prepare this piece by cutting a notch on one end about 1 inch from the tip and
a circular groove around the other end ½ inch up.

Paiute deadfall mangle snare

The trigger is a small branch long enough to extend 1 inch beyond both sides of the upright when it is placed perpendicular to it.

The bait stick should be long enough to touch both the trigger stick (when in the appropriate position) and the rock when it is held parallel to the ground.

The line or cord is attached to the diagonal piece's circular notch and needs to be long enough to wrap around the lower end of the upright while attached to the trigger. Attach the line to the trigger so that it ends up opposite the line coming off the diagonal piece. It should be cut so that when the trap is set, it creates a 45-degree angle between the upper end of the diagonal and upright piece. To arm the Paiute snare, do the following.

1. Tie the line to the circular groove of the diagonal stick.
2. Place the diagonal branch (notch side up) on the upside of the rock, forming a 45-degree angle between the rock and the ground.
3. Put the beveled side of the upright into the notch while maintaining the 45-degree angle. The upright should be placed so it is approximately perpendicular to the ground.
4. Attach the line to the trigger.
5. Run the line (off of the diagonal branch's groove) around the upright so that the trigger is perpendicular to the upright and on the side away from the rock.

6. Hold the trigger in place with the bait stick, which should be placed so that it is parallel to the ground with one end touching the trigger (on the side opposite the line coming off the diagonal stick) and the other touching the lower end of the rock.

7. Place food on the bait stick prior to arming the trigger. When the rodent tries to eat the food, it trips the trigger, causing the rock to fall on it.

Box trap

A box trap is ideal for small game and birds. It keeps the animal alive, thus avoiding the problem of having the meat spoil before it's needed for consumption. To construct a box trap, assemble a box from wood and lines using whatever means are available. Be sure it's big enough to hold the game you intend to catch. Create a two-pin toggle as described for the twitch-up strangle snare above, by carving L-shaped notches in the center of each stick. For the two-pin toggle to work with this trap, it's necessary to whittle both ends until they're flat. Be sure the sticks you use are long enough to create the height necessary for the animal or bird to get into the box. Take time to make a trigger that fits well.

Set the box at the intended snare site. Secure two sticks at opposite ends on the outside of one of the box's sides. Tie a line to each stick, bring the lines under the box, and secure them to the middle of the lower section of your two-pin toggle. Connect the two-pin toggle together, and use it to

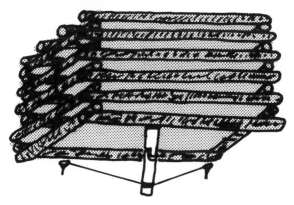

A box trap created using an L-shaped two-pin toggle trigger

raise the side of the box that is opposite the two stakes. Adjust the lines until they're tight and approximately 1 inch above the ground. Bait the trap. When the animal or bird trips the line, it'll be trapped in the snare.

Apache foot snare

The Apache foot snare is a trap that combines an improvised device that can't easily be removed when penetrated with a simple loop snare made from very strong line. This snare is most often used for deer or similar animals and is placed on one side of an obstacle, such as a log. The ideal placement is directly over the depression formed from the animal's front feet as it jumps over the obstacle.

To improvise the device that the animal's foot goes through, gather two saplings, one 20 inches and the other 14 inches, and eight sturdy branches that are ½ inch around and 10 inches long. Lash each sapling together forming two separate circles, and sharpen one end of the eight branches to

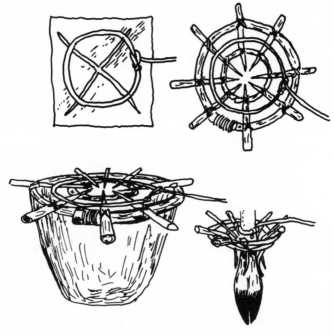

Apache foot snare

a blunt point. Place the smaller circle inside the larger, and then evenly space the branches over both so that the points approach the center of the inner circle. Lash the sharpened sticks to both of the saplings.

To place the snare, dig a small hole at the depression site, lay the circular device over it, and place the snare line over it. When the animal's foot goes through the device, it will be unable to get it out. As it continues forward, the strong, simple loop snare will tighten down on its foot. When constructing a snare like this, I often use a three-strand braid made from parachute cord, but any strong braid will work. The free end of the snare line should be secured to a large tree or other stable structure. Be sure to camouflage the snare with leaves or similar material. Any large animal caught in this snare should be approached with caution.

Skinning and butchering game

In order to eat your catch, you'll first need to skin, gut, and butcher most game. Always do this well away from your camp and your food cache. Before skinning an animal, be sure it is dead. Once you're sure, cut the animal's throat, and collect the blood in a container for later use in a stew. If time is not an issue, wait thirty minutes before starting to skin. This allows the body to cool, which makes it easier to skin and also provides enough time for most parasites to leave the animal's hide.

Glove skinning is the method most often used for skinning small game. Hang the animal from its hind legs, and make a circular cut just above the legs joints. Don't cut through the tendon. To avoid dulling your knife by cutting from the fur side, slide a finger between the hide and muscle, and place your knife next to the muscle so that you cut the hide from the inside. Cut down the inside of each leg, ending close to the genital area, and peel the skin off of the legs until you reach the animal's tail. Firmly slide a finger under the hide between the tail and spine until you have a space that allows you to cut the tail free. Follow the same procedure on the front side. At this point the hide can be pulled down and freed from the animal's membrane with little effort. Avoid squeezing the belly, as this may cause urine to spill onto the meat. Pull the front feet through the hide (inside out) by sliding a finger between the elbow and the membrane and pulling the leg up and free from the rest of the hide. Cut off the feet. The head can either be severed or skinned depending on your talents.

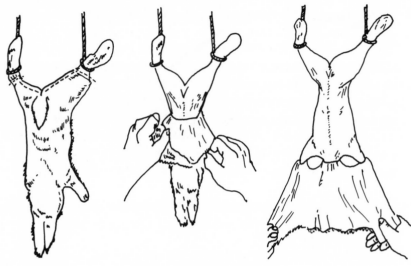

Glove skinning small game

A larger animal can be hung from a tree by its hind legs or skinned while lying on the ground. To hang it by its hind legs, find the tendon that connects the upper and lower leg, and poke a hole between it and the bone. If musk glands are present, remove them. These are usually found at the bend between the upper and lower parts of the hind legs. Free the hide from the animal's genitals by cutting a circular area around them, and then make an incision that runs just under its hide and all the way up to the neck. To avoid cutting the entrails, slide your index and middle finger between the hide and the thin membrane enclosing the entrails. Use the V between the fingers to guide the cut, and push the entrails down and away from the knife. The knife should be held with its backside next to the membrane and the sharp side facing out so that when used, it cuts the hide from the inside. Next, cut around the joint of each extremity. From there, extend the cut down the inside of each leg until it reaches the midline incision. You should attempt to pull the hide off using the same method as for small game. If you end up needing to use your knife, cut toward the meat so as to not damage the hide. Avoid cutting through the entrails or the hide. If skinning on the ground, use the hide to protect the meat, and don't remove it until after you gut and butcher the animal. Once the hide has been removed, it can be tanned and used for clothing, shelter covers, and containers.

To gut an animal, place the carcass belly up on a slope or hang it from a tree by its hind legs. Make a small incision just in front of the anus, and insert your index and middle finger into the cut, spreading them apart to form a V. Slide the knife into the incision between the V formed by your two fingers. Use your fingers to push the internal organs down, away from the knife, and as a guide for the knife as you cut up the abdominal cavity to the breastbone. Avoid cutting the bladder or other internal organs. If they are punctured, wash the meat as soon as possible. Cut around the anus and sex organs so that they will be easily removed with the entrails. Remove the intact bladder by pinching it off close to the opening and cutting it free. Remove the entrails, pulling them down and away from the

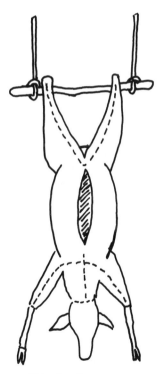

Skinning large game

carcass. To do this you will need to sever the intestines at the anus. Save the liver and kidneys for later consumption. If the liver is spotted, a sign of disease, discard all internal organs and thoroughly cook the meat. Cut through the diaphragm, and reach inside the chest cavity until you can touch the windpipe. Cut or pull the windpipe free, and remove the chest cavity contents. Save the lungs and heart for later consumption. All internal organs can be cooked in any fashion but are best when used in a stew.

If you intend to eat the liver, you'll need to remove the small black sack, the gallbladder, as it's not edible. If it breaks, wash the liver immediately to avoid tainting the meat. Since fat spoils quickly, it should be cut away from the meat and promptly used. The fat is best in soups. To butcher an animal, cut the legs, back, and breast sections free of one another. When you are butchering large game, cut it into meal-size roasts and steaks that can be stored for later use. Cut the rest of the meat along the grain into long, thin strips about ⅛ inch thick, to be preserved by smoking or sun drying. The head meat, tongue, eyes, and brain are all edible, as is the marrow inside bones.

COOKING METHODS

In addition to killing parasites and bacteria, cooking your food can make it more palatable. There are many different ways to prepare game, and some are better than others from a nutritional standpoint. Boiling is best, but only if you drink the broth, which contains many of the nutrients that are cooked out of the food. Fried foods taste great, but frying is probably the worst way to cook something, as a lot of nutrients are lost during the process.

Boiling

Boiling is the best cooking method. If a container is not available, it may be necessary to improvise one. You might use a rock with a bowl-shaped center, but avoid rocks with high moisture content, as they may explode. A thick, hollowed-out piece of wood that can be suspended over the fire may also serve as a container. If your container cannot be suspended over the fire, stone boiling is another option. Use a hot bed of coals to heat up numerous stones. Get them really hot. Set your container of food and water close to your bed of hot stones, and add rocks to it until the water begins to boil. To keep the water boiling, cover the top with bark or another improvised lid, and keep it covered except when removing or adding stones. Don't expect a rolling rapid boil with this process, but a steady slow bubbling should occur.

Baking

Baking is the next preferred method of preparing meat to eat. There are several methods you can use to bake game.

Mud baking

When mud baking, you do not need to scale, skin, or pluck the fish or bird in advance since scales, skin, and feathers will come off the game when the dried mud is removed. Use mud that has a clay texture to it, and tightly seal the fish or bird in it. The tighter the seal, the better it will hold the juices and prevent the meat from drying out. A medium-size bird or trout will usually cook in about fifteen to twenty minutes, depending on the temperature of your coals.

Leaf baking

Wrapping your meat in a nonpoisonous green leaf and placing it on a hot bed of coals will protect, season, and cook the meat. When baking mussels and clams, seaweed is often used; when the shells open they're done. Avoid plants that have a bitter taste.

Underground baking

Underground baking is a good method of cooking larger meals since the dirt will hold the oven's heat. Dig a hole slightly larger than the meal you intend to cook; it needs to be big enough for your food, the base of rocks, and the covering. Line the bottom and sides with rocks, avoiding rocks with high moisture content, which may explode. Start a fire over them. To heat rocks that will be used on top of your food, place enough green branches over the hole to support another layer of rocks, leaving a space to add fuel to the fire. Once the green branches burn through and a hot bed of coals is present, remove the fallen rocks. Place green twigs onto the coals, followed by a layer of wetted green grass or nonpoisonous leaves. Add your meat and vegetables, and cover them with more wet grass or leaves, a thin layer of soil, and the extra hot rocks. The hole is then covered with dirt. Small meals will cook in one to two hours; large meals in five to six hours or perhaps days.

Frying
Place a flat rock on or next to the fire. Avoid rocks with high moisture content, as they may explode. Let it get hot, and cook on it as you would a frying pan.

Broiling
Broiling is ideal for cooking small game over hot coals. Before cooking the animal, sear its flesh with the flames from the fire. This will help keep the juices, containing vital nutrients, inside the animal. Next, run a non-poisonous skewer—a branch that is small, straight, and strong—along the underside of the animal's backbone. Suspend the animal over the coals, using any means available.

FOOD PRESERVATION

Keep It Alive
If possible, keep all animals alive until ready to consume. This ensures that the meat stays fresh. A small rodent or rabbit may attract big game, so be sure to protect it from becoming a coyote's meal instead of yours. This doesn't apply, of course, if you are using the rodent for bait.

Sun Drying
To sun-dry meat, you hang long, thin strips in the sun. To keep it out of other animals' reach, run snare wire or line between two trees. If using snare wire, skewer the line through the top of each piece of meat before attaching it to the second tree. If using other line, hang it first and then drape the strips of meat over it. For best results, the meat should not touch its other side or another piece. It may take one to multiple days to dry, depending on the humidity and temperature. You'll know it is done when the meat is dark and brittle.

Smoking
Smoke long, thin strips of meat in a smoker constructed using the following guidelines.

1. Build a 6-foot-tall tripod from three poles lashed together.
2. Attach snare wire or line around the three poles in a tiered fashion so that the lowest point is at least 2 feet above the ground.
3. If using snare wire, skewer it through the top of each slice of meat before extending it around the inside of the next pole. If using other line, hang it first and then drape the strips of meat over it. For best results, the meat should not touch its other side or another piece.

A smoker is a quick, efficient method of meat preservation.

4. Cover the outer aspect of the tripod with any available material, such as a poncho. Avoid contact between the outer covering and the meat. For proper ventilation, leave a small opening at the top of the tripod.
5. Gather an armload of green deciduous wood, such as alder, willow, or aspen. Prepare it by either breaking the branches into smaller pieces or cutting the bigger pieces into chips.
6. Build a fire next to the tripod. Once a good bed of coals develops, transfer them to the ground in the center of the smoker. Continue transferring coals as needed.
7. To smoke the meat, place small pieces or chips of green wood on the hot coals. Once the green wood begins to heat up, it should create a smoke. Since an actual fire will destroy the smoking process, monitor the wood to ensure that it doesn't flame up. If it does, put it out, but try to avoid disturbing the bed of coals too much. Keep adding chips until the meat is dark and brittle, about twenty-four to forty-eight hours. At this point it is done.

FOOD CACHE

Unless you like to sleep with rodents and perhaps even bigger wildlife, don't store any food in your shelter. During the day, put all food inside a

A tree cache will help protect your food from bears and rodents.

container or cover it. At night, avoid bear and rodent problems by hanging your food in a tree cache. For best results, hang it as high as possible and as far from the trunk as practical.

SURVIVAL TIPS

If you don't have water, don't eat! It takes water to process food, and without water to replace what is lost, you'll accelerate the dehydration process.

Overcome food aversions. If you can't stomach eating a bug, cook it in a stew. In a survival setting bugs may be your only source of carbohydrates, protein, and fats.

Avoid mushrooms. Mushrooms have virtually no nutritional value, and since so many are poisonous, the risk is not worth the benefit.

RETURNING HOME
Meeting Your Signaling and Travel Needs

10

Signaling

During an average year, the U.S. National Park System has around 4,000 search-and-rescue operations. Of those, approximately 50 percent of the missions will involve a seriously injured or ill subject, and in 5 percent of the cases the victim dies.

RULES OF SIGNALING

A properly used signal increases a survivor's chances of being rescued. A signal has two purposes: to attract rescuers to your whereabouts and then help them pinpoint your exact location. When preparing a signal, use the following rules:

1. Stay put: Once you realize you're lost, stay put. Depart only if the area you are in doesn't meet your needs, rescue is not imminent, and you have the navigation skills to get to where you want to go. If you are lost or stranded in a car, plane, or ATV, stay with it; the vehicle will serve as a ground-to-air signal. When a search is activated, rescuers will begin looking for you in your last known location. If for some reason you need to move, be sure to leave a ground-to-air signal pointing in your direction of travel, along with a note telling rescue of your plans. If you do move, go to high ground and find a large clearing to signal from.

2. Properly locate your signal site: Your signal site should be close to your camp or shelter; located in a large clearing that has 360-degree visibility; and be free of shadows.

3. Don't waste a one-time-use signal: Many signals are a one-time-use item and thus should only be ignited when you see or hear potential rescuers and are sure they are headed in your direction.

4. Know and prepare your signal in advance: Since seconds can be the difference between life and death, don't delay in preparing or establishing a signal.

SIGNALS THAT ATTRACT RESCUE

The most effective distress signals for attracting attention are aerial flares, parachute flares, and the cell phone. For longer land trips or when on a boat or plane, the VHF radio or an Emergency Position Indicating Radio Beacon (EPIRB) should be part of your inventory and used to attract rescue to your location.

AERIAL FLARES

An aerial flare is a one-time-use item and should only be used if a rescue team, aircraft, or vessel is sighted. As with all pyrotechnic devices, it is flammable and should be handled with caution. Most aerial flares fire by pulling a chain. In general, you'll hold the launcher so that the firing end—where the flare comes out—is pointed overhead and skyward, allowing the chain to drop straight down. Next, while the flare is pointed skyward, use the free hand to grasp and pull chain sharply down. Make sure the hand holding the launcher is located within the safe area as detailed on the device you are using. For safe use and best results, hold the flare away from your body and perpendicular to the ground. The average aerial flares will have a 500-foot launch altitude, 6-second burn time, and 12,000 candlepower. Under optimal conditions these flares have been sighted up to 30 miles away. Many aerial flares float and are waterproof, and most average in size from a 1-inch diameter to about 4½ inches long (when collapsed). Depending on your needs, they can be purchased as disposable or allow replacement cartridges. The Orion Star-Tracer and the SkyBlazer XLT aerial flares are two good examples that can be found in most sporting or marine stores.

PARACHUTE FLARES

A parachute flare is simply an aerial flare attached to a parachute. The parachute allows for a longer burn time while the flare floats down to earth. Like aerial flares, these signals are a one-time-use item and should be used only if a rescue team, aircraft, or vessel is sighted. They are flammable and should be handled with caution. The Pains Wessex SOLAS Mark 3 parachute flare can reach a height of 1,000 feet and produce a brilliant 30,000 candlepower. The flare's red light drifts down to earth under a parachute and has a burn time of about 40 seconds.

When using an aerial or parachute flare, you need to adjust for any drift created by the wind. You want the flare to ignite directly overhead, so you'll need to point the flare slightly into the wind, usually about 5 to 10 degrees.

CELLULAR PHONES

Although a cellular phone is a great thing to have, it's not without limitations and often doesn't work in remote areas. Do not rely on one as your sole signaling and rescue device. Not only is a cell phone limited by its service area, it is also vulnerable to cold, moisture, sand, and heat. You will need to protect the phone from these hazards by any means available. Cellular phones should not be considered a replacement for other signaling devices.

VHF RADIO

The VHF radio is a quick and easy way to make a distress call. It does not use satellites, which limits how far away it can be picked up. Its normal range varies greatly but is estimated to average between 20 and 60 miles. If a repeater is within that 20- to 60-mile range, however, the signal range can increase significantly. Channel 16 is the recognized emergency channel. The radio should be protected from the moisture and wind, and you're better off having one that can run on alkaline or lithium batteries than one that uses rechargeable batteries. Of course this only holds true if you have packed multiple replacement batteries. In crisis, these radios can transmit a Mayday call using the following: Call MAYDAY, MAYDAY, MAYDAY. Repeat the name of your party or your vessel name and call sign three times. State your present location (give latitude and longitude if you can along with a distance and direction from a known point), the nature of the distress, and the number of people in your group or on board the vessel three times. Repeat this process until you either get a response or are forced to leave your location or vessel.

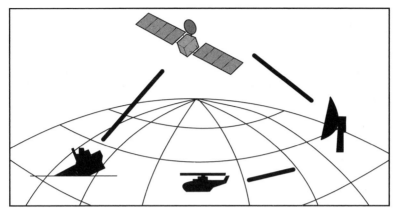

EPIRB transmission

SATELLITE EPIRBS

Emergency Position Indicating Radio Beacons (EPIRBs) are well worth
the cost, and every vessel should carry one. When activated these beacons
quickly and with great accuracy alert rescue to your location. The 406-
MHz EPIRB is the gold standard and by far outperforms the older rescue
beacons, which, if you have them, should be replaced. Once activated,
they automatically transmit a signal on two international distress frequen-
cies picked up by military and civilian aircraft. Most of these devices
float, but make sure you have a good strong lanyard attached before you
even contemplate putting it in the water. Make sure to register the EPIRB
according to the beacon manufacturer's instructions.

SIGNALS THAT PINPOINT YOUR LOCATION

Once help is on the way, handheld red signal flares, orange smoke signals,
signal mirrors, kites, strobe lights, whistles, and ground-to-air signals can
serve as beacons, helping rescuers to pinpoint your position and keep
them on course.

HANDHELD RED SIGNAL FLARE

These signals are a one-time-use item and should only be used if a rescue
team, aircraft, or vessel is sighted. They are flammable and should be
handled with caution. To use one, stand with your back to the wind, and

keep the device pointed away from your face and body during and after lighting. Most red signal flares are ignited by removing the cap and striking the ignition button with the cap's abrasive side. To avoid burns, hold the flare in its safe area, and never hold it overhead. Most devices will burn for 2 minutes, have a candlepower of 500, and are about 1 inch in diameter by 9 inches long. For increased burn time and candlepower, you might consider getting a handheld marine red signal flare. These average a burn time of 3 minutes and have a 700 candlepower. These devices work best when used at night.

ORANGE SMOKE SIGNALS

An orange smoke signal is a one-time-use item and should only be used if a rescue team, aircraft, or vessel is sighted. It is flammable and should be handled with caution. To use one, stand with your back to the wind, and keep the device pointed away from your face and body during and after lighting. Other than wind, snow, and rain, the biggest problem associated with a smoke signal is the cold air that keeps the smoke close to the ground, sometimes dissipating it before it reaches the heights needed to be seen. Two types are the SkyBlazer and the Orion.

SkyBlazer Smoke Signal

The SkyBlazer smoke signal is about the size of a 35-millimeter film container and thus is easy to carry. It's also easy to use, and the directions are on the container. Simply remove its seal, pull the chain, and then place it on the ground—the SkyBlazer smoke signal is not a handheld device. The signal only lasts for forty-five seconds under optimal conditions and produces only a small amount of orange smoke. In order to create a more appropriate quantity of smoke, I have used two at once.

Orion Handheld Orange Smoke Signal

The Orion signal is bigger than the SkyBlazer. It comes in two sizes: marine and wilderness. The marine signal is about the size of a road flare, and the wilderness signal is half that. The Orion, too, has easy-to-read directions right on the signal. Simply remove the cap, and strike the ignition button with the abrasive part of the cap. To avoid burns, hold the flare

A smoke signal is a one-time-use item and should only be used when rescue is sighted.

in its safe area, and never hold it overhead. These signals put out a lot of smoke and last over sixty seconds. If space permits, this is far more effective than the SkyBlazer. Orion also makes a floating orange smoke signal that lasts for four minutes.

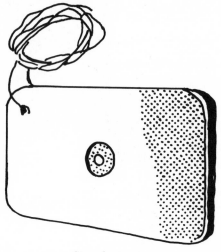

Signal mirror

SIGNAL MIRRORS (WITH SIGHTING HOLE)

On clear, sunny days, signal mirrors have been seen from as far away as 70 to 100 miles. Although the signal mirror is a great signaling device, it requires practice to become proficient in its use. Most signal mirrors have directions on the back, but here are general guidelines on how to use one. Holding the signal mirror between the index finger and thumb of one hand, reflect the sunlight from the mirror onto your other hand. While maintaining the sun's reflection on your free hand, bring the mirror up to eye level and look through the sighting hole. If done properly, you should see a bright white or orange spot of light in the sighting hole. This is commonly called the aim indicator or fireball. Holding the mirror close to your eye, slowly turn it until the aim indicator is on your intended target. If you lose sight of the aim indicator, start over. Since the mirror can be seen from a great distance, sweep the horizon throughout the day, even if no rescuers are in sight. On land, add movement to the signal by slightly wiggling the mirror. At sea, hold the mirror steady so that it stands out from the sparkles created by the water movement. If signaling an aircraft, stop after you're certain the pilot has spotted you, as the flash may impede his or her vision.

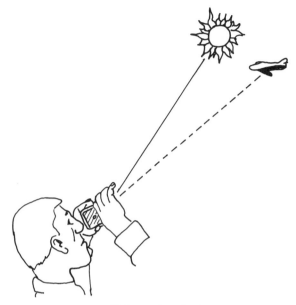

Using a signal mirror

The flash from a signal mirror as seen by a rescue helicopter.

KITE

Kites are a highly visible signal that not only attract attention to your location, but also help rescuers pinpoint where you are. David Instruments' Sky-Alert Parafoil Rescue Kite is a good example. The 28- by 38-inch kite flies in 5 to 25 knots of wind and only requires about 8 to 10 knots to lift another signaling device, such as a strobe or handheld flare. A benefit of this signal is that it can be working for you while you attend to other needs. In addition to providing a great signal, flying the kite can also help alleviate stress.

STROBE LIGHT

A strobe light is a device that fits in the palm of your hand and provides an ongoing intermittent flash. Acr Electronics Personal Rescue Strobe is a good example of this. It delivers a bright flash (250,000 peak lumens) at one-second intervals and can run up to eight hours on AA batteries. It is visible for up to 1 nautical mile on a clear night. As with all battery-operated devices, strobe lights are vulnerable to cold, moisture, sand, and heat; protect the strobe from these hazards by any means available.

WHISTLE

Always carry a whistle on your person. A whistle will never wear out, and its sound travels farther than the screams of the most desperate survivor. If you become lost or separated, immediately begin blowing your whistle in multiple short bursts. Repeat every three to five minutes. If rescue doesn't appear imminent, go about meeting your other survival needs, stopping periodically throughout the day to blow the whistle. It may alert rescue of your location, even if you're unaware of their presence. Storm Whistle's Storm Safety Whistle is a good example. Its unique design makes it the loudest whistle you can buy, even when soaking wet. It is made from plastic and has easy-to-grip ridges.

GROUND-TO-AIR PATTERN SIGNAL

A ground-to-air signal is an extremely effective device that allows you to attend to your other needs, while continuing to alert potential rescuers to your location. Although you can buy a signal panel, I'd suggest purchasing a 3- by 18-foot-long piece of lightweight nylon—orange for winter and white for summer. There are three basic signal designs you should know, and each can be made using the nylon.

V = Need assistance

X = Need medical assistance

↑ = Proceed this way

Once you've created the appropriate signal, stake it out so that it holds its form and doesn't blow away. For optimal effect, follow these guidelines.

Ground-to-air signal as seen by a rescue helicopter.

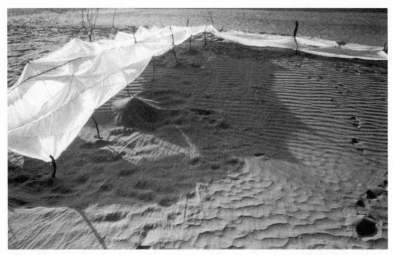

Elevating the ground-to-air signal creates a shadow and makes it appear larger.

1. Size: The ideal size has a ratio of 6 to 1, with its overall size at least 18 feet long by 3 feet wide.
2. Contrast: The signal should contrast the surrounding ground cover, such as orange on white ground and white on brown or green.
3. Angularity: Because nature has no perfect lines, a signal with sharp angles will be more effective.
4. Shadow: In summer, elevate the signal. In winter, stomp or dig an area around the signal about 3 feet wide. If the sun is shinning, either of these methods will create a shadow, which ultimately increases the signal's size.
5. Movement: Setting up a flag next to your signal may create enough movement to catch the attention of a rescue party. It is also advisable to suspend a flag high above your shelter so that it can be seen from all directions by potential rescuers.

IMPROVISED SIGNALS

Many manufactured signals are one-time-use items or are limited by their battery life, and it may be necessary to augment them with an improvised signal. A fire can be as effective as a red flare; a smoke generator works better and lasts longer than an orange smoke signal; an improvised signal mirror can be as useful as a manufactured one; and a ground-to-air signal can be made from materials provided by Mother Nature.

FIRE AS A SIGNAL

During the night, fire is probably the most effective means of signaling available. One large fire will suffice to alert rescue to your location. Don't waste your time, energy, and wood building three fires in a distress triangle, unless rescue is uncertain. Prepare the wood or other fuel for ignition prior to use.

SMOKE GENERATOR

Smoke is an effective signal if used on a clear, calm day. If the weather is bad, however, chances are the smoke will dissipate too quickly to be seen. The rules for a smoke signal are the same as those for a fire signal: You only need one, and prepare the materials for the signal in advance. To

A large fire is an effective night signal.

make the smoke contrast against its surroundings, add any of the following materials to your fire:

To contrast snow: Use tires, oil, or fuel to create black smoke.

To contrast darker backgrounds: Use boughs, grass, green leaves, moss, ferns, or even a small amount of water to create a white smoke.

Set up the smoke generator in advance so that it can be quickly lit when rescue is spotted. To do this, build, but don't light, a tepee fire with a platform and brace, using a lot of tinder and kindling in the process. Then construct a log cabin firelay around the tepee, using fuel that is thumb size and larger. Leave a small, quick access opening that will allow you to reach the tinder when it comes time to light it. Finally, place a heavy bough (or similar material) over the top of the whole thing. The covering should be thick enough to protect the underlying structure from the elements. When done, the generator should look like a haystack. Once rescue has been spotted or appears to be headed in your direction, gently

A smoke signal as seen from the cockpit of a rescue helicopter

pick up one side of the covering, and light the smoke generator. If you have trouble getting it lit, this is one of the rare circumstances where I'd advise using your red signal flare as a heat source.

IMPROVISED SIGNAL MIRRORS

You can create a signal mirror from anything shiny, such as a metal container, coin, credit card, watch, jewelry, or belt buckle. Although an improvised signal mirror can make a great signaling device, it requires practice to become proficient in its use. To use one, follow these steps: Holding the device between the index finger and thumb of one hand, reflect the sunlight from the mirror onto the palm of your other hand. While keeping the reflection on that hand, create a V between your thumb and index finger. Move the light reflection and your hand until the rescue aircraft or other rescuer is in the V. At this point, move the reflected light into the V and onto your intended target. Since the mirror can be seen from great distances, sweep the horizon periodically throughout the day

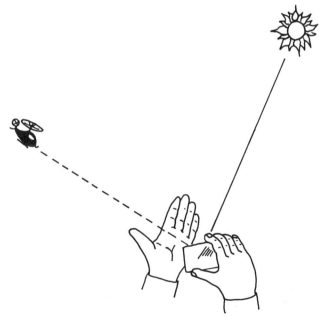

Any shiny reflective material can be used as an improvised signal mirror.

even if no rescue vehicles are in sight. On land, wiggle the mirror slightly to add movement to the signal. At sea, hold the mirror steady to contrast the sparkles created by the natural movement of the water. When signaling an aircraft, stop flashing after you're certain the pilot has spotted you, as it may impede his or her vision.

IMPROVISED GROUND-TO-AIR PATTERN SIGNAL
If you don't have a signal panel, you can improvise one from what Mother Nature provides—boughs, bark, logs, grass, brush, or any other material that contrasts the ground color. Follow the basic guidelines of construction under ground-to-air pattern signal above.

HELICOPTER RESCUE

Helicopter rescues are becoming more prominent as more and more people head into the wilderness. Rescue crews may be civilian, but more often than not they are either military personnel or the Coast Guard. If the helicopter can land, it will. If not, a member of the rescue team will be lowered to your

Helicopter rescue

position. At this point you'll either be hoisted to the helicopter or moved to a better location while in a harness or basket dangling from the helicopter. Secure all loose items before the helicopter lands, or they may be blown away or sucked up into the rotors. Once the helicopter has landed, do not approach it until signaled to do so, and only approach from the downhill front side. This will ensure that the pilot can see you and decrease the chances of being injured or killed by the rotor blades.

SURVIVAL TIPS

Signal often. Since you never know if someone might be in the vicinity, blow your whistle every five to ten minutes, and scan the horizon periodically with your signal mirror.

Always be prepared. To avoid watching rescuers disappear while you're still fumbling with your signals, learn how to use them in advance, and make sure they are ready to use before rescue is near.

11

Travel and Navigation

Navigation is the ability to get from point A to point B using landmarks and references to identify your position and plan a route of travel. As long as you are able to meet your survival needs, stay put. Rescue attempts are far more successful when searching for a stationary survivor. However, there are exceptions. On land, travel should only be considered when one of the following is met.

1. If your present location doesn't have adequate resources to meet your needs, such as for personal protection, sustenance, or signaling.
2. If rescue doesn't appear to be imminent.
3. If you know your location and have the navigational skills to travel to safety.

Hopefully, you established an emergency heading before beginning the adventure. An emergency heading is one that takes you to a well-traveled road, regardless of where you might be during your short trip. On longer trips, this heading might need daily adjustment. If you do travel, leave a ground-to-air signal pointing in the direction of travel and a note detailing your intentions.

At sea, the same rules apply. Unless the vessel is burning, sinking, or poses another threat, stay close to it. If you must travel, consider a heading that takes you toward shipping lanes, land, or rain (you'll need drinkable water).

MAP AND COMPASS

A map and compass are the basic tools that most backcountry travelers use for navigating in the wilderness. Identifying your location, determining direction of travel, and avoiding obstacles all require a good understanding of compass and map nomenclature.

MAP NOMENCLATURE

The particulars of any map's nomenclature can usually be found within its main body and the surrounding margins. For a map to be an effective tool, however, you must become familiar with the one you're using before departing to the wilderness, as there are several different types of maps available. The basic components of most commercial maps are as follows.

Size

If traveling on land, you will most likely use large-scale topical maps. When traveling by air or sea, you will use smaller nautical or aeronautic charts. The exact size of a map or chart is determined by its ratio relationship, also known as its representation fraction. For example, maps or charts with a scale of 1:50,000 have been created so that one unit (any unit of measurement) on the map represents 50,000 units in actual terrain. Maps with a scale of 1:24,000 are considered large-scale maps since they provide much more detail over a small area. Maps with a scale of 1:250,000 are considered small-scale maps since they provide much less detail over a large area. In other words, large-scale maps cover less area and provide much more detail than a small-scale map. The easiest way to identify the relative size (large or small scale) of a map or chart is to understand that the bigger the second number the smaller the scale. Think of it as a fraction; 1:24,000 is equal to $\frac{1}{24,000}$, a bigger fraction than 1:100,000, which is equal to $\frac{1}{100,000}$. In addition to scale, maps often list the latitude and longitude area covered. For example, a 7.5-minute series map covers 7.5 minutes of latitude and 7.5 minutes of longitude, and a 15-minute series map covers 15 minutes of latitude and 15 minutes of longitude. It would take four of the 7.5-minute series maps to cover the same surface area as one 15-minute series map. Several examples of topographic maps are listed here.

Large-Scale Topographic Maps

Large-scale topographic maps use a representation fraction of 1:24,000 (7.5-minute series) where 1 inch equals 0.3946 statute miles (0.610 km). These maps provide much detail and are the map of choice for most backpackers.

Medium-Scale Topographic Maps

Medium-scale topographic maps use a representation fraction of 1:62,500 (15-minute series) where 1 inch equals 0.9864 statute miles (1.588 km). These maps are used for planning long backpacking trips.

Small-Scale Topographic Maps

Small-scale topographic maps use a representation fraction of 1:100,000 (30- by 60-minute series) where one inch equals 1.578 statute miles (2.54 km). These maps are used for planning long-distance travel by vehicle or on foot.

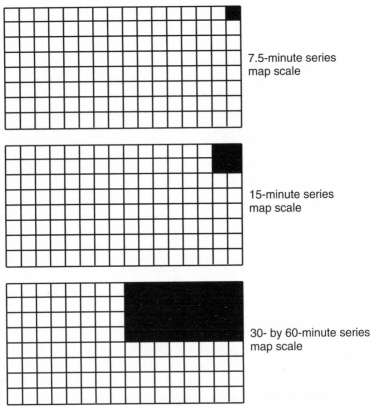

7.5-minute series
map scale

15-minute series
map scale

30- by 60-minute series
map scale

Map scale and series relationship

Colors and symbols

The color and symbols on a map denote different things and are very useful in evaluating the terrain. When evaluating the accuracy of symbols, however, don't forget to check the map's date. Roads, buildings, and other features may have changed since the publish date. Most common colors and their meanings are as follows:

Green = woodland

White = nonforested areas such as rocks, meadows, etc.

Blue = water

Black = man-made structures such as buildings and trails

Red = prominent man-made items such as major roads, etc.

Brown = contour lines (covered below)

Contour lines

Contour lines are imaginary lines (superimposed on a map) that connect points of equal elevation. Charts, unlike maps, rarely use contour lines. Instead they list water depths as numbers and provide information regarding passageways and shallow areas that help the navigator avoid obstacles. Topographical maps use contour lines to reflect the land's elevation changes related to the map's vertical datum (often equivalent to mean sea level). The interval between two contour lines is usually found in the map's margins close to the bar scale. Each map uses a contour interval that best suits its size and the steepness of terrain, and thus the contour interval between two maps is not always the same.

Contour lines are normally brown, and in order to help the navigator calculate larger elevation changes, every fifth line is bold. In addition, in areas that are relatively flat, dashed contour lines might appear between the regular lines. The dashed lines usually represent one-half of the contour lines' regular intervals. Contour lines help provide information related to the terrain's elevation, slope, and shape.

Elevation

Your elevation or that of a destination can be obtained using contour lines. On most maps, the fifth bolded line will provide a number value (in feet or meters) related to mean sea level. Using the fifth line's known elevation allows you to quickly identify an elevation by adding or subtracting the contour interval (distance between each contour line) for each line above or below the referenced line. Maps provide a numeric value for elevation of such items as peaks, road junctions, and benchmarks (surveyor's vertical junction points marked with an X and the letters BM).

Slope
Contour lines help identify the steepness of a slope that may fall within a route of travel. Lines that are close together represent steep terrain; lines far apart represent a more gradual gentle slope.

Shape
Contour shapes help identify various land features like peaks, depressions, saddles, valleys, drainages, and ridgelines.

> *Peaks:* A high point (mountain or hilltop). Contour line forms an enclosed circle.

> *Depressions:* A low point. Contour line forms an enclosed circle with short inward-pointing dashes from the inner surface.

> *Saddle:* A low area between two peaks. Contour lines usually form a U or V between the two peaks. Saddles provide easy passage through mountainous terrain.

> *Valley:* A large low-lying area. Contour lines are similar to a saddle except the low area is much larger than the smaller passage found in a saddle.

> *Drainage:* An area with sharp upward-sloping sides usually found close to a peak. Contour lines form a V pointing toward higher elevation. Year-round or intermittent creeks are often found in drainages.

> *Ridgeline:* An area with sharp downward-sloping sides usually found close to a peak. Contour lines form a V pointing toward lower elevation.

Coordinate systems
Coordinate systems allow us to identify a location using intersecting lines. These systems include angular coordinates (latitude and longitude) and

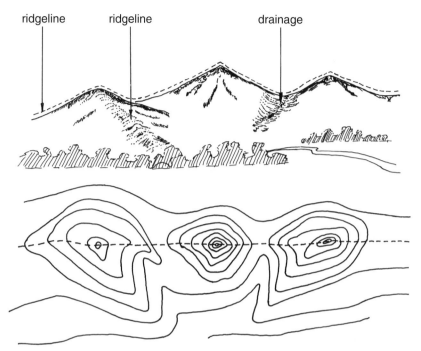

ridgeline   ridgeline   drainage

Contour lines are two-dimensional representations of the three-dimensional terrain.

rectangular coordinates (the most often used rectangular coordinate system is the Universal Transverse Mercator).

Angular coordinates (latitude/longitude)

Parallels of latitude and meridians of longitude are imaginary lines that encircle the globe, creating a crisscross grid system that helps you identify your location.

Latitude lines run east to west and are numbered from 0 to 90 degrees north and south of the equator. The equator has the 0-degree latitude designation (it is the divide between north and south) and, like the rungs of a ladder, latitude lines progress until they reach the north and south poles (90 degrees north latitude and 90 degrees south latitude, respectively). These lines run parallel to one another and are used to measure north and

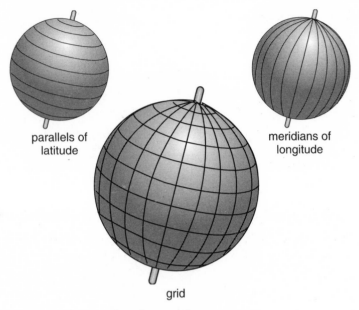

parallels of
latitude

meridians of
longitude

grid

Angular coordinate system

south distances. Latitude is often noted at the extreme ends of the horizontal map edges.

Longitude lines run north and south and are numbered from 0 to 180 degrees east and west of Greenwich, England. The 0-degree longitude line is known as the prime meridian. The 0-degree meridian becomes the 180th east or west meridian once it intersects the extreme north and south sections of the globe. The 180th meridian is also known as the International Date Line. When it is 12:00 at the prime meridian (Greenwich Mean Time), it is 24:00 at the International Date Line. The earth rotates 15 degrees an hour, 180 degrees in twelve hours, and 360 degrees in twenty-four hours. Crossing the International Date Line also changes the date.

Unlike latitude lines, longitude lines are not parallel to one another and therefore cannot be used for measuring distances. Longitude is often noted at the extreme ends of the vertical map edges. Most maps will display longitude and latitude values on the map's vertical and horizontal edges and a large plus sign to indicate locations where latitude and longitude lines cross.

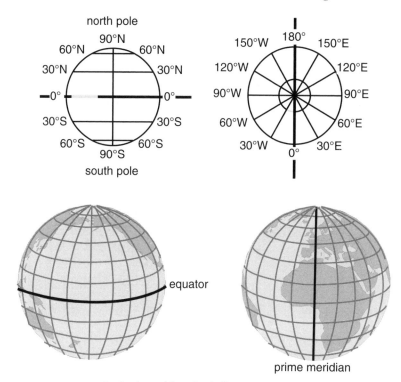

Latitude and longitude line progression

Angular coordinate lines (latitude and longitude) are measured in degrees (°), minutes ('), and seconds ("). There are sixty seconds in one minute and sixty minutes in 1 degree. One minute of 1 degree of all latitudes is equal to 1 nautical mile (approximately 1.15 statute miles) or 1,852 meters, regardless of your location. One degree of all latitudes is equal to 60 nautical miles (69 statute miles). However, since longitude lines are not parallel, but converge at the north and south poles, the distance between one minute of longitude decreases as you move up or down the longitude line—it is greatest at the equator and zero at the poles. With this in mind, you can use a degree or minute of latitude to measure distances but not a degree or minute of longitude, which constantly changes.

It's important to distinguish north from south when defining latitude and east from west for longitude. For example, a latitude of 45° 30' 30"

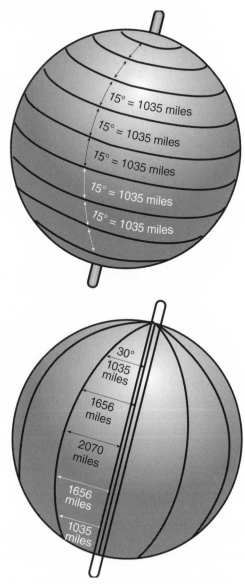

Unlike latitude lines, longitude lines get closer together north or south of the equator.

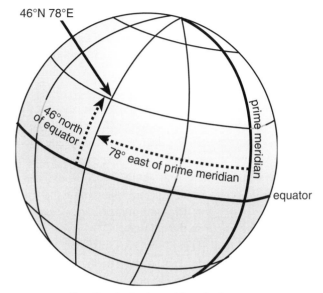

Reading latitude and longitude

north of the equator would read 45 degrees, 30 minutes, and 30 seconds north latitude. If at the same coordinate position south of the equator, it would read 45 degrees, 30 minutes, and 30 seconds south latitude. A latitude line will never be over 90 degrees north or south. A longitude of 120° 30' 30" east of the prime meridian would read as 120 degrees, 30 minutes, and 30 seconds east longitude. If at the same coordinate position west of the prime meridian, it would read 120 degrees, 30 minutes, and 30 seconds west longitude. A longitude line will never be over 180 degrees east or west. Whenever you give latitude and longitude coordinates, always read the latitude first.

Rectangular coordinates
Although there are several types of rectangular coordinate systems, the Universal Transverse Mercator (UTM) system is the one most often used. The Universal Transverse Mercator (UTM) grid system uses a rectangular framework that links its coordinate system to a measurement of distance. The UTM system designates rectangular coordinates onto the world map

between latitudes 84° north and 80° south. Although not an angular system, these large quadrilateral grids are centered exactly on a line of longitude (central meridian) and use latitude and longitude coordinates to establish size.

The UTM system uses sixty zones (columns) that are 6 degrees apart and begin at the 180th meridian, advancing to the east. For example, zone one is located between 174 degrees west longitude and 180 degrees west longitude, zone two between 168 degrees west longitude and 174 degrees west longitude, and so on. Each of the sixty zones has its own origin (located at the equator and its central meridian). Using the central meridian of a zone as its origin ensures that all spots within that zone are within 3 degrees of the center line. The central meridian is exactly 6 degrees of longitude from the origin of the adjoining UTM grids. For example, the central meridian of zone ten is 123 degrees west longitude, zone eleven is 117 degrees west longitude, and so on. The creation of sixty separate zones limits the distortion to less than 0.04 percent, making it an acceptable option, especially for large-scale maps.

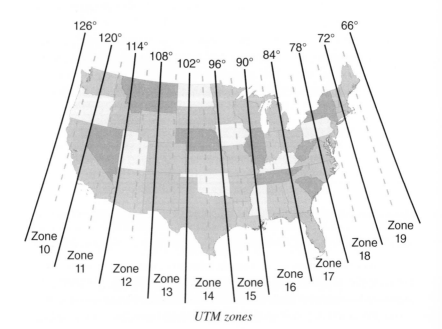

UTM zones

Most U.S. Geological Survey (USGS) maps display the Universal Transverse Mercator (UTM) grid zone in addition to angular coordinate system, allowing you to identify a location by both its latitude and longitude and grid zone coordinates. The map's grid zone is often found within the marginal information at the bottom of the map.

UTM grid coordinates are expressed as a distance in meters to the east (called easting) and to the north (called northing). All easting coordinates relate to the zone's central meridian, which is assigned an easting value of 500,000 meters east. An easting of zero, however, will never occur, since a 6-degree-wide zone is never more than 674,000 meters wide. All northing coordinates relate to the equator, which is given two different values. For locations north of the equator, the equator is assigned the northing value of 0 meters north. To avoid negative numbers, the equator is assigned the northing value of 10,000,000 meters north for locations south of the equator. Since a zone can have two of the same northing values (one north of the equator and one south), it is important to know which hemisphere of the zone you are in (northern or southern). The easting and northing values are arbitrary figures and are therefore often referred to as false easting and false northing.

Coordinates of the UTM system depict an area of precision directly related to the easting and northing value, which represents the bottom left corner of a square. The size of the square depends on the number of digits used and ranges from a 100,000-meter square to a 1-meter square. Within a UTM zone, a combined (easting and northing) three- or four-digit coordinate represents a location to within 100,000 meters of precision. Five or six digits are within 10,000 meters, seven or eight digits are within 1,000 meters, nine or ten digits are within 100 meters, eleven or twelve digits are within 10 meters, and so on. Since the easting distance of a zone is based on a central meridian of 500,000 (false easting) and the zone's total distance (from its western to eastern edge) never reaches 1,000,000 (seven digits), easting values will either drop the first number or start with a 0. In order to avoid confusion, UTM coordinates are always read in order from left to right and bottom to top (easting value first, northing value second). For example, if your UTM designation was 0605000 mE, 5248000 mN (northern hemisphere), your location would be 0605000 easting (605,000 – 500,000 = 105,000 meters east of the central meridian) and 5248000

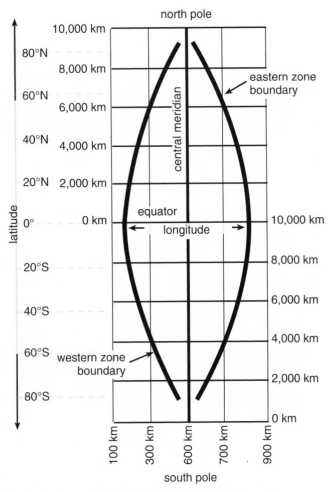

UTM northing and easting

northing (5,248,000 meters north of the equator). It is common to see the coordinates written together as 11 06050005248000 (northern hemisphere), where the grid zone is 11 and the combined coordinates represent 0605000 easting and 5248000 northing. In reality, these coordinates would probably be displayed as 11 6055248 (dropping the easting first zero and the last three zeros of both values). This figure represents the bottom left corner of a 1,000-meter square.

Most USGS topographic maps have a grid overlay or fine blue tic marks every 1,000 meters (1 km) that are located along the maps' outer horizontal and vertical edges. Each marking is labeled relevant to its northing or easting value. To create less clutter, most maps omit the last three zeros and use a smaller type for designations greater than 100,000. For example, if you were located at 607,000 easting and 5,152,000 northing, it would appear as ^{6}07 and ^{51}52 on the map's edge. When using a USGS 7.5-degree quadrangle series (1:24,000 scale) or smaller map, it is doubtful you can calculate a position closer than 10 meters. The closest easting or northing value you will find will usually be a six-digit number (eleven or twelve when easting and northing are combined). In other words, the easting and northing values will drop the last zero. To find the value of the last two digits (after dropping the last zero), use the grid lines or tic marks that are closest to the point you are trying to locate. The easting is the value of the nearest grid line west of your location plus the distance east of that line, and the northing is the value of the nearest grid line south of your location plus the distance north of that line.

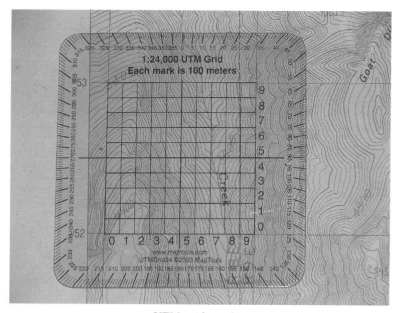

UTM grid overlay

Although you can find a distance or location by eyeballing a map's grid lines, using a UTM grid overlay will provide greater precision. To use the grid overlay, place it on the map with its edges aligned to the map's grid lines. You can determine your UTM location using the tool's markings. If you are located in zone ten and established an easting value of 060750 and a northing value of 515250, it would be written as 10 60750515250 northern hemisphere.

Magnetic Variation

Understanding the relationship between true north, grid north, and magnetic north is extremely important when using a map and compass together. Failing to recognize the differences between them is a potential fatal error.

True north

True north refers to any direction from your location to the north pole. The easiest way to identify this direction on a chart and map is to find a longitude line, since all longitude lines point and converge at true north (and south). You must know the declination angle difference between true north and that found in rectangular coordinate systems (UTM) or a compass, and you must adjust for that difference when appropriate.

Grid north

Grid north refers to the declination difference between true north and a vertical grid line of a rectangular coordinate system (UTM). The grid declination at the central meridian of the UTM system is always zero since it falls on a line of longitude. Grid lines east of the central meridian have a declination to the east, and grid lines to the west of the central meridian have a west declination. All values are relative to true north and increase the farther away from the central meridian and equator you are (see preceding discussion on UTM system related to its origin).

Magnetic north

Magnetic north refers to the direction the compass's magnetic-north-seeking arrow points. Provided there is no magnetic interference, the compass's arrow will point toward Prince of Whales Island located in Northern Canada (magnetic north). Isogonic lines, lines that represent a specific dec-

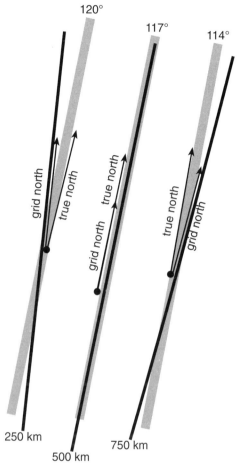

Grid north's relationship to longitude lines

lination's path, provide the angle difference between true north and magnetic north. The only time these lines have a zero value is when your location puts magnetic north directly between you and true north. In such instances, the line is called an agonic line and the declination angle is zero.

The relationship between true north, grid north, and magnetic north is often referred to as *declination* on maps and *variation* on charts. Most maps display the declination as a three-lined diagram that identifies the true north line with a star, magnetic north with a full or half arrow and in

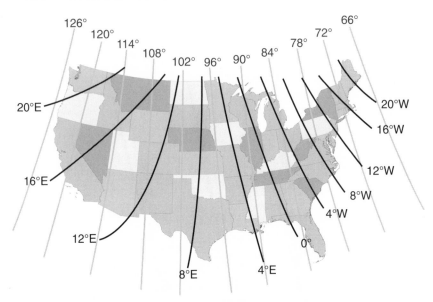

Isogonic lines represent the relationship between magnetic north and true north.

some cases the letters MN, and grid north as a straight line and the letters GN. In addition to the lines, the declination angles between magnetic north and true north, and grid north and true north, are given. The importance of these declination angles is covered in the compass section.

COMPASS NOMENCLATURE

A compass allows the traveler to identify direction, and although there are several types of compasses available, the most common style is the orienteering (base plate) compass. Regardless of the type of orienteering compass you use, it should have a basic design that features a rectangular base plate, circular rotating housing, and a magnetic-north-seeking arrow.

Rectangular base plate

The sides of the base plate have millimeter and inch markings, used to relate a map measurement to that of a relative field distance. The front has a direction-of-travel arrow. The arrow is parallel to the long edge and perpendicular to the short edge. Compass headings are read from the point where the bottom of the direction-of-travel arrow touches the numbers on

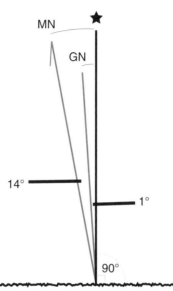

Map declination showing magnetic and grid north west of true north

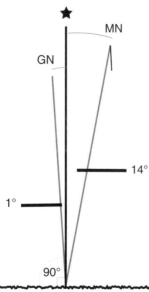

Map declination showing magnetic north east and grid north west of true north

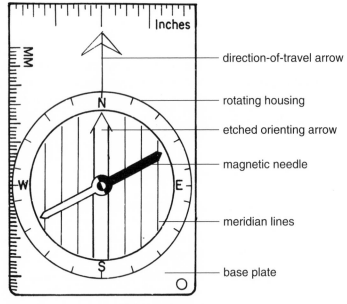

Orienteering compass

the edge of the circular compass housing. If the direction-of-travel arrow is not present or centered on the circular housing, your compass will probably have a stationary index line, sometimes called an index pointer. This nonmoving short white line is located either on the base plate next to the circular housing or inside the circular housing just beneath the moving numbers (it will be centered on the short wall of the base plate and on the same side of the compass as the direction-of-travel arrow). Headings are read where the numbers touch or pass over this line. The direction-of-travel arrow must always point toward the intended destination when a heading is being taken.

Circular housing

A rotating circular housing sits on the base plate. Its outer ring is marked with the four cardinal points (N, S, E, W) and degree lines starting at north and numbered clockwise to 360 degrees. The bottom of the housing has an etched orienting arrow that points toward the north marking on the outer ring.

Magnetic needle

The compass needle sits beneath the circular housing. It floats freely, and one end, which is usually red, points toward magnetic north (not true north). A compass's magnetic-seeking arrow, however, cannot discriminate between magnetic north and other magnetic fields. The magnetic forces affecting a compass are magnetic north, local magnetic field influences, and magnetic interference.

Magnetic north

Compass arrows point to the magnetic north pole, located where the earth's magnetic field is the most concentrated. More specifically, the magnetic pole is located close to 74 degrees north latitude and 101 degrees west longitude (in northern Canada), which is around 1,600 kilometers (1,000 miles) from true north. The difference between true north and mag-

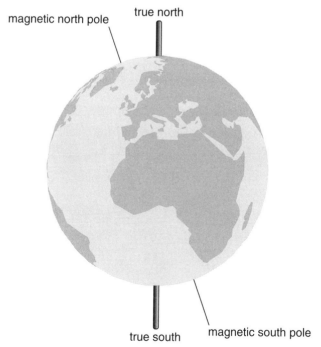

Magnetic north is approximately 1,000 miles from the true north pole.

netic north (called *declination* for maps and *variation* for charts) is different from place to place and year to year due to the earth's never-ending magnetic shifts.

To further explain the difference between magnetic north and true north, take a look at the following illustration. Notice the line that passes through the Great Lakes and along the coast of Florida. This line is an agonic line, and a compass heading of 0 or 360 degrees would point toward both magnetic and true north. In other words, there is no magnetic variation. Lines with a variation between true north and magnetic north are known as isogonic lines. The line that extends through Maine has a variation of 20 degrees west. Note that when this line is extended, the compass bearing of 360 is 20 degrees to the west of true north and the compass heading for true north is actually 20 degrees. The opposite would be true for the line extending through Washington. In this case, a compass bearing of 360 would be 20 degrees east of true north and the compass heading for true north is actually 340 degrees. Because of these variations, adjustments must be made in order to use a map and compass together.

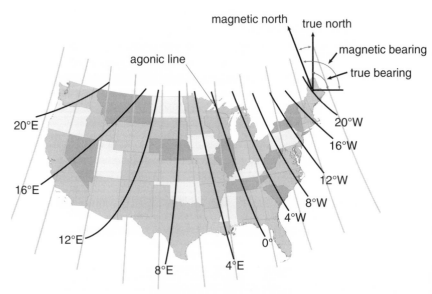

Magnetic north and true north

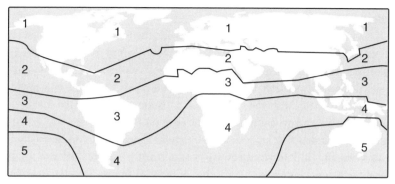

Magnetic fields

Local magnetic field influences

Dips associated with the earth's magnetic field (at various locations) affect the compass's north-seeking arrow. These dips, called magnetic inclination, occur because the earth's magnetic field is almost perpendicular to the earth's surface at either pole. Only at the magnetic equator does the magnetic force run horizontal with the earth's surface. As a result, when close to the poles, the compass's magnetic needle is pulled down and dips away from horizontal. The needle's north end dips down in the northern hemisphere and its south end dips down in the southern hemisphere. To compensate for the dip, compass needles are made with a counterbalance specific to the area of intended use. A compass balanced for one zone would not work well in another zone. Suunto uses the magnetic inclination zones shown in the above illustration for compasses it markets.

Magnetic interference

A compass's magnetic-seeking arrow is a nondiscriminatory device that seeks out any magnetic source. This includes the steel in automobiles, electric currents in buildings, metal fencing, telephone lines, belt buckles, knives, and so on. The compass's magnetic-north-seeking arrow is very susceptible to being pulled away when too close to such objects. It is best to stay a safe distance of 60 or more meters from power lines, 20 meters from vehicles, 10 meters from fencing and telephone lines, and 3 meters from other handheld metal devices.

Beyond the basics

A no-frills orienteering compass will provide the basics as outlined above. Depending on your budget, however, you may elect to purchase an orienteering compass with added features. Perhaps you travel in snow country and desire a clinometer or prefer the added precision found in a mirror compass that can sight the compass on a distant point while the magnetic needle is aligned with the north reference on the dial. Some compasses come with a dial that lets you set the magnetic declination so that a compass heading of 360 points toward true north (for the area you are in). If you are using a compass that can be set for a given magnetic declination, be sure it is set for the correct declination each time you begin a trip. The declination of your last venture may not be the same as your present one.

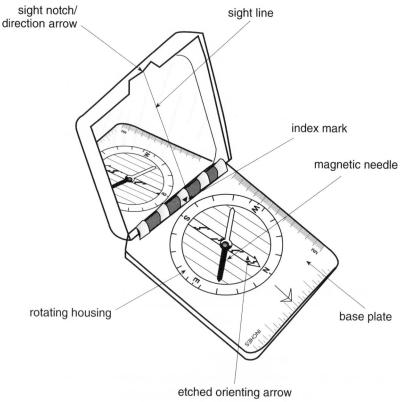

sight notch/
direction arrow

sight line

index mark

magnetic needle

rotating housing

base plate

etched orienting arrow

Mirrored orienteering compass

USING YOUR MAP AND COMPASS TOGETHER

Constant awareness and proper use of your map and compass together are the keys to determining your general and specific location.

Determine general location

Anytime you're traveling in the wilderness you should maintain a constant awareness of your general location, focusing on the surrounding terrain and how it relates to the map you are carrying. If you do this throughout your trip, you shouldn't ever need to use other means of establishing where you are. One way to keep a constant awareness is with dead reckoning. Dead reckoning uses a simple math formula to help you find your present location.

$$\text{Time} \times \text{rate} = \text{distance}$$

Time refers to the amount of time that has passed since you left your last known location.

The rate of speed you travel is usually measured in miles per hour on land or knots per hour at sea. In a vehicle you'll have to remain aware of your speed. The average backpacker travels at a speed of 1 to 3 miles per hour, depending on the weight carried and terrain covered. Take the time to evaluate your speed using known variables. Consider purchasing an electronic pedometer to measure the distance traveled and use it to determine your average rate of speed by applying it to the following formula, where time and distance are known.

$$\text{Distance} \div \text{time} = \text{rate}$$

Once you've determined the distance you've traveled, apply this to your line of travel (heading) from your starting point to figure out your approximate location.

Adjusting your location (latitude and longitude) can be done based on your direction of travel and the distance traveled. There are several other methods you might use to determine your location and direction of travel.

Determining Specific Location

The first step in determining your specific location is to orient the map. Once this is done, you can either shoot a line of position or triangulate to establish a better idea of your whereabouts.

Orienting a Map

Orienting the map aligns its features to those of the surrounding terrain. This process is extremely helpful in determining your specific location.

1. Get to high ground. This will help you to evaluate the terrain once the map is oriented.

2. Open the map and place it on a flat, level surface. If possible, protect it from the dirt and moisture with something such as a poncho.

3. Rotate the circular housing on the compass until the bottom of the direction-of-travel arrow is touching the true north heading. When doing this, you must account for the area's given declination, as outlined above, the difference between magnetic north (MN) and true north (★). True north is north as represented on a map, and magnetic north is the compass heading. In other words, a 360-degree map heading—true north—is not necessarily a 360-degree compass heading. This variation is usually depicted on the bottom of most topographic maps. If magnetic north is located west of true north, which is the case for most of the eastern United States, you would add your declination to 360 degrees. The

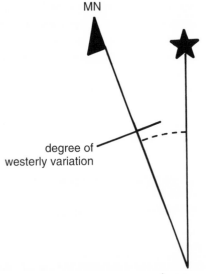

MN

degree of
westerly variation

Westerly magnetic variation

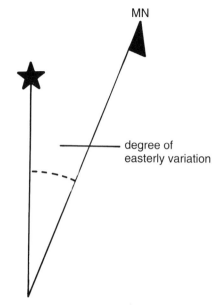

Easterly magnetic variation

resultant bearing would be the compass-heading equivalent to true north at that location. If magnetic north is located east of true north, which is the case for most of the western United States, you would subtract your declination from 360 degrees. The resultant bearing would be the compass-heading equivalent to true north at that location.

4. Set the compass on the map with the edge of the long side resting next to and parallel to the left north-south margins (longitude line). The direction-of-travel arrow should point toward the north end of the map.

5. Holding the compass in place on the map, rotate the map and compass together until the floating magnetic needle is inside the etched orienting arrow on the base plate, with the red portion of the needle forward. This is called boxing the needle.

6. Double-check to ensure that the compass is still set for the variation adjustment, and if correct, weigh down the map edges to keep it in place.

7. At this point, the map is oriented to the lay of the land, and the map features should reflect those of the surrounding terrain.

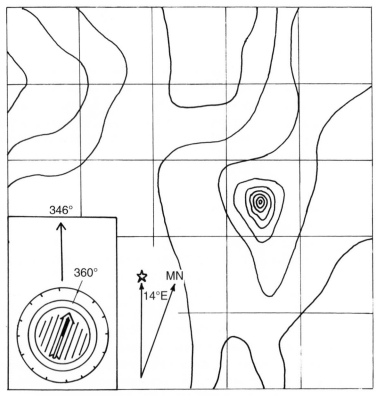

Magnetic variation and orienting the map with a compass

Line of position to determine your location

A single line of position can be used when at least one prominent land feature can be seen. A prominent land feature includes any easily identified
man-made or natural feature. For best results, get to high ground with 360
degrees of visibility.

1. Orient the map as outlined above.
2. Positively identify the prominent land feature. The following guidelines related to contour, distance, and elevation can help in the identification process.

   Contour: Evaluate the landmark's contour, translating it into a
   two-dimensional appearance, and search for a matching contour
   outline on your map.

Distance: Determine the distance from your present position to the landmark to be identified. In treed terrain: From 1 to 3 kilometers (approximately 1 to 2 miles), you should be able to see the individual branches of each tree. From 3 to 5 kilometers (approximately 2 to 3 miles), you should be able to see each individual tree. From 5 to 8 kilometers (approximately 3 to 4 miles), the tree will look like a green plush carpet. At greater than 8 kilometers, not only will the trees appear like a green plush carpet but there will also be a bluish tint to the horizon.

Elevation: Determine your landmark's height as compared with that of your location.

3. Using your orienteering compass, point the direction-of-travel arrow at the identified landmark, and then turn the compass housing until the etched orienting arrow boxes the magnetic needle (red end forward). At the point where the direction-of-travel arrow intersects the compass housing, read and record the magnetic bearing.

4. Before working further with a topographic map, ensure it's still oriented.

5. Place the front left tip of the long edge of the compass (or a straight edge) on the identified map landmark, and while keeping the tip in place, rotate the compass—don't move the map—until the magnetic needle is boxed (red end forward). Double-check that your compass heading is correct for the landmark being used.

6. Lightly pencil a line from the landmark down, following the left edge of the compass base plate or straight edge. You may need to extend the line. If you have a protective plastic cover on your map, you can draw on it to avoid exposing the map to moisture and dirt.

7. Your position should be located on or close to the line. For final position determination, evaluate the surrounding terrain and how it relates to your line, along with believed distances to other land features.

Triangulating to determine your position

Triangulating is a process of identifying your specific location by doing three lines of position. The ideal scenario allows you to positively identify three landmarks that are 120 degrees apart, forming a triangle where the three lines cross. Your position should be located within or around the tri-

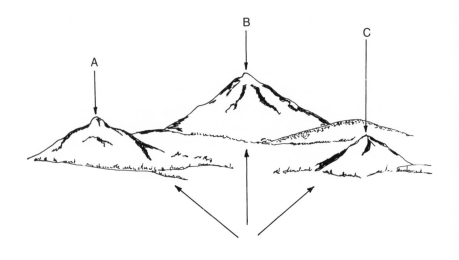

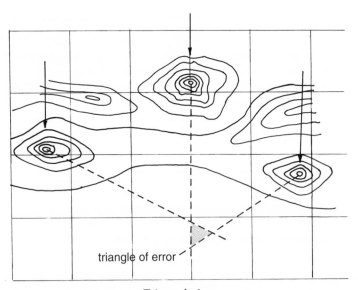

Triangulation

angle. For final position determination, evaluate the surrounding terrain and how it relates to the triangle displayed on the map.

ESTABLISHING A FIELD BEARING
Never travel unless you know both your present position and where you intend to go.

Establishing a field bearing with a map and compass
1. Orient your map to the lay of the land.
2. Lightly draw a pencil line from your present location to your intended destination.
3. Place the top left edge of the compass on your intended destination.
4. Rotate the compass until the left edge is directly on and parallel to the line you drew.
5. Rotate the compass housing—keeping the base of the compass stationary—until the floating magnetic needle is boxed inside the orienting arrow (red portion of the needle forward).
6. Read the compass heading at the point where the bottom of the direction-of-travel arrow touches the numbers of the circular compass housing. This heading is the field bearing to your intended destination.

Establishing a field bearing with only a compass
1. Holding the compass level, point the direction-of-travel arrow directly at the intended destination site.
2. Holding the compass in place, turn its housing until the magnetic needle is boxed directly over and inside the orienting arrow (red portion of the needle forward).
3. Read the heading at the point where the bottom of the direction-of-travel arrow touches the numbers of the circular housing. This heading is the field bearing to your intended destination.

DELIBERATE OFFSET
If your destination is a road, consider a heading with a deliberate offset. In other words, use a field heading several degrees to one side of your final location. Since it is very difficult to be precise in wilderness travel, this offset will help you decide to turn left or right once you intersect the road.

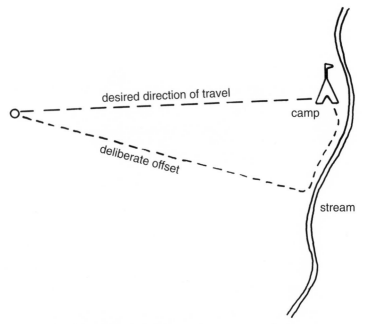

Using a deliberate offset makes it easier to find camp.

MAINTAINING A FIELD BEARING

Point to point
Pick objects in line with your field bearing. Once one point is reached, recheck your bearing and pick another. This method allows the traveler to steer clear of obstacles.

Following the compass
Holding the compass level while keeping the magnetic needle boxed, walk forward in line with the direction-of-travel arrow.

TRAVEL CHECKLIST
1. Heading: Establish the compass heading to your desired location. Once confident of your heading, trust your compass and stay on it.
2. Distance: Determine the total number of kilometers your route will cover.

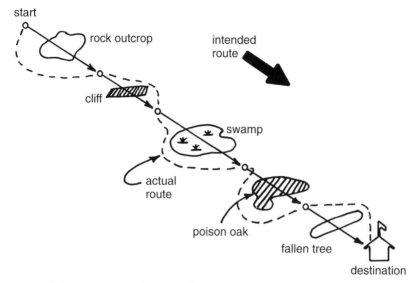

Point-to-point navigation allows you to steer clear of obstacles.

3. Pace count: Estimate the number of paces it will take to reach your final destination (a pace is measured each time the same foot hits the ground). On fairly level terrain, it takes about 650 paces to 1 kilometer. On steep terrain, paces will nearly double for each kilometer.

4. Terrain evaluation: Evaluate your route's major terrain feature, such as a road or clearing, and determine how many paces it takes to each. By doing this, you'll maintain a constant awareness of your location within your route of travel.

5. Point description: Take the time to evaluate the appearance of your final location. This will help when the time comes to evaluate if you have had a successful trip.

6. Estimated arrival time: Estimating your arrival time will help you set realistic goals on the distance to travel each day.

DETERMINING DIRECTION USING THE SUN

When headed into the great unknown, always take a map and compass with you. If by some odd circumstance, however, you find yourself without a map and compass, the sun can be used for establishing cardinal directions.

As a general rule, the sun rises to the east in the morning and sets to the west in the evening. The sun does not, however, follow the same east–west passage from one day to the next, and unless you are on the same latitude as the sun's passage, it will not rise and set directly due east or west. Depending on the time of year, the sun can follow an east–west route anywhere between 23 degrees 27 minutes north and 23 degrees 27 minutes south latitude. The sun reaches its maximum northern and southern route on the longest and shortest days of the year, the solstices (23 degrees 27 minutes north latitude on June 21 and 23 degrees 27 minutes south latitude on December 21). The sun passes directly over the equator during the equinoxes (March 21 and September 23). During the equinox, the lengths of day and night are equal. Regardless of the sun's passage or your location, the sun will be directly overhead, due north or due south of your location, at local apparent noon (when it is at its highest point in the sky and halfway between rising and setting).

STICK AND SHADOW

Near midday, all shadow tips move due east and are accurate within 10 degrees (or thereabout) for two to three hours on either side of local apparent noon (shortest shadow of the day). This is true no matter what your location or the time of year. During morning and evening hours, however, the stick-and-shadow method can be off by a significant amount.

Before midday (local apparent noon) on a flat surface, scrape away debris and vegetation until a 3-foot bare ground surface is all that remains. Find a 4-foot stick and sharpen it at both ends. With the stick perpendicular to the ground, force the downward end into the dirt so that the shadow of the upward end is centered on the area you prepared. Try to get the stick as perpendicular to the ground as you can. Mark the shadow tip with a twig or rock. Every five minutes place another marker at the shadow tip's new location. Watch as the shadow gets shorter and then longer. The shortest shadow occurs when the sun is either due north or south of your location (depending on the hemisphere you're in and the time of year). Draw a line that connects the shadow tips located on each side of the shortest shadow. This line represents east and west. Since the sun rises in the east and sets in the west, the first marking on the shadow line is west and the second one is east. Creating a line perpendicular to the east and west line provides

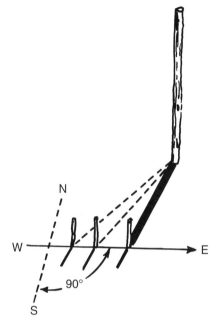

Stick and shadow

a north–south reference. This line should occur close to the location where the shortest shadow was seen. The constantly changing relationship between the earth and sun creates obstacles when using a stick and shadow in the tropic and polar regions.

Tropic region
During the summer solstice, the sun's rays shine directly over the tropic of Cancer (23 degrees 27 minutes north); during the winter solstice the sun's rays shine directly over the tropic of Capricorn (23 degrees 27 minutes south). Between these dates, the sun could be north or south of the equator (depending on the season) anywhere between 23 degrees 27 minutes north and south. This poses no problem—simply realize that the first shadow is west and that the subsequent shadows move toward the east. A perpendicular line to the east–west line allows you to find north and south.

Temperate region

The stick-and-shadow method works best in the temperate latitudes (between 23 degrees 27 minutes and 66 degrees 33 minutes north and south latitude). The shadow always moves from west to east (opposite the sun's movement, which is from the east to the west), and the sun is always due south in the northern hemisphere and due north in the southern hemisphere at local apparent noon (shortest shadow of the day).

Polar region

Beginning with the summer solstice, latitudes above 66 degrees 33 minutes north (Arctic Circle) may never see the sunset, and latitudes below 66 degrees 33 minutes south (Antarctic Circle) may never see the sunrise. On the flip side, during the winter solstice things change and latitudes within the Arctic Circle may never see the sunrise, and latitudes within the Antarctic Circle may never see the sunset. The sun's position on the horizon and its constant presence—or lack thereof—make the stick-and-shadow method impractical in regions greater than 66 degrees 33 minutes north and south latitude.

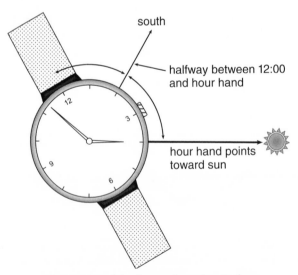

Using a watch in the northern hemisphere

DETERMINING DIRECTION USING A WATCH
A watch can be used to find cardinal directions. Like the stick and shadow, this method should be used within one to two hours of local apparent noon.

Using a watch in the northern hemisphere
Keeping the watch level, point its hour hand toward the sun, and draw an imaginary line between its hour hand and 12 o'clock (1 o'clock if daylight savings time). The line represents a gross southern heading. With a known southern heading, a second line drawn perpendicular to the first is all that's needed to establish directions.

Using a watch in the southern hemisphere
Keeping the watch level, point it's 12 o'clock symbol (1 o'clock if daylight savings time) toward the sun, and draw an imaginary line midway between

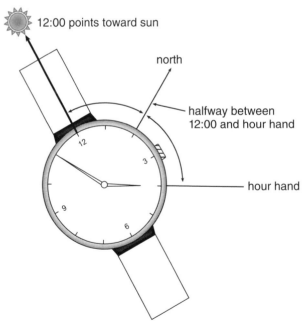

Using a watch in the southern hemisphere

the 12 o'clock symbol and the hour hand. The line represents a gross northern heading. With a known northern heading, a second line drawn perpendicular to the first is all that's needed to establish directions.

LOCAL APPARENT NOON

At local apparent noon, the sun has reached its highest point and will be due south if you are in the northern hemisphere and due north if in the southern hemisphere. Local apparent noon is not necessarily the same as a 12:00 reading on your watch—it is unlikely that the sun will always be highest at this time or even close to it. There are several methods of determining local apparent noon. In order for these methods to work, the horizon height used must be the same for the first recording (sometimes called sunrise) and for the second (sometimes called sunset).

To establish local apparent noon, record the exact sunrise and sunset times, based on the twenty-four-hour clock, add them together, and divide the total by 2. Sunrise is when the top of the sun first appears on the horizon; sunset is when the top of the sun disappears on the horizon. This is based on a nonobscured view of the horizon. The resultant figure is your local apparent noon—when the sun is directly north or south depending on your hemisphere.

Time of sunrise + time of sunset ÷ 2 = local apparent noon

For example, if sunrise was at 0720 hr and sunset at 1930 hr:

0720 + 1930 = 2650 ÷ 2 = 1325 hr

In this example, 1325 hour, 1:25 P.M., is local apparent noon, and this figure can be used to help you determine your cardinal directions, since the sun should be directly north or south of you at that time. Given that the sun moves 15 degrees an hour, you can maintain a course by simply establishing the cardinal directions and then using the sun to adjust your heading throughout the day. If the horizon is obscured by shadows, a kamal device could be used to achieve the same result.

Kamal

This device allows you to create a new horizon above any cloud or haze that obscures your view. Create one by attaching a string to something flat, such as a credit card, and tying a knot in the free end of the string. Place the knot on the string so that the line is tight when the flat plate is held out with an extended arm. To use, place the knot between your teeth, and hold the flat plate out so that its bottom touches the horizon. Your sunrise is when the top of the sun first appears at the top of the card; sunset is when the top of the sun disappears below the top of the card. If more height is needed, use a larger card. The recorded figures can be used to determine local apparent noon in the same fashion as described above.

DETERMINING DIRECTION USING THE STARS

NORTHERN HEMISPHERE
In the northern hemisphere, Cassiopeia and the Big Dipper are very useful tools for helping you find Polaris, the North Star. The Big Dipper looks like a cup with a long handle. Cassiopeia is made up of five stars that form a large W, with its opening facing the Big Dipper. The Big Dipper and Cassiopeia rotate counterclockwise around Polaris, and halfway between these constellations, Polaris can be found. It is located at the very end of the Little Dipper's handle. Contrary to popular belief, it is not the brightest star in the sky but instead is rather dull. Between 5 and 50 degrees north latitude, Polaris is within 1 degree of true north, and at latitudes between 50 and 60 degrees north, it may be off as much as 2 degrees. Cassiopeia provides the key to this variance.

Polaris is due north (360- or 0-degree heading) when Cassiopeia is directly above or below its location.

Polaris is at a 001-degree heading when Cassiopeia is to its right (002 degrees above 50 degrees north).

Polaris is at a 359-degree heading when Cassiopeia is to its left (358 degrees above 50 degrees north).

When both constellations cannot be seen, you can still find Polaris or determine your cardinal directions with one of the following methods.

Big Dipper
Two stars form the front end of the Big Dipper's cup. Extend a line from the uppermost of these two stars approximately four to five times the distance between them to find Polaris.

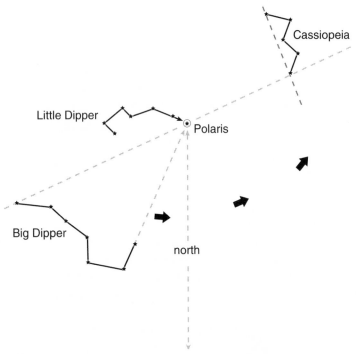

The Big Dipper and Cassiopeia are useful tools for finding the North Star.

Cassiopeia

From Cassiopeia's trailing star, extend a line out approximately two times the distance measured between the leading and trailing stars that form the W to find Polaris.

Orion's Belt

Orion the Hunter circles the earth directly above the equator. The leading star of Orion's Belt, called Mintaka, rises exactly due east and sets exactly due west. The belt is formed by three close stars in line at the center of the constellation. Unless you are located at the equator, however, Orion will not rise directly due east or set due west of you. If you know your latitude and have an unobstructed view of the horizon, however, you can calculate Orion's rising and setting direction. The rising angle equals 90 degrees minus your latitude. This heading (the rising angle of Mintaka as compared to your location) can be used to establish cardinal directions.

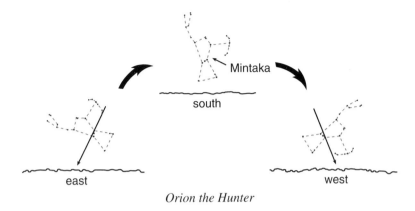

Orion the Hunter

SOUTHERN HEMISPHERE

To determine the cardinal directions in the southern hemisphere, use the Southern Cross, a constellation with four bright stars that look as though they are the tips of a cross, and the Pointer Stars. The False Cross looks similar to the Southern Cross and may create confusion. The False Cross

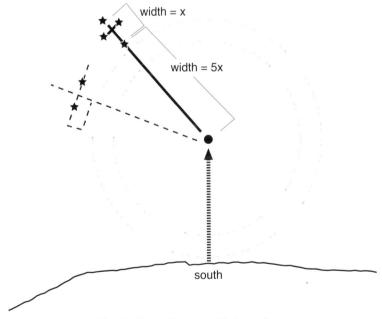

The Southern Cross and Pointer Stars

is less bright than the Southern Cross, and its stars are more widely spaced. In fact, the southern and eastern arms of the actual Southern Cross are two of the brightest stars in the sky. The Pointer Stars are two stars that are side by side and in close proximity to the Southern Cross. To establish a southern heading, extend an imaginary line from the top through the bottom of the cross. Draw another imaginary line perpendicular to the center of the Pointer Stars. At the point where the lines intersect, draw a third line straight down toward the ground; this line represents a southern direction.

NIGHT VERSION OF THE STICK AND SHADOW

At night most travelers will use Polaris (the North Star) or the Southern Cross and Pointer Stars to determine their cardinal directions. When these constellations cannot be found, however, you may opt to use stars—located away from the celestial poles—to create cardinal directions. Since these stars generally move from east to west, they can provide the same east–west line as shown with the stick and shadow. Find a straight 5-foot-long stick, and push it into the ground at a slight angle. Tie a piece of line to the top of the stick, ensuring that it is long enough to reach the ground with lots to spare. Lying on your back, position yourself so that you can

Night version of the stick and shadow

pull the cord taut, and hold it next to your temple. Move your body around until the taunt line is pointing directly at the selected, noncircumpolar star or planet. At this point, the line represents the star's shadow. Place a rock at the place where the line touches the ground, and repeat the process every ten minutes or so. Similar to the stick-and-shadow technique, the first mark is west and the second one is east. A perpendicular line will aid you in determining north and south.

GLOBAL POSITIONING SYSTEM (GPS)

A Global Positioning System (GPS) is a tool that can augment solid navigation skills but should *never* replace them. Learn how to use a map and compass before ever laying hands on a GPS. The GPS is an electronic device that works by capturing a satellite's signal. To identify your location, given in latitude and longitude coordinates, it must lock onto three satellites; to identify your altitude, it must lock onto four satellites. As with all electronic devices, a GPS is vulnerable to heat, cold, moisture, and sand. Even though satellite signals are now easier than ever to capture, there are still times when a signal cannot be obtained. In such instances, the GPS is nothing more than added weight in the pack. It's a great tool, but don't rely on it for your sole source of navigation.

ADDITIONAL INFORMATION ON TRAVEL

Before departing into the outdoors, leave an itinerary with someone you can trust (see chapter 5 for a sample trip plan). Set up check-in times that let them know you are ok. This insurance is key to a short survival stay versus a long one. If you don't check in, this person can let rescuers know your intended route of travel and initiate a search long before you'd otherwise be missed.

BASIC TRAVEL TECHNIQUES

Conserve your energy

To conserve energy, maintain a constant steady pace, take frequent rest breaks throughout the day, and avoid overheating by wearing your clothes loose and layered. When going uphill, stand straight, shorten steps, and use the rest step (covered below). When going downhill, keep the knees slightly bent and walk with slow, small, controlled steps. When trails are available, use them, provided they are in line with your direction of travel. Traveling off-trail expends much more energy. Avoid traveling in the desert or deep snow unless absolutely necessary.

Breaking trail and setting the pace

If you are in a team, the person breaking trail is working harder than anyone else, and this job needs to be traded off at regular intervals between the members of a team. The leader should always set a pace that is comfortable for all team members.

Kick stepping

When in snow, sand, or scree (small rocks), kick stepping will make your ascent much easier. Using the weight of your leg, swing the toe of your boot into the ground's surface, creating a step that supports at least the ball of your foot if going straight up, or at least half of your foot if traversing. When going uphill, lean forward until your body is perpendicular to the earth's natural surface, not that of the hill.

Plunge stepping (down climbing)

Plunge stepping is similar to kick stepping, except you are going downhill and kicking your heels rather than your toes into the slope. Slightly bend the knees, and lean backward until your body is perpendicular to the ground at the base of the hill, not that of the hill.

Traversing

Traversing, or diagonal climbing, is a quick and easy method for getting up or down a hill. When traversing a hill, it may be necessary to slightly shorten your strides as the grade changes. This same technique can be used to descend a hill.

Rest stepping

When walking uphill, use a rest step, which is done by locking the knee with each step. This process takes the weight off the muscle, allowing it to rest, and places it on the skeletal system. For best results, you'll need to take a short pause with each step.

Using a ridgeline to your advantage

When traveling in mountainous terrain, try to stay on the ridgeline as much as you can. It's better to travel a little farther than to deal with the constant up-and-down travel associated with frequent elevation changes.

Terrain issues

Cornices

Cornices are usually formed on the downwind or leeward side of a ridge. This happens as a result of the wind blowing snow off and over the windward side of a cliff, depositing it on the downwind side. If you are approaching a peak from the windward side, you may not be aware that a cornice exists. Since wind patterns are similar throughout an area, take the time to look at the downwind side of other peaks in your location. Try to identify a cornice in advance, and stay well below its potential fracture line. If you're unsure of whether a cornice exists, keep your elevation well below the peak, going no higher than two-thirds of the way up the ridge. If

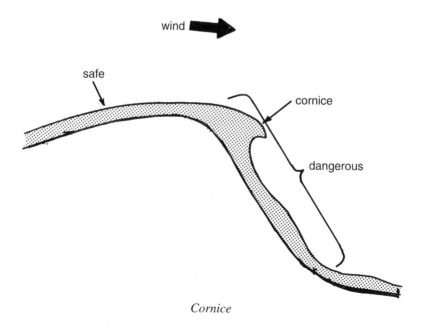

Cornice

approaching from the leeward side, look for wavelike formations that extend from the peak, and avoid these areas.

Glaciers and crevasses

A glacier is basically a snow and ice river that forms over many years. It is created when snow is in a location that doesn't allow it to melt before the next year's snowfall. Each year, new layers are added to the top of the glacier, and it loses some of its lower region as it melts away. The place at which it melts occurs where the glacier is low enough that no new snow can accumulate and the temperatures are high enough to cause melting. Crevasses are cracks in a glacier that result when a glacier stretches or bends too fast. They often run about 100 feet deep. On occasion, low elevation glaciers will completely fracture at a crevasse, causing an ice avalanche, which can be deadly. These usually occur during late summer and early fall. Unless you have achieved specific training in glacier travel, you should avoid these areas. If no other option exists, cross close to the top where the glacier is more stable.

Creeks

If you need to cross a small creek, loosen your pack's shoulder straps and undo your waistband so you can quickly remove the pack if you fall. Try to find a sturdy, naturally occurring bridge formed by a fallen tree or large dry rocks that span the creek's surface. If snow is on the ground, cross at a shaded area where there is a large amount of snow and no water can be seen. Use a pole to evaluate the snow's depth and stability before taking each step. Cross one person at a time. For larger creeks where no bridge or road crossing is available, cross the stream in a shallow area by way of a diagonal downstream route. For added stability, use a long walking staff for support. You can also decrease the current's impact on your legs by placing the stick on the upstream side of your position to form a V with you in its center.

Frozen bodies of water

Avoid crossing large bodies of ice—the risk associated with breaking through is too high. Always go around a lake. If you are approaching a river and you have no other choice but to cross, however, cross on the outside of bends or at a straight stretch where the water is apt to be shallow. Avoid areas that have anything sticking up or out of the ice, such as logs, stumps, or rocks, since the radiant heat from the object will have weakened the ice directly next to it.

Trees and rocks

In snowy conditions, trees and rocks can present problems for the backcountry traveler. Steep-sided wells form around rocks and tree trunks due to wind and the radiant heat that these objects produce. To avoid falling into these deep air pockets, avoid walking too close to trees and rocks. Tree branches hoard snow, which gladly drops down the back of your neck when you pass by. When you have to pass under a tree, either shake the branches first or walk behind someone else.

Rocky peaks

Although it might be tempting to climb a mildly sloping rocky peak, be careful. People often start to climb up a rock only to discover that it is too difficult to reach the top. At this point most people try to down climb, and many are surprised to find that the route down is much more difficult than it was going up. If the down climb becomes too hard, you may slip and get hurt or become stranded on the rock.

Canyons and similar structures

Canyons often present a maze, and unless you have good navigation skills, it is easy to get lost. Before entering a canyon make sure you can get back out. Do your research. Avoid canyons during peak flash flood seasons. A flash flood in a canyon has the same potential as an avalanche for sweeping you away and taking your life.

Dunes

Sand dunes form as a result of the wind's movement off the sand. It is far easier to hike on the windward side of a slope, where the sand is packed and more stable. On the leeward side, the sand is soft, and it requires far greater work to get from one point to another.

SURVIVAL TIPS

If you don't have navigation skills, stay put. Your survivability and odds of rescue depend on it.

Before departing, always establish an emergency heading to the nearest well-traveled road that will remain constant no matter where you are.

IMPROVISING TO MEET YOUR NEEDS

12

Improvising

With creativity and imagination, you can improvise the basic survival necessities. The only limiting factor is your imagination.

FIVE STEPS OF IMPROVISING

When working through the improvising process, the following five-step guide helps you make the best choice.

1. Determine your need.
2. Inventory your available materials, man-made and natural.
3. Consider the different options of how you might meet your need.
4. Pick one, based on its efficient use of time, energy, and materials.
5. Proceed with the plan, ensuring that the final product is safe and durable.

For example, you're lost in a temperate forest during a cool spring evening, it's 8 P.M., and you're in need of a shelter.

1. Determine your need: You need a shelter.
2. Inventory your available materials:
   a. Man-made: You have line, a tarp, a poncho, and a large plastic bag.
   b. Natural: In the general area, you can see trees, branches, leaves, and cattails.
3. Consider the different options of how you might meet your need:
   a. Construct a tarp shelter.
   b. Construct a poncho shelter.
   c. Construct a shelter using the plastic bag.
   d. Find a good tree well (may even incorporate your tarp into the lower boughs to add to the natural protection).
   e. Construct a natural shelter using cattail leaves to provide the outer covering.

4. Pick one, based on its efficient use of time, energy, and materials:
    a. Time. Options *a* through *d* require little time to construct.
    b. Energy. Options *a* through *d* require very little energy.
    c. Materials. Options *a, b,* and *c* would require materials that could be put to better use. Options *d* and *e* are good choices, since they spare your man-made resources. Option *d* would use material in an appropriate fashion, provided the tarp was not necessary to meet any of your other needs.
5. Proceed with the plan, ensuring that the final product is safe and durable: Construct the shelter, ensuring that it meets the criteria in the section on personal protection.

TOOLS OF IMPROVISING

Improvising can turn an uncomfortable survival stay into one of luxury. The ability to tie knots is extremely valuable during the improvising process.

CORDAGE

Since line is key to holding improvised items together, you may at times need to improvise some cordage. Improvised cordage can be made from various materials such as cattail or yucca leaves, grasses, dried inner bark from some trees, animal products such as rawhide and sinew, or various man-made products such as parachute line or twine. The best rope-making materials have four basic characteristics: The fibers need to be long enough for ease of work, strong enough to pull on without breaking, pliable enough to tie a knot in without breaking, and have a grip that allows them to bite into one another when twisted together. Any materials that meet these criteria should work.

The first step to making cordage is to create long single strands of your selected material. Twist the material between your thigh and palm, adding additional fibers to its free end to create one long continuous cord. This spun cord is then used in making two-strand, three-strand, and four-strand braids.

Two-strand braid

The two-strand braid is an excellent all-around line that can be used for many tasks. If a lot of weight will be applied to the line, however, a four-strand braid would be a better option. Follow these steps to make a two-strand braid.

1. Grasp a piece of spun cord between the thumb and forefinger of your left hand, with two-thirds of its length on one side and a third on the other.
2. With the thumb and pointer finger of your right hand, grasp the strand that is farthest away from you. Twist it clockwise until tight, and then move it counterclockwise over the other strand. It is now the closer of the two.
3. Twist the second strand clockwise until tight, and then move it counter-clockwise over the first strand.
4. Repeat this process until done.
5. Splicing will need to be done as you go, and this is the reason for the two-thirds and one-third split. If you were to splice both lines at the same location, it would cause a significant compromise at that point. Splicing is simply adding line to one side. Make sure to have plenty of overlap between the preceding line and the new one, and to use line of similar diameter.
6. To prevent the line from unraveling, finish the free end with an over-hand knot.

    If you are in a hurry, there is a quicker alternative.

good braid

bad braid

A properly spun two-strand braid has even tension throughout.

1. Using spun cord, grab one end between the thumb and forefinger of your left hand, and roll it in one direction on your thigh with your right palm.
2. Repeat this process until the whole line is done and is tight.
3. Still holding the line at one end with your left hand, grasp the other end with your right hand.
4. Place the middle between your teeth, move your hands together, and tightly hold both ends in one hand.
5. Release the line from your mouth. The tension created by rolling the line on your leg will cause the two strands to spin together.

Three-strand braid

A three-strand braid is ideal for making straps and belts. Follow these steps to make a three-strand braid.

1. Tie the three lines together at one end, and lay them out so that they are side by side.

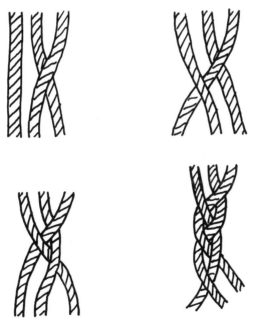

Three-strand braid

2. Pass the right-side strand over the middle strand.
3. Pass the left-side strand over the new middle strand.
4. Repeat this process, alternating from side to side—right over middle, left over middle—until done.
5. To prevent the line from unraveling, tie the end.

Four-strand braid

A four-strand braid is ideal for use as a rope. It provides the strength and shape desired and is far superior for this purpose than either the two-strand or three-strand braid. To make a four-strand braid, follow these steps.

1. Tie the four lines together at one end, and lay them out so they are side by side.
2. Pass the right-hand strand over the strand immediately to its left.
3. Pass the left-hand strand under the strand directly to its right and over the original right hand strand.

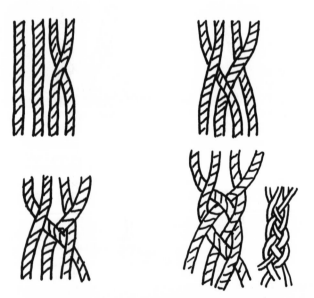

Four-strand braid

4. Repeat this process alternating from side to side—right strand over the strand immediately to its left, left strand under the strand immediately to its right and over the next one.
5. Splice in new material as needed.

KNOTS
Several knots can be tied using man-made or improvised line.

Square knot

The square knot connects two ropes of equal diameter.

Double sheet bend

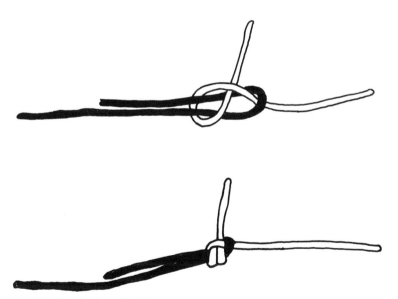

The double sheet bend connects two ropes of different diameters.

Improved clinch knot

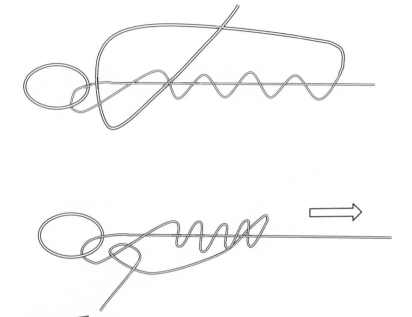

The improved clinch knot is used to attach a hook to a line.

Overhand fixed loop

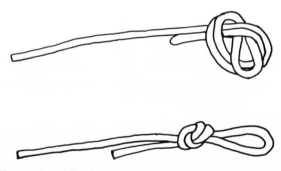

The overhand fixed loop has multiple uses in a survival setting.

Bowline

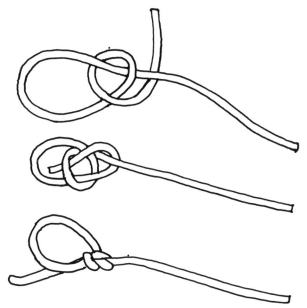

The bowline is much easier to untie after you use it than the overhand fixed loop.

Double half hitch

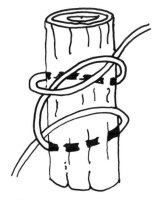

The double half hitch secures a line to a stationary object.

LASHES

Square lash

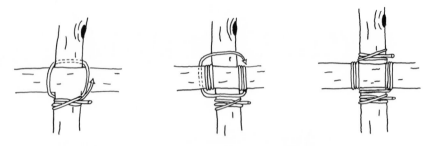

The square lash secures two perpendicular poles together.

Shear lash

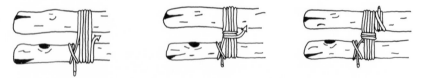

The shear lash attaches several parallel poles together.

SURVIVAL SKILLS FOR CHILDREN

13

Children and Survival

Every year search-and-rescue teams spend countless hours searching for lost children. Sadly, many of these missions end in tragedy; the children are never seen again or found dead. Could a few simple steps have changed their fates? If you intend to take your children to the woods, take the time to discuss safety issues and make sure they always carry certain items that will aid in their survival.

SAFETY ISSUES

ADULT SUPERVISION
Children should never go on a hike without adult supervision. You wouldn't take them into the heart of a major city and let them out of your sight. You shouldn't allow this to happen in the wilderness either.

STAY ON THE TRAIL
There is absolutely no reason for children to be off-trail. If your children need to go to the bathroom, make sure they can see the trail or you while they take care of their personal business. They are not experienced with a map and compass, and it doesn't take much for them to get turned around and headed in the wrong direction.

EXPOSURE ISSUES
Dress your children appropriately for the environment you are in. Make sure they understand the loose-and-layered approach and use it throughout the day.

Before taking your children into the outdoors, take the time to discuss safety issues.

HYDRATION

In mild conditions, children need at least 1 to 2 quarts of water a day. Don't expect them to get that amount from a water fountain. Have them carry a CamelBak that has a 2- to 3-liter water storage capacity. During the day, make sure to check how much your child has consumed. People have died from heatstroke with a half-filled water bladder inside their CamelBak. The CamelBak can also be used to carry a small survival kit.

SURVIVAL KIT

Create a survival kit that will help your children stay warm and signal for rescue. With your children, inventory this kit before each trip and discuss how each item is used. Make sure your children have this on at all times, even when walking from camp to the car. As a minimum this kit should contain the following.

MANDATORY ITEMS

Whistle
The whistle can provide a great means of alerting others to your location. The whistle should be attached to the body as a necklace or tied to a belt loop and inserted inside a pocket.

Garbage bag
An industrial-size garbage bag can be used for protection from the wind, rain, and cold by making holes for the head and arms. To decrease heat lost from the head, create the hood when making the head hole. Show your children how to do this before departing home. Make sure your children know to not place their heads inside the garbage bag!

Petzel headlamp
These small flashlights can be used to decrease the fear associated with a dark night and can be used as a signal.

Hat and socks
To prevent heat loss from the head, feet, and hands. During cold times, the socks can be worn on the hands or the feet (if the ones being worn get wet).

Water
Staying hydrated is very important. Water can be carried in a CamelBak or a water bottle that is attached to your child using carabiners or lines.

Energy bar
This item helps a child's will to survive. Please take the time, however, to discuss how important water is, and remind them that if they don't have water, they shouldn't eat.

HIGHLY SUGGESTED ITEMS
Most of the items listed here should not be given to your children unless you have properly trained them on their use. Without training, they are nothing more than dead weight and serve no purpose. Some items might even be harmful in the untrained hand.

Signal mirror
When used correctly, the signal mirror is probably the most effective signaling device there is.

Solar blanket
Although flimsy, these blankets can add a layer of protection, making a long, cold night more comfortable.

Iodine tablets
Iodine is lightweight and does a pretty good job at purifying water (see chapter 9 for details).

Folding blade knife
The knife is a great tool for improvising and building fires, but it can also cause debilitating cuts that compromise a survival situation.

Waterproof matches and lighter
Anyone can start a forest fire! Building a fire to warm yourself and signal for help, however, requires skill. If you teach your children the art of fire craft, remind them that fire is the third line of personal protection, and they need to meet their clothing and shelter needs first.

Tinder
Cotton balls saturated with petroleum jelly (carried in a sealable plastic bag) make great tinder, provided you pull the fibers apart, creating the edges necessary to light.

OTHER SUGGESTIONS
The size of your children's survival kits depends on how much they can carry. The list is unlimited. Take the time to review chapter 4 on survival

and medical kits and incorporate as much as you safely can into your children's kits.

STEPS OF SURVIVAL

Don't expect your children to have innate survival skills. As parents, it is your responsibility to prepare them for the outdoors, teaching them how to stay found. At the same time, you need to love them, and let them know you won't be mad if they get lost. Take the time to educate them on what to do if they get separated from you. Do this every morning, and quiz them several times during the trip, especially after stopping to rest or eat.

The steps of survival for a child are not much different than those outlined in chapter 6. They have the same basic needs that we have. The following algorithm can be applied for children.

1. Stop: Children will often panic when lost, running frantically through the wilderness screaming for help. During this time, they are moving farther and farther away from the place where rescue efforts will begin. Make sure your children understand how important this step is, and how moving makes it much harder for you to find them.

2. Meet Your Needs: For adults, I advocate the five survival essentials (health, personal protection, sustenance, signaling, and travel). Children, however, need to focus on four things to help ensure their survival (for greater detail on the following survival needs, refer to the appropriate chapters).

   a. Clothing: Clothes are the first line of personal protection. Make sure your children understand the basics on clothing care and use. Keeping clothes clean and dry and wearing them in a loose and layered manner is the key to how clothes insulate your children from hot or cold conditions. Discuss how a hat and dry socks will decrease heat loss and keep them warm. Make sure they understand the difference between playing in the sandbox and being in the woods.

   b. Shelter: Shelter is the second line of personal protection. Using a tree well and a plastic garbage bag or solar blanket can provide enough protection to survive most nights. Take the time to review how to use a garbage bag and solar panel, and when hiking, point out a good tree well, and have your children climb inside so they can see how comfortable it can be.

Greg Davenport's three-step approach for children

    c. Signaling: The minute your children stop, they need to immediately begin blowing their whistle and continue doing it in short bursts every three to five minutes until rescue arrives. If they have a signal mirror, they should flash the horizon every five to ten minutes. If they don't have either, they can use a big stick and pound on a tree; this unnatural noise will attract rescuers to their location.

    d. Water: Don't have your children ration their water. They should drink it. Better to be hydrated early on than dehydrated throughout the whole process. If they can see a creek from the trail, they should collect more water. They should not, however, wander around looking for a water source. Doing this takes them farther away from the rescue team and makes it harder to find them.

3. Keep the Faith: Let your children know that if they ever get lost, you'll be looking for them. Knowing this helps motivate them to do whatever it takes until you find them, such as stay put, stay dry, and signal for help. If you are a spiritual family, discuss your faith and how they can turn to it for comfort.

Index

Page numbers in italics indicate illustrations.

acute mountain sickness, 61
airway, breathing, circulation (ABCs),
    50–51
altimeter, 31
altitude illnesses, 60–61
    acute mountain sickness, 61
    high altitude cerebral edema
        (HACE), 62–63
    high altitude pulmonary edema
        (HAPE), 61–62
animal bites, 66
axes, 25–26
    felling and cutting trees with,
        26–28

backpacks, 16–18, *17, 18*
batteries, tips for protecting, 32
berry rule, 158–59
birds
    as food source, 174–77
    methods of procuring, 175–77, *176*
    preparing, 177
bivouac bags, 19–20, *20*, 92
blankets
    all-weather, 22
    fleece or quilted, 22
bleeding (hemorrhage), treatment
        options for, 51–52, *52*

blisters, 56
bolas, 178–79, *179*
boots, 84
    fabric, 84
    leather, 84
    rubber, 85
bowel disturbances, 63
bugs, *see* insects
burns, 55–56

CamelBak, 19
children
    safety issues concerning, 278–79
    survival kit for, 279–82
    three-step approach for, 282–83,
        283
climates, 2
    desert, 5–7
    ice, 3–4
    rain forests, 8–9
    snow, 2–3
    temperate forests, 9–10
clothing, 74–90
    adjusting, to maintain body temper-
        ature, 74–77
    caring for and wearing, 81–82
    COLDER principle for, 81–82, 105
    eye protection, 87

clothing, *continued*
  footwear, 84–85
  gaiters, 86
  gloves and mittens, 85
  headgear, 86
  improvised, 87–90
  insulating layer of, 77
  natural fabrics for, 78
  outdoor, 82–87
  outer shell of, 77–78
  synthetic fabrics for, 78–79
  tips, 136
  wicking layer of, 77
cold injuries
  frostbite, 59–60
  hypothermia, 59
COLDER principle, 81–82, 105
compasses, 236–42, *238, 242*
  with added features, 242, *242*
  circular housing, 238
  magnetic fields and, 241, *241*
  magnetic interference and, 241
  magnetic needle, 239
  magnetic north and, *239*, 239–40,
    240
  rectangular base plate, 238
  using, with maps, 243–50
  see also maps; navigation
conduction, 74–75
convection, 75–76
cooking methods, 196
  baking, 197–98
  boiling, 196–97
  broiling, 198
  frying, 198
cordage, 269–73
  four-strand braid, *272*, 272–73
  knots, 273–75
  lashes, 276
  three-strand braid, *271*, 271–72
  two-strand braid, 269–71, *270*
CPR, 50–51
crustaceans, as food source, 162–63

Davenport, Greg, *49, 72, 82*
dehydration, 48–49
desalting, tablets, 148
Diamox, 61, 62
dislocations, 55

edibility test for plants, universal,
    156–58, *157*
emergencies, life-threatening, 50–57
  six steps for treating, 50
  see also injuries, traumatic
evaporation, 76
eye
  injuries, 56
  protection, 87, 90

fabrics
  coatings, 79–80, *80*
  natural, 78
  synthetic, 78–79
fire, 74, 112–35
  beds, 135
  bundle, *135*
  fuel, 115–22, *120, 121, 122*
  heat sources, 112–13, 122–32, 134
  kindling, 118, *119*
  man-made heat sources, 112–13
  platform and brace, *114*, 114–15
  reflectors, *133*, 133–34
  site preparation, 113–14
  steps to building, 132–33
  tinder, 115–18
  tips, 136
  triangle, *113*
fish
  to avoid, 165–66
  methods of procuring, 166–74
  preparing, 174
fish hook injuries, 57
fishing
  barehanded, 168–69
  chop, 169
  with fish traps, *173*, 173–74

gill net, *171*, 171–72, *172*
scoop net, 172–73
spear, 169–70, *170*
tackle, 166–68, *167, 168*
when and where to go, 166
foods, 155
   the berry rule, 158–59
   birds, 174–77
   cache, *200*, 200–1
   cooking methods for, 196–98
   crustaceans, 162–63
   fish, 165–74
   game, 177–96
   insects, 161–62
   mollusks, 164
   mushrooms, tip concerning, 201
   plants, 156–60
   preserving, 198–200
   snakes, 164–65
   to take, 155–56
   universal edibility test for plants,
      156–58, *157*
footwear, 84–85
   improvised, 88
fractures, treating, 54, *54*
frostbite, 59–60

gaiters, 86
   improvised, 88
game, 177
   handheld weapons for procuring,
      178–81
   skinning and butchering, 193–96,
      194, 195
   snares and traps for procuring,
      181–93
gear, 16
   altimeter, 31
   axes, 25–28
   backpacking stoves, 28–29
   backpacks, 16–18
   bivouac bags, 19–20
   blankets, 22

CamelBak, 19
cooking pots, 29–30
Global Positioning System (GPS),
   30–31
headlamps, 29
knives, 22–25
miscellaneous, 32
ponchos, 22
saws, 25
sleeping bags, 20–21
sleeping pads, 21
snowshoes, 31–32
tents, 19
tips, 32
Global Positioning System (GPS),
   30–31, 261
gloves and mittens, 85
Gobi Desert, *7*
goggles, improvised, 90, *90*

headgear, 86
headlamps, 29
health, 48
   environmental injuries and ill-
      nesses, 57–69
   general, 48–50
   six steps for life-threatening emer-
      gencies, 50
   survival stress, 70–73
   tips, 73
   traumatic injuries, 50–57
heat exhaustion, 58
heat injuries, 57
   heat exhaustion, 58
   heat rash, 57
   heatstroke, 58
   hyponatremia, 58–59
   muscle cramps, 58
   sunburn, 57
heat rash, 57
heat sources
   battery and steel wool, 126
   bow and drill, 127–29, *128, 129*

heat sources, *continued*
  flint and steel, *125*, 125–26
  glass, convex shaped, 126
  hand drill, 130–31, *131*
  lighters, 123
  maintaining, 134, *135*
  man-made, 122–26
  matches, 123
  metal match, 123–25, *124*
  natural friction-based, 126–32
  pyrotechnics, 126
heatstroke, 58
helicopter rescues, *218*, 218–19
hemorrhage, *see* bleeding
high altitude cerebral edema (HACE),
    62–63
high altitude pulmonary edema
    (HAPE), 61–62
hydration, importance of, 48–49
hyponatremia, 58–59
hypothermia, 59

illnesses, environmental
  altitude, 60–63
  bowel disturbances, 63
  cold or flu, 69
improvising
  clothing, 87–90
  cordage, 269–73
  five-step approach to, 44–45,
    268–69
  footwear, 88
  gaiters, 88
  goggles, 90
  knots, 273–75
  lashes, 276
  snowshoes, 88–89
  tools of, 269–76
infections, 56
injuries, environmental
  animal bites, 66
  cold, 59–60
  heat, 57–59

immersion (trench foot), 60
insect bites and stings, 66–69
lizard bites, 65–66
snakebites, 63–65
snow and sun blindness, 60
injuries, traumatic, 50
  abdominal, 53
  airway, breathing, circulation
    (ABCs), 50–51
  bleeding (hemorrhage), 51–52
  blisters, 56
  burns, 55–56
  chest, 53–54
  dislocations, 55
  eye, 56
  fish hook, 57
  fractures, 54
  head, 53
  shock, 52–53
  six steps for life-threatening emer-
    gencies, 50
  spinal, 53
  sprains and strains, 55
  thorns, splinters, and spines, 57
  wounds, lacerations and infections,
    56
insect bites and stings, 66–69
insects
  as food source, 161–62
  nutritional value of various, *161*
  tip concerning, 201

kindling, 118, *119*
knives, 22–25, *24*
  sharpening, 23
knots
  bowline, *275*
  double half hitch, *275*
  double sheet bend, *273*
  improved clinch, *169, 274*
  overhand fixed loop, *274*
  square, *273*

lacerations, 56
lashes
 shear, *276*
 square, *276*
lizard bites, 65–66

mammals, as food source, *see* game
maps, 221–36
 angular coordinate system, 225–29
 colors and symbols, 223
 contour lines, 223–24, *225*
 latitude and longitude, 225–29, *226,*
  227, 228, 229
 magnetic variation, 234–36, *235,*
  236, 237
 orienting, *244,* 244–45, *245, 246*
 rectangular coordinates, 229–34
 size, 221–22, *222*
 Universal Transverse Mercator
  (UTM) system, 229–34, *230,*
  232, 233
 using, with compasses, 243–50
 see also compasses; navigation
medical kits, suggested items for, *37*
mittens, *see* gloves and mittens
mollusks, as food source, 164
muscle cramps, 58
mushrooms, 201

navigation, 220
 checklist, 250–51
 deliberate offset, 249–50, *250*
 determining general location, 243
 determining specific location,
  243–49
 establishing and maintaining a field
  bearing, 249, 250, *251*
 line of position to determine location, 246–47
 orienting a map, *244,* 244–45, *245,*
  246
 triangulating to determine location,
  247–49, *248*

 using Global Positioning System
  (GPS), 261
 using map and compass, 243–50
 using the stars, 257–61, *258, 259*
 using stick and shadow, 252–53,
  254, 260, 260–61
 using the sun, 251–53, 254
 using a watch, 254–57, *255*
 see also travel

Ojibwa bird snare, 175, *176*
Ostrem, Jared, 161

pants, rain, 83–84
parkas, 83–84
plants, 156
 the berry rule, 158–59
 edible parts of, 159–60
 universal edibility test for, 156–58,
  157
ponchos, 22
pots, cooking, 29–30
preservation methods, 198
 smoking, 198–200, *199*
 sun drying, 198

radiation, 74, *75*
respiration, 76–77
reverse osmosis water maker, 149–50
rodent skewers, 181, *181*

saltwater, conversion methods for,
 148–50
saws
 Pocket Chain, 25
 Sven, 25
scent, human, method of hiding, 183
scorpions, 69
shelters, 74, 90
 A-frame, 96, *96,* 102, *103*
 A-tent, 95, *95*
 bivouac bags, 92
 campsite selection, 90–92

shelters, *continued*
  caves, 111–12
  desert/shade, 98, *99*
  design, basics of, 92–94
  hobo, 110, *111*
  lean-to, 96–97, *97, 98, 104*, 104–5
  molded dome, *108*, 108–9
  natural, 98–112
  snow A-frame, 106–8, *107*
  snow cave, 105, *106*
  tarp, 94–98
  tents, 92
  tips, 136
  tree pit, 100, *101*
  tropical hut, 109, *110*
  wickiup, 100–2, *102*
shock, 52–53
signaling, rules of, 204–5
signals
  aerial flares, 205
  cellular phones, 206
  Emergency Position Indicating
    Radio Beacons (EPIRBs), 207
  fire, 215, *215*
  ground-to-air pattern, 212–14, *213,
    214*, 218
  handheld red signal flares, 207–8
  improvised, 214–18
  kites, 212
  mirrors, 210, *210, 211, 217*, 217–18
  orange smoke, 208–9, *209*
  parachute flares, 205–6
  radios, VHF, 206
  smoke generator, 215–17, *216*
  strobe lights, 212
  that attract rescue, 205–7
  that pinpoint location, 207–14
  tips, 219
  whistles, 212
sleeping bags, 20–21
  construction designs, *21*
sleeping pads, 21

slingshots, improvised, 180, *181*
snakebites, 63–65
  hemotoxic, 63–64
  neurotoxic, 64
snakes
  as food source, 164–65
  procuring, *165*
snares and traps, 181
  Apache foot snare, *192*, 192–93
  box trap, 191–92, *192*
  figure-four mangle snare, *187*,
    187–99, *188, 189*
  paiute deadfall mangle snare,
    189–91, *190*
  simple loop snare, *182*, 182–84, *183*
  squirrel pole, 184, *185*
  twitch-up strangle snare, 185–86,
    186
snow blindness, 60
snowshoes, 31–32
  improvised, 88–89, *89*
socks, 85
solar stills, 148, *149*
spears, 169–70, *170*, 178
spiders
  black widow, 67–68, *68*
  brown recluse, 68–69, *69*
splinters, 57
sprains and strains, 55
stoves, backpacking, 28–29
stress, 70
  environmental influences, 70
  overcoming, 71–73
  physical and psychological, 70–71
sun blindness, 60
sunburn, 57
survival
  children's, 278–83
  factors that influence, 42, *43*
  five essentials of, 43
  identifying and prioritizing essen-
    tials, 43–44

improvising to meet your needs,
44–45
recognizing situation, 42–43
six Ps of, 70–71
three-step approach to, 42–45, *44*,
71–73, 282–83, *283*
survival kits, 33–36
for children, 279–82
essentials, *34*
small cargo pocket kit items, 35–36

temperature, body, maintaining,
74–77, *75, 76*
tents, 19, 92
commercial, *92*
tinder, 115
manmade, 115–16, *116*
natural, 116–18, *117, 118*
transpiration bag, *145*, 145–46
traps, *see* snares and traps
travel, 220
itinerary, 261
techniques, 261–65
terrain issues, *263*, 263–65
tips, 266
see also navigation
travel itinerary, 38–40
trees, felling and cutting, *26*, 26–27,
27, 28
trench foot, 60

Van Dyk, John, 161
vegetation bag, 144, *144*

water, 137
condensation, 143–45
dispelling myths about, 138
filters, 150, 151
ground, *141*, 141–42
indicators, 138–39
precipitation, forms of, 142–43
purification, 151–54
requirements, 137
saltwater conversion methods,
148–50
sources and procurement, 139–50
storage, 154–55
surface, 140, *140*
tips, 201
from vegetation, 146–48
water generators, snow, *143*
weather, 11
forecasting, using barometric pressure, 12–13
forecasting, using clouds, 13–15
fronts, 11–12
map, *12*
pressure systems, 11
reports, 11–12
weighted clubs, 179, *180*
wounds, 56